Philosophy and Pluralism

ROYAL INSTITUTE OF PHILOSOPHY SUPPLEMENT: 40

EDITED BY

David Archard

Published by the Press Syndicate of the University of Cambridge
The Pitt Building, Trumpington Street, Cambridge, CB2 1RP
40 West 20th Street, New York, NY 10011-4211, USA
10 Stamford Road, Oakleigh, Melbourne 3166, Australia

A catalogue record for this book is available from the British Library

Library of Congress Cataloguing in Publication Data applied for

ISBN 0 521 56750 5 (paperback)
ISSN 1358-2461

Origination by Michael Heath Ltd, Reigate, Surrey
Printed in Great Britain by the University Press, Cambridge

Contents

Contents

Notes on Contributors

Catherine Audard was educated at the Ecole Normale Supérieure in Paris and teaches philosophy at the London School of Economics. She is also a Directeur de Programme at the Collège International de Philosophie in Paris. She has translated John Rawls's books into French and has written numerous articles on justice and liberalism. She is currently editing an Anthology of Utilitarianism in French and writing a book on citizenship and moral individualism.

Harry Bunting is a Lecturer in Philosophy at the University of Ulster at Jordanstown. He has published articles on ethics and political philosophy, and is currently writing a book on moral relativism.

J. D. G. Evans is Professor of Logic and Metaphysics at the Queen's University of Belfast. He is the author of *Aristotle* and *Aristotle's Concept of Dialectic*, editor of *Moral Philosophy and Contemporary Problems*, and has written many articles on the history of philosophy, especially Greek philosophy, and on the nature and applications of philosophy. He is currently chairman of the UK National Committee for Philosophy and chairman of the Belfast Branch of the Royal Institute of Philosophy.

Keith Graham is Reader in Philosophy at the University of Bristol. He is the author of *J. L. Austin: A Critique of Ordinary Language Philosophy*, *The Battle of Democracy*, and *Karl Marx, Our Contemporary*, and has contributed to numerous edited collections and philosophy and politics journals. He is currently working on problems of identity and political allegiance.

Attracta Ingram is Lecturer in Politics at University College Dublin. She is author of *A Political Theory of Rights* (1994) and co-editor of *Justice and Legal Theory in Ireland* (1995). She has published recent articles on federalism and constitutional patriotism, and is currently working on normative issues of state and nation.

C. J. McKnight has been a lecturer in Philosophy at Queen's University of Belfast since 1976. He was co-editor (with Marcel Stchedroff) of *Philosophy in its Variety* (1980). He has written on applied ethics in the *Journal of Medical Ethics* and *Philosophy Now*.

Susan Mendus is Senior Lecturer in Politics and Director of the Morrell Studies in Toleration Programme at the University of York. She is author of *Toleration and the Limits of Liberalism* (1989) and co-editor (with John Horton) of *After MacIntyre: Critical Perspectives on the Work of Alasdair MacIntyre* (1994). Her main academic interests are in liberal political philosophy, feminist theory, and the philosophy of Kant. She is currently working on a book on conceptions of the self in political philosophy.

Tariq Modood is a Senior Fellow at the Policy Studies Institute, London. He is the author of *Not Easy Being British: Colour, Culture and Citizenship*, and has published extensively on ethnic relations in Britain. He is currently the principal researcher on the Fourth National Survey of Ethnic Minorities.

Alan Montefiore retired in 1994 after more than thirty years as Fellow and Tutor in Philosophy at Balliol College, Oxford. He has written on a wide variety of philosophical topics, and recent books include the edited collection *Philosophy in France Today* (1993), and *Goals, No-Goals and Own Goals* (1989) and *The Political Responsibility of Intellectuals* (1991) both of which he co-edited and contributed to. He is currently working on making a book out of accumulated material on personal and cultural identity.

Dermot Moran is Professor of Philosophy (Logic and Metaphysics) at University College Dublin. He is Editor of the *International Journal of Philosophical Studies* and author of *The Philosophy of John Scottus Eriugena* (1989). He is currently completing a number of studies on intentionality.

Terry O'Keeffe is Professor of Philosophy and Dean of the Faculty of Humanities at the University of Ulster. He has written widely on philosophy of religion, particularly on Paul Tillich, and is currently working on a series of articles on religious experience.

Bhikhu Parekh is Professor of Political Theory in the University of Hull. He is the author of several books including *Hannah Arendt and the Search for a New Political Philosophy*, *Marx's Theory of Ideology*, *Contemporary Political Thinkers*, and *Gandhi's Political Philosophy*. He has written a number of articles on such issues as the nature of national identity and nationalism. He is currently writing a book on the philosophical foundations of multiculturalism.

Anthony Skillen wrote *Ruling Illusions* in 1977. As well as continuing to publish on political themes, he has recently written articles on sport, epistemology, ethics, and on literary realism, the subject of his next book. He is Reader in Philosophy at the University of Kent at Canterbury.

John Skorupski is Professor of Moral Philosophy at the University of St Andrews. His most recent book is *English-Language Philosophy 1750–1945*.

Introduction

DAVID ARCHARD

As befits a volume devoted to the topic of pluralism the contributing pieces collected here are varied. Their concern is with very different kinds of difference, and their conclusions range from an insistence that pluralism is both inevitable and desirable to a belief that it is unsustainable and perhaps remediable. The starting point for any discussion of pluralism is a recognition that we inhabit a world of differences. These differences are exhibited in moral outlooks, cultural identities, ways of life, religious beliefs, and even modes of philosophy. The mere fact of such differences is salient but unremarkable. What preoccupies philosophers is the question of the conclusions that are to be drawn from a proper recognition of this fact. And the central issue at dispute for philosophers is whether the fact of difference—plurality—licences a view—pluralism—that it is legitimate, rather than just inevitable, that such difference should persist.

It simplifies but does not necessarily exaggerate matters to suggest that philosophers are torn between two impulses. On the one hand, there is the conviction that the goal of philosophical argumentation is convergence upon a single agreed answer. Truth is one, and so too, it has been felt, is the good. Difference is a sign of failure, evidence that mistakes have been made somewhere by someone. To maintain otherwise is inconsistent with how one must understand the nature of truth or morality. On the other hand, the claims of philosophical modesty press a contrary view, and the dangers which attend insistence upon the correctness of only one answer underline the value of remaining modest. That different conclusions are reached by equally sincere, conscientious reasoners is discomfiting to the assumption that difference is attributable to palpable error; that conflict and intolerance can result from a refusal to moderate or modify one's own claims in the face of disagreement is enough to expose the high price of monism.

These impulses are strongly felt and they are likely to exert a pull at whatever level the discussion of pluralism is conducted. For instance, someone who defends principles which might regulate the satisfactory negotiation of difference is likely to be asked what status these principles have and what assurance their author can have that there is only one such set of principles. Or again, someone who argues that, in the final analysis, equally rational inquirers will come up with different answers to the question of how things are is likely to be asked what continued confidence she can have in the rational warrant for her own particular view.

Those unsympathetic to monism are also anxious to distinguish pluralism from relativism. That no single correct answer can be agreed upon does not mean that each and every answer is true. Nevertheless, those unsympathetic to pluralism will continue to demand that it be clearly distinguished from relativism without any confidence that this can be achieved. That it is agreed there can be no agreement would suggest that in the final analysis any answer is as good as any other. Both sides to the dispute may nevertheless agree that the question is not whether agreement *can* be secured, but rather whether there is any reason to think that one *should* seek to secure it. The contributions collected here take up these matters in the areas of philosophy, religion, morality, and politics.

The opening papers in this volume consider whether philosophy itself is or is not plural. This is understood to be more than simply a matter of variations in style or emphasis or subject matter. Alan Montefiore examines the question of whether there are different, culturally specific philosophies and suggests that, insofar as philosophy is a discursive subject, there are forces peculiar to each contextualised unit of philosophical discourse which are resistant to translation across different units. Dermot Moran takes the concept of intentionality as a case study in philosophical difference. Central to both of what have been called the 'Continental' and 'Analytic' traditions of philosophy, intentionality has nevertheless been given a different significance in each. For continental philosophy intentionality is a defining feature of consciousness or the mental; for analytic philosophy it is an important property of sentences. Despite their divergent starting points, Moran detects a present convergence of viewpoints and willingness sympathetically to explore the differences.

The two papers by Anthony Skillen and David Evans look to the work of past philosophers for insights into pluralism. Skillen offers a sustained exegesis of William James's essay 'On a Certain Blindness'. The blindness of which James speaks is that of practically engrossed human beings to the richness of other lives. Nevertheless Skillen detects a certain ambiguity in James concerning the source of that richness, between the individuality of another's meaningful existence or the cultural values that underpin occupations which may otherwise be strange to us. David Evans argues that Aristotle is no simple pluralist, as is often maintained, but rather a realist who recognises that the differences between cultural contexts are essential elements in the construal of objective value. In this way Aristotle offers an alternative to the normative monism of Plato without slipping into relativism.

Terry O'Keeffe examines the question of religion and pluralism. Inasmuch as any one religion lays claim to have possession of a single truth, and single path to human salvation, it is disposed to intolerance of other religions which make similar claims. Yet any moderation of that claim in the name of tolerance seems inconsistent with the very nature of religious truth. O'Keeffe considers the various ways in which this problem has been treated, paying particular attention to the difficulties of definitive interpretation of any canonical text which lies at the source of religious claims to truth.

The next three contributions address the central issue of moral pluralism, one that preoccupies philosophers more than any other instance of pluralism and one that has also received a great deal of attention in recent years. Moral pluralism is interesting not only in its own right, but for the relation it bears to political liberalism. Harry Bunting offers a critique of various twentieth century defences of moral relativism, from the comparatively neglected work of Westermark to the influential internalism of Gilbert Harman and Bernard Williams. Bunting considers what merit there might be in relativism, and concludes that the position is ultimately an unsatisfactory one. Christopher McKnight scrutinises the claim of Isaiah Berlin, perhaps the most influential defender of pluralism, to offer a non-relativist account of how values can conflict and yet in some sense be objective. He finds that this is possible only insofar as ethics is not conceived as a search for the correct description of moral reality. John Skorupski also attempts to make clear what pluralism claims. That a moral theory needs to be relative to situation and circumstance does not establish the truth of pluralism. Inasmuch as normative judgements are genuine judgements a person's making one entails her commitment to the convergence of others upon that judgement. The idea that there are, as the value-pluralist claims, genuine moral dilemmas ultimately conflicts with our understanding of morality as a single, sovereign source of law.

The remaining contributions are in different ways concerned with how we should respond at the social or political level to the facts of plurality and the claims of the pluralist. Bhikhu Parekh detects a deep anti-pluralist bias in Western thought, from the Greeks through Christianity to contemporary liberalism. This bias reveals itself in an implausible moral monism which asserts that the good is single and human nature uniform. Such a monism is not only indefensible but has shown itself intolerant of, and missionary in its zeal to eliminate difference. Keith Graham argues that the scope of the plurality, which is central to much contemporary political philosophy, is narrower than is assumed or alleged. This is because there are constraints on all human deliberation about the best way to live. These constraints are of necessity, having to do with who and what each of us is, and of precondition, having to do with what is presupposed of any choice of life. Graham further argues that the materiality of our nature and condition falls under both constraints.

Attracta Ingram and Catherine Audard both inspect the credentials of what is currently the most influential and distinguished response within Western political philosophy to the problem of plurality, that is the existence within liberal democratic societies of permanent disagreement on fundamental religious, philosophical and moral matters. This response is due to John Rawls in his 1993 *Political Liberalism*. Rawls believes that an overlapping consensus on the principles of a well-ordered, fair society is possible between defenders of reasonable, if conflicting and incompatible, comprehensive doctrines of the good. Ingram seeks to elucidate the senses in which reasonable must be understood if such a consensus is to be possible, and finds merit in Rawls's hope that liberalism can be defended on grounds that are not philosophically liberal all the way down, as it were. Nevertheless this is so only if a moral cosmopolitanism which affirms the equal rationality of all is accepted. Catherine Audard contrasts Rawls's political liberalism with the republicanism which has defined the French political project. In offering a 'thicker' notion of citizenship, and one which seeks to constitute a community in a substantive notion of civic membership, republicanism is distinct from political liberalism. Nevertheless, the implementation of such secularist ideals is not without its problems, and Audard considers the French responses to ethnic and religious diversity.

Tariq Modood insists that any theory of ethnic diversity should be sensitive to the specific national context and shows how, for Britain at least, racial discrimination is not a unitary form of disadvantage. Racism may be compounded by particular cultural stereotypings of different ethnic groups. He examines the implications for an ideal of multiculturalism in also challenging the assumption that the public order can be neutral and blind to ethnic or cultural divisions.

Finally Susan Mendus examines the paradox whereby liberalism, born out of a recognition of conflicting values and apparently sensitive to the tragedy of loss which must attend such a conflict of values, has tamed that conflict. It has done so by sharply distinguishing the public from the private, and the sphere of justice from that of mere misfortune. In further prioritising the political so understood it has restricted the space within which individuals can understand the successes and failures of their own lives. Ironically then, in eliminating the tragic in its previous form liberalism has reinstated a new form of tragedy whereby one's personal fate can only be construed in a limited and obfuscating manner.

These papers were first given at a conference of the Royal Institute of Philosophy organised by the University of Ulster and the Belfast Branch of the Royal Institute of Philosophy and held at the Causeway Coast Hotel, Portrush, from 20 to 23 April 1995. Thanks are due to all those who assisted in the organisation and conduct of this conference, especially colleagues in the Department of Philosophy and Politics, the University of Ulster. Thanks too are due to the Northern Ireland Tourist Board who made possible a lunch and coach trip around the North Antrim Coast for the speakers.

Philosophy in Different Cultural Contexts

ALAN MONTEFIORE

The question to which I seek here to address myself may be formulated in the following way. Is philosophy to be thought of as essentially one and the same subject in all its different manifestations, carried on, certainly, in noticeably differing ways by different people at different times and in different places, but to be understood nevertheless as consisting of one overall body of knowledge? Or should the term 'philosophy' be regarded rather as standing for a 'family resemblance concept', and the family in question as containing among its members some who may be hardly capable of establishing any mutually agreed channels of communication with each other? In what follows I shall try to display, if not necessarily to disentangle, some of the underlying complexities on which, as it seems to me, answers to these questions may depend.

Geographically or culturally based distinguishing labels are, of course, in common use in philosophy. Greek philosophy, German philosophy, American philosophy, Oxford philosophy, 'Continental', Indian, Chinese, Bulgarian, Jewish, Québecois, Nova Scotian, Islamic, Parisian, London, Belfast, Dublin, Coleraine philosophy. ... Where, if anywhere, has my list started to take on an arbitrary implausibility of its own? Again no-one finds it in the least strange to talk, for example, of Ancient, Medieval, eighteenth century or twentieth century philosophy. But are these ways of picking out particular tracts of philosophy in principle any different from such references as one may make to Hume's or Russell's philosophy or to that of the 'first' or 'second' Wittgenstein?

In fact none of these references is altogether without its problems. It is true that there exists no commonly accepted distinction between a first and a second Hume, or a first and a second Russell, such as exists in the case of Wittgenstein or that, more controversially perhaps, of Heidegger; but no-one would suppose that Russell's philosophical views remained essentially unchanged over the life-time course of his writings, and although I myself should not, some might wish to argue that even the differences between the Treatise and the Enquiries are best seen as amounting to a change in 'Hume's philosophy'. There are, in any case, no clearly determinate criteria of individuation and identity for 'philosophies' in this or, indeed, any other sense. Another way of looking at the situation would be to say that it is in any case philosophies rather than philosophers as such that one should try to relate to or distinguish from each other. Thus there are, for instance, those who find it more helpful to try and show how one may trace out in Locke the contrasting influences of both empiricism and rationalism rather than to seek one overall way of characterising a peculiarly Lockean philosophy—other than that of characterising it as just such a mixture. None of the interpretative issues involved is uninteresting or unimportant. But once they have been argued out, nothing much more, it would seem, is going to depend on just where one draws the labelling line between what one is prepared to distinguish as 'one philosophy' rather than another.

Should one say the same of geographically or historically based labels? If, for example, one speaks of French or Irish chemistry, it would usually be something more than just a way of referring to a number of individual scientists happening to share a given nationality. Schools of chemistry (or physics or geology or mathematics) will tend to develop around particular authorities in their field and, in the first instance at any rate, the work carried on by teams working in certain particular laboratories. Why do they work on the particular topics and in the particular manner that they do? Obviously, there will be no one overall answer to such a question, but the factors involved may run from interests and habits of thought and work formed under the influence of their own teachers of a former generation of (naturally) French or Irish scientists to those of whatever body, very often nowadays governmental, may have been responsible for their funding. Clearly, where interests and habits are passed on from one generation to another, recognisable traditions may be formed. Moreover, other culturally specific factors may interact with the more obviously scientific, commercial or governmental ones. There is, for instance, likely to be more funding available for oenological research in a wine-producing country than in one where the staple alcoholic drinks are beer, schnapps or whiskey. Even so, it remains the case that the results of chemical or other scientific research must always be submissible to fellow-chemists of any other country or tradition for testing and for confirmation or rejection. That a particular discovery may have been made thanks to the inspiration or backing that a particular group of scientists may have derived from their national traditions or from their own government's funding can in no way mark out the content of that discovery as having any particular national characteristic. Newton's Laws of Motion are as such no more British than is Heisenberg's Uncertainty Principle German.

How does this situation compare with that of literature or history? So far as idiom goes, German history is, of course, history of Germany, while German literature is, on the contrary, literature written in German by, typically if not necessarily invariably, native German-speakers. Whatever is written in one language may, certainly, be translated into another. It is, however, a commonplace that in even the very best translations, while something may indeed be gained, something else is inevitably lost. Arthur Waley's English translations of ancient Chinese poems provide one excellent example. They may be regarded as constituting in their own right admirable contributions to English literature as such, and may quite certainly be highly appreciated by readers without any knowledge of Chinese, whether ancient or modern. But the idea that they might be regarded as precise aesthetic equivalents of the originals simply makes no very precise sense. Statements of any given scientific claim, whatever the language in which they may be formulated, must in principle present themselves as extensionally equivalent; so far as ancient Chinese poems are concerned, however, the very notion of extensional equivalence has no appropriate application.

None of this, of course, is to deny that there have been, and no doubt still are, many natural languages which, as they stand or stood, lack or have lacked the resources necessary for the adequate translation of the concepts of, say, quantum mechanics; such resources are built up over time, the time of the development of the relevant language and of the culture of those whose language it is. The point is rather that one has to assume that the theory in question, if properly applicable at all, must be equally applicable everywhere and in the terms of whatever the language into which it *may* be translated. One may (or may not) be able to provide convincing explanations in cultural, social, historical or economic terms for the fact that Newtonian mechanics was first developed in England, but to the extent that it is true or applicable (*whatever* exactly that may mean), it must be so throughout all the macrophysical dimensions of this world; and it must be testable as to the range of its applicability by anyone possessing the relevant competence, no matter what his natural language, his cultural tradition, his religion or his political or ideological allegiance. There is, by way of contrast, no sense to the suggestion that ancient Chinese poems—or poems of any other language or time—might be so tested. Their appreciation by one reader is in no way threatened by a failure to appreciate them by others. And in so far as they are capable of translation at all, their worth as poems in whatever the language of their translation has to be judged afresh in terms of whatever criteria of appreciation may be thought appropriate to translations of poetry in that language.

Where does philosophy stand in relation to science or literature? This is itself, of course, a characteristically philosophical question. To ask where science in general stands in relation to philosophy or the Arts is clearly not to ask a scientific question in the sense of one whose answer may be accounted a contribution to scientific knowledge; paradoxically enough it amounts, on the contrary, to asking very much the same philosophical question all over again. Whatever answers a chemist, biologist or physicist may propose to questions of this sort will add nothing to his knowledge of chemistry, biology or physics. If he feels that he owes it, as it were, to the clear-minded pursuit of his subject thus to reflect on its nature, we could reasonably say that this only shows his sensitivity to the way in which every intellectual pursuit secretes its own urge to philosophy, that is, to the reflexive need to reflect on the nature of what one is doing.

The situation is much the same with regard to the social sciences, despite the familiar fact that some of them at least may rightly be held to be reflexive in the sense that social scientists themselves, together with the ways in which their own activity may modify the nature of whatever they are studying, may be held to be among the proper objects of their own enquiries. It remains the case, however, that questions concerning the nature or status of the social sciences belong to the philosophy of the social sciences rather than to social science as such, just as questions relating to the nature and status of the natural sciences belong to the philosophy of science. Indeed, in so far as people are led to reflect on the nature and status of what they may be doing they may be said to be embarked on the philosophy of that aspect of their life's engagement; it is when one starts to reflect further on what one is doing in so reflecting, when philosophy starts to reflect not only on this aspect of living or studying or that but more specifically on the nature and status of that very reflection, that it thus becomes not only reflective, but evidently and explicitly reflexive.

Suppose that one asks rather where literature stands in relation to philosophy and the sciences? Put this way the question is a curiously lop-sided one. The fact is that the term 'literature' does not function in the same way as the other two. In its probably most general contemporary usage it may be taken to refer to what the *OED* characterises as 'literary work or production' or 'the realm of letters', where 'literary' means 'of or pertaining to, or of the nature of, literature, polite-learning, or books and written compositions'; or again 'literary productions as a whole; the writings of a country or period, or of the world in general'. In the broadest possible sense, then, anything that is written down may be brought under the head of literature, though this broadest possible sense would normally be hemmed in by a number of tacitly excluding clauses. For example, lecture notes, transitory everyday correspondence, much advertising copy, etc., etc. would not normally be classed as literature; and in most contexts most of what is to be found in at any rate the popular press would probably likewise be excluded. The category of 'polite-learning' has no doubt fallen pretty much into disuse, but it remains true that the term 'literature' typically retains some sort of vaguely honorific force. At any rate, the point of immediate relevance lies in the fact that, whatever may be the case in regard to graffiti, passports, railway tickets and the like, the term 'literature' can quite naturally be used to cover both philosophical and scientific writings—there is nothing in the least odd about chemists, geologists or philosophers referring each other to 'the available literature' on some aspect or another of their subject. If, then, all philosophical writings, or at least those with any claim to relative permanence (as opposed, for instance, to merely satisfying some examination requirement) are themselves to be counted as falling within the overall field of literature, what sense is left to the question as to where literature stands in relation to philosophy? The relevant questions must rather be: (i), whether a given text is to be regarded from a literary or from a philosophical point of view: (ii), whether these view-points are entirely independent of each other: and, (iii), whether, if they are not thus independent, the philosophical status of the text might not actually depend on its literary qualities.

What, then, is it to look at a text from 'a literary point of view'? It is, I here take it, to look at it in an attempt to give some account of the overall effects that it may be expected to produce (or may have been intended to produce) on its various potential readers—even perhaps on a fictionally 'ideal reader'—and of the ways in which such effects may have been brought about. Some of them, of course, may be 'propositional effects', that is to say, effects sustaining or productive of beliefs of one sort or another. But there will always be a whole diversity of non-propositional effects as well, many of them of what we may call aesthetic significance, but others perhaps of a more directly practical nature, for instance moral, political or psychological. There may also be effects of echo, association or recall; and if some of these are conscious, others may be below the threshold of explicit awareness. What, if anything might these non-propositional effects have to do with the philosophical point of a philosophical text?

At this point we find ourselves approaching an area of potentially major philosophical disagreements. Everyone will no doubt accept that speech acts never come singly, so to speak, or even in determinably finite groups. As with every other form of action, every time I produce some unit of discourse I can necessarily be seen as doing many different things at the same time. I produce a series of sounds or of marks on paper, say, or on a computer screen; I produce a series of words and sentences in, say, English or French; I make assertions, ask questions, give instructions; I swear allegiance, I take the oath in a Court of Law, I make a promise, I give my assent to my own marriage in the appropriate ceremonial context; I betray secrets, I amuse, I surprise, I insult, I persuade, I embarrass, I frighten, I shock, I make some political point, I appear to suggest or to reject all manner of not explicitly avowable complicities; and so on and so on. Some of these actions I perform in virtue of certain formally recognisable conventions governing the use of the appropriate words and phrases in certain standard contexts; others I perform in virtue of less formal, tacit, but still widely recognisable conventions of the society to which I belong. Of many of these actions I am or can readily be made consciously aware; but of many others I have no conscious awareness—indeed, I may not even be in possession of all the relevant concepts or classifications, under which my action might nevertheless entirely appropriately be brought. None of this would any speech act theorist seek in any way to deny. Nor would he wish to suggest that in producing philosophical texts or in discussing philosophical issues I should not equally be doing many other things at the same time; boring or enraging my audience, earning my living, redeeming a promise, displaying my own incompetence, supporting or discomforting some colleague, undermining or providing direct or indirect support for one political cause or another ... The question is rather whether the undeniable fact of the multiple other-sidedness of any philosophical act that I may perform should be seen as having any bearing on the nature and validity of the philosophical act as such?

There are, it would seem, powerful reasons for giving strikingly different answers to this question. We have already noted that any philosopher must in principle acknowledge that every act of philosophical production, including his own, must involve the performance of many other non-philosophical acts at the same time. The crucial question is whether he can claim properly to have taken on board the apparently acknowledged implications of his own theory if he does not then seek to guide his own philosophical activity in the light of his fullest understanding of all that it entails, that is, in the light of his fullest understanding not only of the meanings but also of the diverse forces of his own philosophical utterances. Having been philosophically brought up in an analytic version of the classical philosophical tradition, my own natural instinct would be to suppose that I could, for example, very well acknowledge that my attempt to discuss the relations between value judgements and statements of fact before an audience of so-called dissident philosophers in Prague in the 1980s constituted in that context a clearly political act as well without allowing my understanding of that fact to influence in any way the terms of my discussion. But, whether agreeing or not, one can understand the viewpoint of those who would take it to be a mark of philosophical bad faith, of a lack of integrity in the fullest sense of that word, were one not to try and guide one's conduct in the light of one's best understanding of *all* that one was doing—were one to pretend, as it were not to be engaging in a politically significant activity, while knowing that, like it or not, that was a main point of what one was trying to do in that particular context.

Suppose that one takes some version of this second view. It must mean that in elaborating one's text—the text, as one might say, of one's discourse, be it written or spoken, improvised or well prepared—one must in all philosophical responsibility pay as much heed to its likely overall impact on its intended (and perhaps also unintended, but predictable) readership or audience as to the strict logic of its argument or the truth of the assertions contained within it. One will, of course, know that even in the best of cases this overall impact can have no calculable or even incalculably determinate limits, nor can one ever hope to anticipate or even retrospectively know its fullest extent. One will never, it goes without saying, be wholly indifferent to questions of truth or validity; but one is likely to see them as having at best a place of special attention among questions of many other kinds, of style, of occasion and of context. Indeed, certain kinds of intended effect might best be achieved through the use of apparent or even formally evident contradictions, of unanswerable question and paradox, of words or phrases that suggest rather than assert certain associations, or of some other manner of non-assertoric affirmation. In short, one is likely to be as much concerned with the effects of one's discourse on its listeners or readers as with the lines of argument that it embodies considered 'in their own right'.

When philosophers come to understand the point of what they

are trying to do in this way, when the implications of their own *arguments* lead them to shape the language of its expression in ways that belong to another form of rhetoric, they become what according to certain readers of philosophical texts they have in fact been all along—that is, the producers of a whole range of verbal effects, which in speech may indeed be characterised under the once wholly honourable title of rhetoric and in writing may be characterised as literature. From this point of view philosophy may be seen more as a form of literature than as a form of science. The production of literary effects, many of which must be in principle incalculable, is hardly to be viewed as 'eine strenge Wissenschaft'.

The relevance of all this to the question with which we started lies in the fact that while meanings may in the last resort always be translated, reconstituted or explained in other terms, the forces that attach to the differential use of words and to speech acts in general are largely non-transferable, but are peculiar to the languages to which they belong and to the contexts of their production. Moreover, as many linguists would argue, there is, on the (relatively broad?) margins, in principle no unique or theoretically razor-sharp way of drawing a boundary line between meaning and force. Thus while those who regard philosophy as more akin to logic or science (or who prefer to see philosophy in this perspective) will naturally regard it as constituting essentially one and the same subject throughout the history and dispersal of its different manifestations, those who regard it as more akin to literature may see it rather as consisting in a more or less loosely interconnected family of discourses, with perhaps a fairly tight core of very closely related family members at its centre and with an outer penumbra of cousins so distant that there may be reasonable dispute as to whether they should be counted as members of the family at all. The further removed from the centre, the less straightforwardly evident the relationship; and the more local the nature of the forces that give any particular discourse its effective shape.

Another way of characterising this situation would be to reserve the title of philosophy for the inner most distinctively cognitive core of family members, while treating remoter members as belonging to such more or less related families as philosophical literature, sermons, essays, poetry and so on. It would be untrue to the whole spirit of this 'presentation', however, if I were now simply to say that nothing need turn on how one uses one's classificatory labels for these different forms of writing, provided that one understands the underlying issues at stake. It may be true that nothing strictly cognitive need be at stake. But the whole issue turns, of course, on the degree to which the so-called strictly cognitive aspects of what may confidently be recognised as philosophical discourse may be dissected out, as it were, from all the other forces at work within and around it. If they cannot be cleanly disentangled in this way, it is only to be expected that the use of one set of terms rather than another to characterise all these different aspects and forces in relation to each other, will itself carry its own distinctive ensemble of forces. (What, for example, of the varied associative resonance that my present use of the word 'discourse' may have for different readers/listeners depending on the contexts in which they may have encountered it before? Does the explicit reflexivity of my 'discourse' at this point somehow contribute to certifying it as (pretentiously would-be?) philosophical? Or am I merely indulging in a lazy stretch of free-wheeling?)

What can be said at any rate is that writers as surface different as Wittgenstein and Derrida (not to mention Nietzsche and Heidegger) have both made extensive use of non-assertoric, non-thetic, forms of writing with a view to modifying the view-points, grasp or orientation of their readers and not only what one might call the propositional contents of their beliefs. Not all of their techniques depend, certainly, on forces peculiar to the speech or language in which they are writing. Questions and commands, for example, are in principle as translatable from one language into another as are the statements that correspond to them. Many other linguistic forces, however, are far from being so readily transposable. The echoes that they may carry, the associations that they may awake, the forces of the metaphors peculiar to each particular language, the overtones or undertones of insult or approbation, of scorn, derision or enhancement, the practical as well as the 'merely' symbolically suggestive implications of bringing different things or activities together—or of keeping them apart—under one set of classifications rather than another, all these are aspects of a 'discourse' that may well vary significantly from one conversational context to another.

Suppose that one is unwilling, perhaps even in effect culturally unable, to classify under the head of philosophy any text or performance that is not primarily directed towards a certain type of analysis or argument. One effect of this might be to disqualify from inclusion within the acceptable limits of a philosophy syllabus many or most of the texts of such writers as, say, Nietzsche and Derrida or even, indeed, Wittgenstein; and to disqualify from employment within philosophy departments so denominated all such candidates as might specialise in such authors or, even worse, actually write like them. To this it may, of course, be replied that this is a policy matter, susceptible of explicit formulation—in such terms, indeed, as those which I have just employed—and in no way fated to remain a matter of covert suggestion, always inevitably implied but never openly statable. Moreover, none of this implies anything as to the suitability of such texts for inclusion within the syllabus, or specialists in them for employment within the establishment, of any other Faculty or Department. This reply is, it seems to me, an entirely fair one—in so far as it goes. But then the issues may always return as disputes about the proper analysis and understanding within such a context of the use of the terms 'analysis' and 'argument' themselves. And so on and so on. The situation is not so much that there are certain linguistic forces whose nature must remain an ultimate mystery towards which it is only possible to gesture, and whose most likely effects can never be explicitly stated or explained, as that it is principle impossible so to liberate oneself from the whole panoply of forces of the language that one is employing at any one time as to be able ever to provide an exhaustively explicit account of them all at once. The door to further regress will always remain, if not exactly wide open, at least significantly ajar.

The situation as I see it, then, may be summed up in the following way. Any unit of discourse whatsoever is bound to contain within it some complex and never exhaustively determinable interplay of what we may here characterise as meanings and forces. This must be as true of philosophical discourse as of any other. Meanings are, broadly speaking, translatable, or at least explainable or reconstructible, both within and across different languages. The same is true of certain central linguistic forces, the explicitly interrogative, imperative, permissive; for this very reason, no doubt, there may be some theoretical uncertainty as to how best to fit them into the distinction between meaning and force, or, indeed, whether this is the best way of dealing with the matter at all. Many other often very influential forces, however, will, to one degree or another, be peculiar to the particular languages and 'language games' to which they attach. Their nature may in principle be explained in other terms; but to explain is not to reproduce. Literature, as we may most appropriately understand the term, involves the exploitation of such forces; science characteristically does not. To the extent, then, that philosophical writing is assimilated to 'other' forms of 'literature', it is bound to vary in its impact and import according to the languages and contexts of its expression; to the extent that it is assimilated to science, it is to be regarded as forming essentially one common body of discourse, and its internal differences as arising from differences in interest and opinion rather than as differences in what it is about. On a Hegelian view, no doubt (in a very broad sense of that term), the essential rationality of philosophical discourse, taken over the whole of its historically evolving diversity, must lie in the way in which it tends always towards the integration of its particular expressions into the overall unity of the reciprocally interlocking dependence of both meanings and forces on each other. It seems to me, however, to be more appropriate to the nature of the case to borrow rather the language of negative dialectics to say that it is the peculiar characteristic of philosophical reflection thus to exist in always potentially unstable tension between the opposite but inseparable poles of the universal and the particular.

Finally, I cannot properly evade the appropriately philosophical question of the status of this very discussion. In so far as I have any privileged authority in the matter, it would seem to me to consist principally of attempted analysis and argument. To that extent it belongs, or so I should hope, to that part or aspect of philosophy that is in principle translatable into and arguable in any other language possessing the necessary conceptual resources. But its argument is also an argument for the thesis according to which explicit argumentation and conclusion never constitute the whole message (or messages) of any text or discourse, be it philosophical or of some other kind; and for the further thesis that there can in principle be no apodeictically conclusive definition of determinate frontiers between that in the overall message which is of philosophical relevance and that which is not. To that extent it may be accounted an argument that tends towards some measure of auto-deconstruction. However, I should also wish to argue that if this move towards auto-deconstruction is allowed to go too far, to escape all control, as it were, it will eventually transform itself into a form of auto-destruction; and this may be represented as an argument for the thesis that there will always remain a central area of philosophical discourse that is to regarded as occupying the same sort of field within whatever the language or culture of its appearance, even though it must always expect to find itself continuous on its outlying margins with areas, which may themselves be largely peculiar to each their own diversely special contexts.

How far my own argument, and the terms in which I have tried to express it, moves itself towards such outlying or marginal areas is, of course, a fair question, but one to which, at the time of writing, I am in principle, as it would seem to me, to be in no proper position to give a proper answer—unless, of course, this is itself to be accounted as one.

A Case for Philosophical Pluralism: The Problem of Intentionality

DERMOT MORAN

In what sense can we speak of pluralism regarding the philosophical traditions or styles crudely characterised as 'Continental' and 'Analytic'? Do these traditions address the *same* philosophical problems in different ways, or pose *different* problems altogether? What, if anything, do these traditions share?

Studying philosophical pluralism means examining each area and each issue separately to avoid unhappy generalisations about traditions, their methods, starting points, and presuppositions. Here I propose examining philosophical pluralism with respect to a single issue: intentionality. In what sense can intentionality serve as a test case for pluralism? Intentionality is in a sense privileged by being located both at the origins of Continental phenomenology and quite centrally in contemporary analytic philosophy of mind. Highlighted in certain strands of both traditions (e.g. Husserl, Searle), it is downplayed or displaced in other strands (e.g. Derrida, Quine). Its historical role and its contemporary locus, then, may be sufficient reasons for examining intentionality as an interesting case of pluralism.

It is no longer credible to do philosophy without attention to the history of philosophy (Dummett, 1993), and analytic philosophy has become more conscious of its historical lineage. The *historical* roots and configurations of the concepts associated with intentionality offer a fruitful way of examining pluralism. Concepts have histories; or, better, concepts *are* their histories. Furthermore, these histories are not autonomous, there is almost always some cross-fertilisation, some shared influences. Our study of pluralism, then, opens with some reflections on the history of the problematic of intentionality.

The Concept of Intentionality

Intentionality is not a unitary phenomenon but rather a complex cluster of issues: the 'aboutness' of our beliefs and desires; the puzzling fact that some at least of our mental states possess semantic content; the 'mark of the mental'. No physical phenomenon, it is claimed, exhibits intentionality. Physical things do not refer beyond themselves, they are not intrinsically 'about' anything else. Acts like striking John take real objects, mental acts like imagining Martians have their objects immanently. Intentionality has been seen as the central identifying feature of all consciousness (e.g. by Husserl), or, minimally and controversially, as describing that whereby one part of the world refers to another part of the world, how one thing can carry information about another (Dretske, 1981). Not all these views can be reconciled.

Continental philosophy (Husserl, Heidegger, Sartre, Merleau-Ponty) saw intentionality as a fundamental feature of human consciousness, a *phenomenon* requiring description. The aim was to *describe* the phenomenon by peeling away the network of everyday and metaphysical presuppositions which disguise or distort it.

Absent from early twentieth-century analytic philosophy, intentionality emerges as a problem only with the work of Chisholm (1956; 1957; 1958), Anscombe (1958; 1968) and Sellars. In their accounts of intentionality, analytic philosophers perform a classical analytical manoeuvre: shifting from examining consciousness and its objects directly to the analysing the grammar and logic of *sentences* involving intentions (Chisholm's 'sentences about believing', 'intentional idioms'). Analytic philosophers (excepting Searle and Dretske) make a characteristic methodological decision to analyse *talk* about intentional phenomena rather that looking directly at intentional phenomena themselves.

For recent, avowedly naturalistic, analytic philosophy, intentionality stands as a challenge to the programme of scientific reduction. Intentionality is a phenomenon to be brought under scientific *explanation*, rather than characterised in its own terms (this, analytic philosophers believe, Brentano already adequately achieved). The problem is: given materialism, how can there be intentionality (Haugeland, 1990)?

Analytic philosophers reject post-Brentanian Continental discussions of intentionality as embedded in an alien metaphysical outlook, incorporating idealistic presuppositions, and involving the postulation of mysterious entities (Meinongian non-existent objects) or mysterious mental powers ('noetic rays'). Alternatively, the Continental tradition is simply ignored.

Different terminological traditions have evolved, each side accusing the other of jargon. Much of the disparagement can be dispelled by carefully situating the terminology in its tradition and seeing the parallels. As there is no neutral metalanguage, a pluralist discussion of intentionality must allow that technical vocabularies emerge within overall conceptual schemes. Nevertheless, among some recent philosophers, a shift can be detected away from purely linguistic, propositional formulations to the terminology of psychological and mental states, recognising pre-linguistic or non-linguistic intentional acts, e.g. perception.

There is remarkable convergence regarding intentionality's historical lineage. Analytic and Continental philosophers agree that Franz Brentano is the source of modern discussions of intentionality. The divergence between traditions arises after Brentano. Brentano's significance for analytic philosophy is that he offered a criterion for recognising the mental domain and sharply distinguishing it from the physical. Thus Chisholm sees Brentano as putting intentionality forward as *the* criterion of the mental: All and only mental phenomena are intentional. If intentionality is irreducible, how can physicalism and materialism explain the mental? Analytic philosophers begin from Chisholm's formulations and rarely go behind Chisholm to Brentano's own text.

Continental philosophy, on the other hand, looks back to Husserl as founder of a method for exploring the essential structures of consciousness. Husserl's initial and abiding problem is how objectivity arises from subjectivity, i.e. how objective, timeless truths (e.g. ideal mathematical truths) arise from within transient, subjective, psychological states. To explain this he initially drew on Brentano but soon criticised him.

Brentano's Classification of Physical and Psychical Phenomena

Brentano never advanced the thesis that intentionality is the mark of the mental, meaning the *ontological* claim that reality is divided into two domains—the mental and the physical. Brentano (1973) sought to delimit a new science: empirical, *descriptive psychology* (later *descriptive phenomenology*).[1] 'My psychological standpoint in empirical; experience alone is my teacher' (ibid. p. xv). Against those who saw psychology as the study of psychophysical laws, Brentano maintained that description precedes causal explanation. Traditionally, psychology studied the soul as 'the substantial bearer of presentations' (ibid. p. 5). Brentano wishes to study just presen-

[1] The first edition was published in 1874 in two books, with three other books to follow. The Foreword to the 1874 Edition (p. xv) also promised a Sixth Book on 'the relationship between mind and body'. Only some of the projected books were actually completed, though not in that precise form. The second edition of *Psychology* (1924) produced by Oskar Kraus contains these as additional essays and notes.

tations (*Vorstellungen*), appearances (*Erscheinungen*), phenomena (*Phänomene*).

For Brentano, everything psychological either is a presentation (*Vorstellung*) or is founded on a presentation. I *hear* a tone, I *judge* it is a musical note, and I *experience pleasure* at the sound. The judgement and the pleasure are based on the presentation of the tone. Moreover Brentano is interested in the presentative act not the object of the act.

Brentano distinguishes the appearances of consciousness into two kinds:

> All the data (*Erscheinungen*) of our consciousness are divided into two great classes—the class of physical and the class of mental phenomena. (Ibid., p. 77)

Brentano denies that the physical and psychological sciences divide the entire field of science between them. The study of psychological facts overlaps the empirical sciences (ibid., p. 6). Furthermore, physical events can have mental effects and vice-versa. According to Brentano, physical sciences study specifically the causal relations ('forces') between real objects and our sense organs (ibid., pp. 98–99). The physical sciences deal with phenomena that present themselves in sensation alone, whereas the domain of mental phenomena include items that present themselves in imagination and other psychological modes. Our knowledge of physical phenomena is always fallible. We infer the existence and nature of these physical objects whereas we are directly and infallibly acquainted with our own experiences. Physical phenomena are of interest to psychology only in so far as they provide the content for mental acts (ibid., p. 100). Brentano, then, is scarcely concerned with classifying the nature of the physical at all. Psychology, in the first instance, studies the data of apodictic, self-conscious acts, the domain of inner perception. Brentano's invocation of the traditional distinction between external and inner perception is crucial. We *know* our inner mental perceptions infallibly and apodictically. The phenomena of inner perception (*innere Wahrnehmung*) are given in a manner which made them self-transparent or self-conscious, whereas we can only *theorise* about physical phenomena:

> We have no experience of that which truly exists, in and of itself, and that which we do experience is not true. The truth of physical phenomena is, as they say, only a relative truth. (Ibid. p. 19).

'Our mental phenomena are the things which are most our own' (ibid., p. 20). They are as they appear to be.

Brentano's classification of mental and physical phenomena is riddled with ambiguities. For example, Brentano sometimes uses the term 'phenomena' simply for the manifest facts that present themselves, e.g. the phenomena of magnetism or the 'inorganic phenomena' of chemistry (ibid. p. 50). Sometimes, however, the term 'phenomena' is used to refer to presentations as appearances in consciousness, the manifest phenomenological aspect of experience.

His distinction between physical and psychical phenomena is best approached through the traditional distinction between outer perception and inner perception. The psychological domain consists of *acts* which themselves can be made the direct objects of other psychic acts in inner perception (*innere Wahrnehmung*). One cannot be wrong about one's immediate, inner experience of hearing, or seeming to be hearing, having hearing presentations. Psychical phenomena always have what Brentano calls 'real existence' (*eine wirkliche Existenz*), indubitable self-givenness. 'Physical' phenomena are the contents of mental acts—tones I hear, colours I see, images—and have only 'a phenomenal and intentional existence' (ibid., p. 92). This reverses normal philosophical usage, whereby primarily the physical has real existence. Brentano even states that 'physical phenomena can only exist phenomenally' (ibid., p. 92); 'we deny to physical phenomena any existence other than intentional existence' (ibid., p. 94). Our knowledge of them is always partial and fallible. Brentano withholds judgement as to whether physical phenomena (colours, sounds) have real, extra-perceptual existence. Spatio-temporal objects as such are not experienced directly. They are posits, theoretical constructs located in a world which 'resembles' or is 'similar to' one which has three spatial dimensions and flows in one direction in time (ibid. p. 100). Physical *objects* inhabit scientific theory; Physical *phenomena* are the manifest, phenomenal, immediate 'objects' of sensory awareness:

> Examples of physical phenomena ... are a colour, a figure, a landscape which I see, a chord which I hear, warmth, cold, odour which I sense; as well as similar images which appear in the imagination. (Ibid. pp. 79–80).

Sense qualities, imaginings, all are 'physical phenomena'. Brentano fluctuates between referring to physical phenomena and real physical things (the landscape?). His terminology is broad: *Gegenstand*, *Objekt*, *Realität*, *ein Reales* all refer to the objective domain in a complex of different senses. The texts are ambiguous and Brentano's views shifted continuously. Continental philosophers highlight Brentano's background metaphysical assumptions; analytic philosophers generally ignore the philosophical context of 'Brentano's thesis'. This means that Brentano's confusions of intentional content, object and real thing, continue to haunt contemporary discussion.

Brentano is *not* offering an ontological distinction which divides the physical from the non-physical so as to cut nature at the joints. Contemporary physicalists who cite Brentano's thesis as implying this are simply mistaken. Brentano (like Husserl) leaves entirely open the question whether intentional phenomena ultimately have a physical substratum. He acknowledges that physiological processes are similar in type to chemical and physical processes (except more complex), but rejects as crude any suggestion that mental phenomena can be constructed out of, for example, physiological data of the nervous system (ibid. p. 52). Mental phenomena must first be understood by being described in their own phenomenological terms. Brentano's real aim is to distinguish the 'phenomenological' components within the psychological event, namely the act and its correlative object.

Brentano considers a number of possible criteria for distinguishing mental from physical phenomena but arrives finally at intentionality as the key factor:

> Every mental phenomenon is characterized by what the Scholastics of the Middle Ages called the intentional (or mental) inexistence of an object, and what we might call, though not wholly unambiguously, reference to a content, direction towards an object (which is not here to be understood as meaning a thing) or immanent objectivity. Every mental phenomenon includes something as object within itself, although they do not all do so in the same way. In presentation something is presented, in judgment something is affirmed or denied, in love loved, in hate hated, in desire desired and so on. (Ibid., p.88)

In this paragraph a number of different and possibly conflicting formulations feature:

- the notion of mental inexistence (*intentionale, mentale Inexistenz*)
- relatedness to a content (*die Beziehung auf einen Inhalt*)
- directedness to an object (*die Richtung auf ein Objekt*)
- immanent objectivity (*die immanente Gegenständlichkeit*)

It is not clear how Brentano thought of these characterisations.

Are they different ways of saying the same thing? Is each one a separate but sufficient condition for intentionality, none being necessary in itself? Or are they taken together necessary and sufficient conditions of intentionality? Brentano's characterisations have been criticised for veering between the ontological and the semantic. Chisholm, dissatisfied with Brentano's criteria, offers a number of reformulations. Husserl and Heidegger follow Twardowski in criticising Brentano for failing to keep the notions of *content* and *object* distinct. What is asserted is not the same as the object referred to. Brentano's notion of content is unclear, indeed he acknowledges the ambiguity of the term. Does content include both the immanent, private, subjective, psychological part of the act (e.g. the sensation, aspect or mode of presentation) and also the propositional or semantic content? Husserl distinguished between the real and ideal contents of the act. Dummett (1990, p. 84) maintains that 'content' for Brentano meant 'propositional content' as in Frege, but Husserl's and Heidegger's criticisms that Brentano failed to recognise that objects are given under aspects, under a description, suggest that 'content' may cover a whole series of items in Brentano's account (including mode of presentation, sensations, etc.). Brentano's phrase the 'intentional inexistence of the object' appears to posit a new species of non-existent objects immanent in consciousness. This was criticised widely. After 1905, Brentano sought to avoid immanentism. In the 1911 Foreword to the Second Edition of *Psychology*, he stated: 'I am no longer of the opinion that mental relation can have something other than a thing as its object' (Brentano, 1973, p. xix), meaning thereby that he rules out all but existent objects. The later Brentano endorses a realism whereby the intentional act refers to the real thing possessing real existence or else does not refer at all.

When I promise to marry someone, Brentano says, it is a real person that I promise to marry and not an intentional object. Similarly, Brentano (1966, p. 78) says that when one thinks about a horse, it is an actual horse one is thinking about and not the 'thought about horse'. But even here Brentano's terminology remained imprecise, the term 'object' (*Objekt*) is ambiguous between the direct content of the act and the external object:

> It has never been my view that the *immanent* object is identical with the '*object of thought*' (*vorgestelltes Objekt*). What we think about is the object or thing and not the 'object of thought'. (Brentano, 1966, p. 77)

Brentano's mature view of the intentional relation is *adverbial* (Bell, 1990), what Scholastics called the *modus essendi* view. Irreal entities do not exist, they are modifications of the intending mind. The Scholastics understood inexistence (*in-esse*) as the manner a quality inheres in a substance. A non-existent intentional object is really a modification of the subject and need not exist at all in any sense (Aquila, 1977, p. 2). Similarly, the object of the act is transcendent but may be ideal (ibid. p. 13).

Brentano's account of the intentional relation remains unsatisfying. What is the nature of this supposedly irreducible intentional relation? Brentano's account of relation has also been criticised (Chisholm, 1958; Aquila, 1977). Chisholm (1957, pp. 169-70) asks what relation holds between two things when one of them need not exist? Brentano (1973, p. 272) himself rejects the notion of the intentional relation as something that arises when two really existing things are put together, e.g. as spatial distance arises between two objects. Brentano (ibid.) himself dropped relation in favour of something 'relation-like' (*Relativliches*), a property. It is a relation which makes one of the relata an object, something over and against a subject. Husserl and Heidegger criticise the relational account of intentionality. It is not a relation between two things, i.e. a subject and a physical thing (Heidegger, 1982, p. 60), or between a mental act and its own immanent content (ibid. p. 61). Intentionality is not a relation at all, for Heidegger (1985), it is that feature whereby we are already out in the world not a *relation* with the world.

Brentano's ambiguities concerning the intentional relation and object haunt the later tradition. Analytic and Continental discussions of intentionality perpetuate many of the ambiguities and false promises of Brentano's original insight. To see this, we need to sketch the *Wirkungsgeschichte* of 'Brentano's thesis'.

Husserl, Heidegger and the Continental Tradition of Intentionality

Husserl rejects Brentano's account of the structure of the act, the intentional relation, and the intentional object, while retaining the concept of *descriptive phenomenology*. Husserl makes intentionality central to consciousness, but criticises Brentano for ignoring the fact that different kinds of acts have different essential structures. Brentano's division of mental acts into presentations, judgements and phenomena of love and hate is rejected by Husserl (1970, p. 554) who recognises a complex series of acts with different intentional structures, some embedded in and modified by other acts. To *see* the Berlin Schloss, to *judge* about it, to *delight* in its architectural beauty, to *cherish the wish* that one could do so, are distinct experiences with distinct modes of intention (ibid. pp. 559–60), characterisable in different phenomenological terms. One act can itself become the object of another act (I can *remember thinking* X). Acts can be complex wholes, not divisible into different component acts (ibid. p. 574). Husserlian intentional acts have essential structures which open out towards each other, allowing intrinsic possibilities; indeed, the essence of the act can be conceived of as a structure of possibilities.

Husserl rejects Brentano's 'intentional inexistence of the object':

> The 'immanent', 'mental object' is not therefore part of the descriptive or real make-up (*Bestand*) of the experience, it is in truth not really immanent or mental. But it also does not exist extramentally, it does not exist at all (ibid., pp. 558–59).

Husserl is a direct realist about the object intended in perception. I see the object and not my sensations. Sensations (later called 'hyletic data') accompany and form part of the 'matter' of the act of seeing the real object. Furthermore, each shift of perspective yields a new 'content' to my experience of seeing the box, i.e. I see it from a different angle, in a different light, and so on, but nevertheless, the object—the box—itself remains constant. Sensations and perceptual aspects are a necessary part of my experience of the box but are not what I directly experience. Husserl distinguishes the matter (*Materie*) or the content of the act from the 'act quality' (the act of judging, interrogating—the specific propositional attitude that is being adopted). Different contents can pick out the same object and similarly the same mental content can refer to different objects in different acts. Husserl retains Brentano's distinction between outer and inner perception. There is an *aspectual* moment—what Husserl calls an *Abschattung*, an adumbration or profile. A physical thing is always experienced aspectually in profiles. Inner experiences are given absolutely and apodictically and not onesidedly in profiles: 'A mental process of feeling is not adumbrated' (Husserl, 1983, p. 96). Husserl and Brentano remain Cartesian in this respect.

In writings (1967, 1983, 1989) after the *Logical Investigations* Husserl develops a new noetic-noematic structure for intentional acts. The 'noema' (literally: the meant) is the *object as intended* and is part of the structure of the intentional act, graspable only in a special act of attention. It encapsulates the possibilities that accrue to an object and determines reference to the object (as in Frege). The sameness of the object across different adumbrations is the work of the noema and of the synthesising nature of the noetic acts. Even non-linguistic acts have noemas and hence the noema is an extension of the notion of meaning to all acts. The nature of Husserl's noema has been the subject of much critical debate—especially compared to Frege on sense and reference. Føllesdal see the noema as an abstract entity—a meaning—and not an object as such. Others (Sokolowski, 1984) see the noema as an *aspect* of the object, the object as it presents itself in the act. This aspect can be seen either as a real dimension of the object, or as something abstract that indicates the object. Husserl's views have importance for recent discussions of mental content. Føllesdal (1969, 1990, 1993, 1994), Mohanty (1964, 1972, 1981, 1982), Dummett (1990), and Dreyfus and Hall (1982) all see Husserl as offering an alternative and indeed more complex structure than Frege's *Sinn* and *Bedeutung*.

Heidegger criticises both Husserl and Brentano for remaining imprisoned in a Cartesian standpoint. For Heidegger, intentionality is not the problem of the relation between the isolated subject and transcendent objects in the world. This misreads the true phenomenology of our lived experiences. We encounter objects in pragmatic engagements or comportments (*Verhaltene*) with the environment. It is only because I encounter something environmentally and pre-conceptually that I am later able to make it the focus of theoretical objectification, turning an environmental thing (*Umweltding*) into a natural thing (*Naturding*). e.g. 'flowers' are given as gifts, says Heidegger (1985, p. 37), whereas 'plants' are the domain of botany. Brentano and Husserl wrongly privileged theoretical activities over lived engagements. Husserl had become preoccupied with method for gaining access to the transcendental sphere of the *a priori* structures of consciousness. Heidegger moves more towards the intersubjective, pragmatic domain of linguistic behaviour and its interpretation. Heidegger's mature work abandons intentionality altogether, in favour of the nature of our dwelling in the linguistic and significative domain (being-in-the-world).

In summary, Husserl provides an elaborate, nuanced description of the complex structures of intentional acts. In particular he inserts a noema between the act and its transcendent object. Husserl regarded the reduction as his greatest achievement. After Husserl (e.g. in Merleau-Ponty) there was a growing recognition of the impossibility of reduction. Thus in Continental philosophy of the mid-twentieth century the theme of intentionality gradually gets displaced, receiving a death blow in Derrida's deconstruction.

The Analytic Discussion of Intentionality

Analytic accounts of intentionality are more diversified than Continental, because inspired by a wider range of philosophical intuitions and perspectives. Accounts range from those which see intentionality as irreducible (Searle, 1983), to instrumentalist intentional stance accounts (Dennett, 1987), to reductionist accounts inspired by information theory (Dretske, 1981), to evolutionary and biologically based accounts (Millikan, 1984), to eliminationist programmes (Churchland, 1981, 1984; Stich, 1983), to interpretationist accounts (Putnam, 1991). There are realists, irrealists, internalists, externalists.

Analytic commentators start from Chisholm's reconstruction of Brentano. Chisholm calls attention to peculiar logical features of sentences employing intentional idioms. He argue that sentences expressing psychological states exhibit intensionality (chiefly: failure of existential generalisation, and failure of substitution of identicals, referential opacity). For Chisholm, this raises a challenge for the naturalistic explanation of the mind. Unfortunately, as Chisholm himself and others realised (Lycan, 1969; O'Connor, 1967), these intensional characteristics of sentences do not pick out all and only *psychological* states (or sentences embodying intentional verbs). Many non-psychological verbs observe intensionality, e.g., verbs expressing tense ('Mary Smith will become Mrs Jones'), modal verbs, verbs expressing relations, and verbs such as 'I owe John ten pounds'. Chisholm's redeployment of Brentano does not succeed in providing criteria for picking out the mental. Yet analytic commentators continue to see Brentano's thesis as distinguishing two different orders—the mental and the physical and see the challenge as incorporating mental events into a naturalistic account of the world. Thus while Dennett and Searle disagree, they share many of the same assumptions.

Daniel Dennett (1969) begins with Chisholm's formulation of Brentano's challenge. Dennett dissolves Chisholm's problem by embracing naturalism while allowing intentionality as a pragmatic, explanatory stance. Behaviour is explained by attributing beliefs and desires *as if* the behaviour were rational. To say the cat *saw* the mouse is a successful way of making intelligible the behaviour and predicting its outcome. For Dennett the intentional stance is immensely powerful and indispensable and, in that sense, irreducible. Nevertheless, intentionally-construed behaviour is actually produced by innumerable, non-intentional events going on at the physical level. In a sense, the intentional supervenes on the physical. Behaviour at the macroscopic level is best predicted intentionally because most intentional systems approximate to rationality. Nevertheless, at the microscopic level, events obey the laws of physics. There is no mystery or threat posed by allowing intentionality in explanation. It does not introduce new ghostly entities with magical powers. It is an ontologically neutral *stance*, an indispensable mode of explanation for humans (e.g. in law, economics, etc.). To an extent then Dennett agrees with eliminationists like Paul Churchland, and to an extent he agrees with non-reductionists like Searle. He denies he is strictly an *instrumentalist* in the ascription of mental states. Rather he is more like a pan-psychist, there is nothing mysterious about minds, because everything, more or less usefully, can be described in mentalist terms. The progress from non-mental to mental is a matter of complexity not a difference in kind. There is no *underived* intentionality, our intentionality is derived as a late and complex product of evolutionary forces.

Searle, too, seeks to naturalise intentionality ('biological naturalism') but, *contra* Dennett, Searle asserts the irreducibility of intrinsic intentional states. Searle (1992) attacks materialist and behaviourist attempts to explain away the mental as caught in a Cartesian 'conceptual dualism'. Intentionality is a real property of minds, albeit physically based: 'mental phenomena are caused by neurophysiological processes in the brain and are themselves features of the brain' (ibid. p. 1). In this sense, he agrees with Dennett that the basic processes are physical and that many of the macrophenomena are explicable in terms of the microphenomena (ibid. p. 87). But there are genuine 'higher-order' properties not found at the lower levels (e.g. water is a fluid due to molecular behaviour, no molecule itself has fluid properties). Mental properties causally supervene on physical properties (Searle and Dennett agree). Searle sees no reason to hold the mental cannot also be physical. Consciousness, for Searle, is an *emergent higher-level* property of the brain.

Searle's account of intentional states (Searle,1983), using strategies drawn from the study of speech acts whereby intentional states consist of representative content in a psychological mode, is an analytic version of Husserl's account. Like Husserl, Searle distinguishes between real objects in the world, and the presentative contents of our psychological modes. Both Husserl and Searle are realists: When I think of President Carter, I am thinking of the real person and not some intentionally inexistent object. Like Husserl too, different kinds of intentional states (perceiving, imagining, remembering, etc.) represent their conditions of satisfaction in different ways. Searle, like Husserl, recognises that an intentional state always takes place against a Background of non-intentional practices and in a Network of other states.

Continental Versus Analytic—The Case for Pluralism

Having sketched -very broadly—the Continental and Analytic discussions on intentionality, what are the lessons for pluralism? Pluralism consists in tolerating different approaches while seeking a common answer to at least some shared problems. Pluralism in philosophy cannot mean abandoning the search for truth in favour of peaceful co-existence. It is precisely the acceptance of the project of seeking the truth (even if disagreeing about the universality of truth across different forms of life) that allows philosophical projects to be compared.

The history of intentionality suggests the possibility of convergence of traditions. Husserl complicates Brentano's picture while seeking to develop a science of subjectivity. Heidegger criticises the unexamined Cartesian metaphysical assumptions underlying this project. Analytic philosophers harden Brentano's' original classification into a distinction between two ontological realms—the mental and the physical, and seek to treat the intentional objectively. Searle challenges the broadly Cartesian metaphysical assumptions underlying this orthodoxy. There is considerable suspicion of Cartesiansism in both accounts. The whole subject–object account needs to be radically rethought and here there is a coming together of traditions.

Increasingly, there is evidence of willingness to explore the other tradition's resources, e.g. Dummett's (1990) comparison of Frege and Husserl. Just as Chisholm revived Brentano for analytic philosophy, so Føllesdal translates Husserl's account of the noema into terms comprehensible to an analytic audience, leading to a rethinking of Frege's account of sense and reference.

On both sides, too, there are figures closer to the other side than to their own. Searle's defence of irreducible, intrinsic pre-linguistic intentionality parallels Husserl; his rejection of the unconscious mirrors Brentano's and Sartre's views. Dreyfus (1995) has championed Heidegger's externalist account of intentionality against both Husserl's and Searle's internalism. Heidegger and Putnam both challenge internal representationalist accounts of consciousness (as given in Fodor, 1981). Fodor accepts (partially flippantly) Heideggerian Dasein; Stich acknowledges parallels between his position and Derrida's deconstruction.

On the other hand, considering intentionality is the founding concept of Continental phenomenology, it is surprising how little discussion of the theme occurs in recent Continental publications (except in Husserl exegesis). Since Merleau-Ponty, there is no Continental support for behaviourism or for scientific reductionism or materialism. Continental philosophy is inherently anti-reductionist (though it shows no great knowledge of different concepts of scientific reduction) and is not stirred by the naturalist programme. Continental philosophers seem baffled by analytic discussions of mental causation, supervenience, epiphenomenalism and qualia. Yet they have much to gain from analytic discussions of these problems, if only to define precisely how the Continental tradition stands in relation to them and to redress that tradition's anti-science bias. The recently formed European Society for Analytic Philosophy and the activities of the CREA philosophers in Paris may soon render the convenient labels of 'Analytic' and 'Continental' useless for all practical purposes. This in itself would be a step forward for genuine pluralism by forcing a rethink of conceptual boundaries.

In intentionality, each side has its own best supporting cases. Practical activities such as playing sports support the account of intentional behaviour which avoids positing intentional contents or noemata at all. On the other hand, daydreaming, hallucinating and other private experiences seem best treated by internalist accounts of the intentional object. Philosophy of mind, like moral philosophy, must begin by respecting the full complexity of the phenomena. Genuine pluralism is an openness to consider the best cases of the opponent and allows that opponent to explain her case in her own terms. Both sides can benefit by critical scrutiny of Brentano's classification and its subsequent history. Our case study of intentionality gives some hope for the success of such philosophical pluralism.[2]

[2] I am grateful to Daniel Dennett, Alan Montefiore and William Lyons for comments on earlier drafts of this paper and to Hubert L. Dreyfus, Kevin Mulligan and Richard Kearney for discussion of the issues.

William James, 'A Certain Blindness' and an Uncertain Pluralism

ANTHONY SKILLEN

'Pluralism' may be an ambiguous term. But it is not the multitude of the word's meanings but the multitude of sorts of thing that 'pluralists' might be claiming to be not-single-but-plural that generates unclarity about what any 'pluralist' position amounts to. Take ethics: a 'pluralist' might be maintaining, as against say an ethical hedonist of a Benthamite sort, that there is more than one sort of thing 'good in itself'. Another 'pluralist' might maintain that there is more than one sort of life that counts as a 'good way of life'. Or that not all moral duties are forms of the duty to be truthful. Or that there is more than one framework in terms of which experiences, actions or lives can properly be assessed. There is a problem in understanding what it is that is supposed to be counted: one-or-many of what? While the value today of William James's popular essays in what we might now call 'value pluralism' far exceeds their role in illustrating this difficulty, they do exemplify it. James of course described himself as a 'pluralist'; he was on the flagship of that movement. But just to what extent and in what respects remains unclear.

Richard Rorty (1989, p. 38) has brought to contemporary attention James' 'On a Certain Blindness in Human Beings' (in James, 1917a, pp. 229ff). While this essay, to which James himself attached importance as an expression of the 'pluralistic or individualistic philosophy', was given the keynote place in C. M. Bakewell's 1917 selection of James's philosophical papers (James, 1917b), it was delivered as the first of a pair of addresses (to women students), in 1896. And so it is appropriate to trace his argument through both 'A Certain Blindness' and 'What Makes a Life Significant'. This task is not easy. James's complexity and sense of diversity defy even his own attempts at summary. But there are also substantial obscurities in James's 'line', expressed in apparently inconsistent formulations and unacknowledged changes of direction, that go beyond dialectical and rhetorical shifts of emphasis.

The 'blindness' James initially diagnoses is that which is the consequence of humans' 'practical' engulfment in their own lives, such that the lives of others appear empty and beneath due respect or appreciation. Having sought partially to open our eyes to the richness there may be in others' lives, pursuits and passions, James moves on in his second lecture to seek principles of 'significance', 'value', 'worth'. His line, therefore, is not in a clear sense 'relativistic', for he often wants to insist on 'truths', 'facts', 'realities' in other practices to which 'spectators' are blind ('stupid', 'ignorant', 'unjust'), hence intolerant. Moreover, in the vast 'external' diversity of the 'phenomena' of human involvement, he finds in his second lecture but two 'inner' constituents of significance and worth. In the name of these two criteria he passes judgement on blinkered outlooks and on lives short-measured in significance—even though blinkering is inevitable, and even though there may be more significance in everyday lives than we are prone to acknowledge. James's vision is a generous, not an uncritical one. But what does it amount to?

> The spectator's judgement is sure to miss the root of the matter, and to possess no truth. The subject judged knows a part of the world of reality which the judging spectator fails to see, knows more while the spectator knows less, and wherever there is conflict of opinion and difference of vision; we are bound to believe that the truer side is the side that feels the more, and not the side that feels the less. (James, 1917a, p. 231)

We can see here part of the difficulty to which I alluded at the beginning. James is ascribing to 'us' a monomania that follows from the fact that we are each caught up in our (pre)occupations. Each of us is 'blind' to the vision that is the light in others' eyes; as subjective agents we are deficient spectators of others' subjective agency. To be a 'pluralist' in that way, as James's phrase 'pluralistic or individualistic philosophy' implies, would be to assert the central moral significance of the fact of human individuality—and of the hugely multiple individual 'pebbles on the beach'. On the other hand, James's formulation suggests a different concern: not so much with the number of individuals mutually blind as with the mutual incomprehension and devaluation among different kinds of preoccupation and prioritisation. To be a 'pluralist' in that way, as James's phrase 'conflict of opinion and difference of vision' implies, would be to argue for the central moral significance of the fact that we accord to our lives a validity that occludes the fact that others' visions and valuings are likely to be as well anchored as our own. Pluralism of the first sort would be a counter to Tweedledee's tendency to ignore even Tweedledum's point of view. Pluralism of the second sort would be a counter to

Tweedledee and Tweedledum's shared contempt for Alice's way of seeing and feeling things. James's 'pluralism', as we shall confirm, shuffles between these.

Although James's argument is formulated above in general terms, its burden is carried, through both addresses, in a series of brilliantly lit examples, which expose the dismissive shallowness of the spectator (our prejudicially blind selves) in the face of a richness that, through vivifying description, we are able, as far as a 'spectator' can, to appreciate. Thus we are made to feel, as we look on those with whom we cohabit, that we have been like a dog watching in frustrated stupidity its inert master, who seems 'like a senseless statue', but is in fact immersed in a 'most moving romance' (ibid. p. 230).

James offers a personal paradigm: he had come across 'hideous' hillbilly farms, scarring the heads of valleys in the beautiful North Carolina mountains—an 'ulcer' of stumps, rude cabins, corn, and zig-zag fences—'ugly' squats. Contemplating what seems to him a cultureless life unredeemed by romantic attachment to nature, James was confronted by the locals' pride in their achievement:

> Because to me the clearings spoke of nought but denudation, I thought that to those whose sturdy arms and obedient axes had made them that they could tell no other story. But when *they* looked on the hideous stumps, what they thought of was personal victory. The chips, the girdled trees, and the vile split rails spoke of honest sweat, persistent toil and final reward. The cabin was a warrant of safety for self and wife and babes. In short, the clearing, which to me was a mere ugly picture on the retina, was to them a symbol redolent with moral memories and sang a very paean of duty, struggle and success.
>
> I had been as blind to the peculiar ideality of their conditions as they certainly would also have been to the ideality of mine, had they had a peep at my strange indoor academic ways of life at Cambridge. (Ibid. pp. 233–234)

James generalises:

> Whenever a process of life communicates an eagerness to him who lives it, there the life becomes genuinely significant. (Ibid. p. 234)

What we have so far might seem a sort of 'feeling-tone' criterion of value. This is a tempting interpretation, in the light of James's official Humean dichotomy of 'idea' and 'affect', but especially of the way in which he presents this example. The picture is one where 'the spectator' observes an apparent eyesore. But this phenomenon is connected in the 'agent's' mind with a dense network of cultivating practices, and is hence experienced as having a value lent by those associations. One senses behind James's words, but does not have adequately expressed by him, something more: a revaluing, re-visionary, experience on James's own part—a new appreciation of these farms and the lives that belong to them, a new way of looking at these fences and stumps as part of a mutually appropriate complex; a richer recognition of the ways in which this can be seen as having beauty, as something other than vandalism; as embodying the values of love, care, intelligence, courage, and industrious enterprise. But all that is explicit in James is that if they are 'into it', it's as valuable as anything can be.

In terms of the ambiguity I have already attributed to James, then, we seem to have two sorts of emphasis: one or other individuals' visions screened behind diverse practices, the other on the prejudice that occludes the value in alien practices. 'Individualistic' pluralism says: there is a devoted human being there, whatever you might think of his or her occupation; 'qualitative' pluralism says: there turn out to be values in that occupation whatever you might think of it. 'Individualistic' blindness is a kind of egoistic solipsism; 'qualitative' blindness a kind of egotistical prejudice.

Notwithstanding these ambiguities, we are getting, it seems, a lecture in pragmatism's pluralism, in the need for those caught up in one network of activity to be open-hearted about networks from whose inner personal significance ('ideality') they are necessarily estranged, confined as 'observers' are to their external or 'phenomenal' appearance.

> Our inner secrets must remain for the most part impenetrable by others, for beings as essentially practical as we are are necessarily short of sight. But if we cannot gain much positive insight into one another, cannot we at least use our sense of our own blindness to make us more cautious in going over the dark places? Cannot we escape some of those hideous ancestral intolerances and cruelties and positive reversals of the truth? (Ibid. p. 268)

That James's moral liberalism is part of the metaphysical Pluralism of which he was such a seminal exponent can be seen in the famous 'banquet' metaphor with which he had elsewhere expounded that doctrine. According to this, the infinite complexity of the more-or-less interconnecting processes that constitute the world is such as to reduce description to the status of a beggar at the feast:

> Why may not the world be a sort of republican banquet of this sort, where all the qualities of being respect one another's personal sacredness, yet sit at the common table of space and time?
>
> To me this view seems deeply probable. Things cohere, but the fact of cohesion itself implies but few conditions, and leaves the rest of their qualifications undeterminate. (James, 1897, p. 270)

We are part of this banquet, as well as spectators of it, and so each of us can only know what is presented to us. 'Coldly' you 'snub' me as 'warmly' you attend to her. You savour eagerly what tastes to me a fetid mush. God only knows what's going on under the table. For James the metaphor is as true of our mutual understanding as it is of our understanding of the world at large. The 'practicalities' which confine us disclose to us aspects of things and of each other, and, necessarily restrictive as they are, block off or block out other aspects. If we each recognise this blinkering as our common lot, at the same time crediting that others' involvements are as apt to disclose 'truths' as are our own, we are moved to a sort of melancholy delight in the awareness of lights of other consciousnesses with respect to whose illuminations we must be more-or-less in the dark.

James does not leave things thus. In his second lecture, he sets out to delineate two 'principles to make our tolerances less chaotic' (James, 1917b, p. 268). But it would be a feeble exegesis that moved to discuss these principles without looking at the examples and descriptions through which James moves to his final 'position'. For, as the scare-quotes imply, that position is intended to be no more than an unstable, and at times rhetorical, summary of the illustrations and commentaries he assembles to create 'living awareness' in his listeners. I shall not present or discuss these lengthily-quoted examples in detail, but the overall flavour of them can be conveyed *seriatim*. First, then, the literary illustrations that occupy most of 'A Certain Blindness':

> Robert Louis Stevenson, 'The Lantern Bearers'—
>
> Say that we came, in such a realistic romance on some such business as that of my lantern bearers on the links, and described the boys as very cold, spat upon by flurries of rain, and drearily surrounded, all of which they were; and their talk as silly and indecent, which it certainly was. To the eye of the observer they *are* wet and cold and drearily surrounded; but ask themselves, and they are in the very heaven of a recondite

pleasure, the ground of which is an ill-smelling lantern. (James, 1917a, p. 239)

Josiah Royce—
everywhere the same conscious, burning, wilful life is found ... real as these impulses which even now throb in thine own little selfish heart. (Ibid. p. 242)

De Sénnacour's novel *Obermann*—
I know not what shape, what analogy, what secret relation it was that made me see in this flower a limitless beauty. (Ibid. p. 243)

Wordsworth's *Prelude*—
To every natural form, rock, fruit or flower
Even the loose stones that cover the highway
I gave a moral life. (Ibid. p. 244)

Richard Jeffries 'The Story of my Heart'—
Who could have imagined the whirlwind of passion that was going on in me as I reclined there! (Ibid. p. 247)

Walt Whitman on the Brooklyn Ferry—
And you who shall cross from shore to shore
years hence
are more to me, and more in my meditations, than you might suppose. (Ibid. p. 249)

Benvenuto Cellini, *Vita*—
Oh how much more happy for this present life of mine (in a dungeon) than for all those things remembered! (Ibid. p. 254)

Tolstoy, *War and Peace*—
Later in life he (Peter) always recurred with joy to this month of captivity... (Ibid. p. 255)

R. W. Emerson—
Crossing a bare common ... I have enjoyed a perfect exhilaration. I am glad to the brink of fear. (Ibid. p. 257)

Lotze, *Microcosmus*—A Native American Chieftain quoted:
Blind that they (the white people) are, they lose it all! But we live in the present. (Ibid. p. 259)

W. H. Hudson 'Idle Days in Patagonia'—
All day there would be no sound, not even the rustling of a leaf. (Ibid. p. 262)

The non-blind reader must have noticed something. James had started out reprimanding his own aesthetic soul for its contempt for the rough practicalities of hillbilly life and had generalised from this reprimand to delineate a universal predicament: humans are, as practical beings, intimate with but an aspect of things and blind to the underlying and personal meanings in the practices of others. The matter seemed almost to be one of the unavailability to us of otherwise situated minds—and to them of our minds. But now, instead of a certain blindness in all human beings, we have a blindness in *certain* human beings. Namely, *practical* human beings! James seems to have slipped from 'pragmatist' generality to a critique of the 'practical outlook' and its blindness to a specific vision—the Romantic Vision, now seen as grasping something 'far more deeply interfused' than is available to ordinary people caught up in the petty business of everyday modern life. Instead of 'pluralism' then, we have a valorisation of the sorts of experience that James himself generally inclined to see and to crave as 'religious'. This slide, in fact, occurs virtually in one breath:

> Our deadness towards all but one particular kind of joy would thus be a price we inevitably have to pay for being *practical creatures*. Only in some pitiful dreamer, some philosopher, poet, or romancer, or when the *common practical man* becomes a lover does the hard externality give way ... (Ibid. p. 241)

That James's slide is a sustained one can be seen in the fact that the romantic visions catalogued are contrasted with, in sequence: 'thine own selfish heart', 'neighbours tightly and narrowly intent on their own affairs' (Wordsworth's Lakeland hillbillies?), 'the usual standards of commercial value', 'the distinctions which it takes a hard-working conventional man a lifetime to build up', 'your ordinary Brooklynite or New Yorker leading a life of too much luxury', 'the jaded and unquickened eye'—and so on. And James affirms explicitly the invidiousness of his comparison: the romantic soul, he insists, with its 'responsive sensibilities' and its capacity for mystic rapture has the truth:

> Yet so blind and dead does the clamour of our own practical interests make us to all other things, that it seems almost as if it were necessary to become worthless as a practical being, if one is to hope to attain any breadth of insight into the impersonal world of worths as such, to have any perception of life's meaning on a large objective scale. (Ibid. p. 247)
>
> There is life, and there, a step away, death. There is the only kind of beauty there ever was. (Ibid. p. 253)

So, not only does James shuffle between two sorts of pluralism; he appears, to have slid, towards almost mystical romanticism, away from a pluralist position altogether. But it is one thing for a 'pluralist' to tell his audience that their's is not the only way, truth and light. It is another to pretend to tell them that their's is a blind alley. It is as if James has whispered first in the quivering poet's ear, then in the cauliflower organ of the phlegmatic hillbilly: 'Your life is vain—look at that man over there.'

Such is the romantic burden of the texts-within-the-text. Yet, without apology, James rounds his first lecture off by repeating its 'official' toleration message—that all individuals' perspectives are peculiar, hence both privileged and blinkered at the same time. From a 'meta-perspectival' position then, James has moved to advance, through a succession of paradigms, a particular perspective—before harking back to a multi-perspectivist pluralism. And it is to discipline this 'chaotic' pan-tolerationism that he directs his energies in the second lecture 'What Makes a Life Significant'. (No question mark in the basic edition by the way—*pace* his biographer Bernard P. Brennan (Brennan, 1968, p. 160).)

Whereas the foil to James's list of romantic visionaries had been the dull practical man, it is the pleasant world of Chautauqua, a lakeside summer retreat in New York State at which James had lectured in July 1896, that haunts the quest of 'What Makes a Life Significant'. Let us follow him on his journey; here is Chautauqua:

> Sobriety and industry, intelligence and goodness, orderliness and ideality, prosperity and cheerfulness pervade the air ... You have perpetually running soda water fountains, and daily popular lectures from distinguished men. You have the best of company, and yet no effort. You have no zymotic diseases, no poverty, no crime, no police. You have culture, you have kindness, you have cheapness, you have equality, you have the best fruits of what mankind has fought and bled and striven for under the name of civilization for centuries. You have, in short, a foretaste of what human society might be, were it all in the light, with no suffering and no dark corners. (James, 1917b, p. 270)

Yet, after a week, James emerged from this paradise with a sense of escaping from a nightmare of 'atrocious harmlessness':

> Let me take my chances again in the big outside worldly wilderness with all its sins and sufferings. There are the heights and the depths, the precipices and the steep ideals, the gleams of the

> awful and the intimate; and there is more hope and help a thousand times than in this dead level and quintessence of every mediocrity. (Ibid. pp. 270–271)[1]

—'a self-contradiction and paradox'—utopia as a tedious hell; realised ideals as a lifeless trough. James tries to explain his reaction: Chautauqua was without 'precipitousness', 'strenuousness', 'danger', hence without 'strength', 'sweat', 'struggle' or 'heroism' to 'inspire'. In the train home, James dwells pessimistically on the gentle fairnesses of modern civilization, hankering now, not for the idyllic contemplative romanticism apparently forgotten from 'A Certain Blindness', but for a lost age of romantic action-heroes. Of the generously corrective discussion of the hillbilly life there is no echo regarding the Chautauqua pilgrims. He is snapped out of this melancholy by the sight of some construction workers atop a 'sky-scaling iron construction' in Buffalo.

> And I now perceived by a flash of insight that I had been steeping myself in pure ancestral blindness, and looking at life with the eyes of a remote spectator. Wishing for heroism and the spectacle of human nature on the rack, I had never noticed the great fields of heroism lying around me, I had failed to see it present and alive. ... there it was before me in the daily lives of the labouring classes ... the demand for courage (and 'patient endurance') is incessant; and the supply never fails. (Ibid. pp. 274–275)

Gripped by the insight, James is moved (he reports) to deem this, 'unconscious', 'unexpectant of decoration or recognition', the only genuine virtue; 'these are our soldiers, thought I'—as he is reminded of the 'humble-hearted' and 'dutiful' peasants he had come across in Austria. Pluralism *seems* forgotten.

James (for we are now with him on two sorts of journey) now associates the idea of the unrecognized 'underground' heroism of

[1] James had written in even stronger terms about Chautauqua to his wife. He had been 'meeting minds so earnest and helpless that it takes them half an hour to get from one idea to its immediately adjacent neighbour'—'they lie down on it like a cow on a doormat, so that you can get neither in nor out with them'. After a week of bread-baking and guru-worship he found himself in Buffalo 'glad to get into something less blameless but more admiration-worthy. The flash of a pistol, a dagger, or a devilish eye, anything to break the unlovely level of 10,000 good people—a crime, murder, elopement, anything would do' (*The Letters of William James*, ed. Henry James (William's son), (Boston, Atlantic: Monthly Press, 1920, p. 43). James used to supplement his HArvard and London income by tours giving lectures of the sort we are looking at.

workers and peasants with that of the virtues of 'courage, patience and kindness' that human beings universally value regardless of the 'phenomenal surface' of social position (ibid. p. 278). He muses in a 'levelling spirit' that the 'common inner meaning' to human activity can be seen only by looking *through* the plurality of external appearances. Thus looking, we find that we still lack the sufficient conditions of significance; courage and patience, virtues though they remain, are compatible with a life of blindly compelled drudgery, without pride or responsibility in the work done, 'longing for the signal to quit work and for our wages at the end' (quoting Walter Wykoff's account of the life of an unskilled labourer) (Ibid. p. 286). What is missing from these honest wage-slaves? Not, according to James, the affluent comforts of a Chautauquan existence:

> A man might in truth live like an unskilled labourer, and do the work of one, and yet count as one of the noblest of God's creatures. Quite possibly there were some such persons in the gang that our author describes; but the current of their souls ran underground, and *he* (Wykoff) *is too stooped in the ancestral blindness to understand it*.
>
> If there *were* any such morally exceptional individuals, however, what made them different from the rest? It can only have been this—that their souls worked and endured in obedience to some inner *ideal*, while their comrades were not actuated by anything worthy of that name. These ideals of other lives are *among the secrets that we can almost never penetrate* although something about the man may often tell us when they are there. (Ibid. p. 288)

James speculates on political or religious or ascetic missions and meanings, of which unskilled working life might for exceptional individuals be obscurely expressive. When it is so, we have a life, not just embodying 'virtue', but one inspired by a personal conscious 'ideal'. Only when virtue is so animated do we have the 'fusion' or 'marriage' that constitutes 'significance' of an 'objective' sort. (Ibid. p. 294). Otherwise we have either drudgery or sentimentality. 'Living awareness' of the fact that 'significant lives' can exist all around us, then, brings with it 'tolerance, reverence and love for others'—a sympathetic, imaginative connection across disparate external ways of life. And yet, by implication, the 'unthinking' life of the merely 'practical' 'average' person (whatever their social position) is downgraded!

I have followed what James himself belatedly describes as a journey of 'beating and tacking on my part'. (Ibid. p. 295) The journey ends in a surprising place: a peroration on the 'labour-question'. The class antagonists, James says, are 'blind to the internal significance of the lives of the other half', regarding each other 'as they might regard a set of dangerously gesticulating automata'. Each 'ignores the fact that happiness and unhappiness and significance are a vital mystery' that behind the contrasting externals they may share virtues and ideals in common:

> No outward changes of condition in life can keep the nightingale of its (life's) eternal meanings from singing in all sort of different men's hearts. That is the fact to remember. If we could not only admit it with our lips but really and truly believe it, how our antipathies and dreads of each other would soften down! If the poor and the rich could look at each other in this way, *sub specie aeternitatis*, how gentle would grow their dispute! What tolerance and good humour, what willingness to live and let live would come into the world! (Ibid. p. 301)

Let us return to the question I raised at the beginning concerning the nature of the units that James wanted us to count as plural. Is it to the life-of-the-capitalist (enterprising, clever, patient, as ruthless to self as to others...) that the militant worker is blind, and is the capitalist correlatively as blind to the life-of-the-worker (courageous, enduring, solidary, heroic...)? Have we two, mutually blind (if mutually implicated), ways of life here? Or is it rather that what we have is two or more individuals who, being so socially situated as to focus on certain external aspects of each other (ruthlessness/obstinacy; greed/greed!), are blind to the individual spirit possibly dwelling behind these 'external' phenomena. Is it this blindness that James is most concerned with: to the individual 'vitality' that lies (or may lie) 'mysteriously' behind the diverse masking of ways of life. In other words, is not James's 'unit' the radically individual soul or subject? If this is so, it helps resolve the puzzlement I expressed about James's initiating example of the hillbillies and his apparent lack of revaluation, having accepted that the hillbillies were vibrantly engaged in it, of their mode of living. It also helps make sense of James's invocation of romantic visions which place the individual subject, active or passive, at the centre of value. Here, perhaps, James could be said to have lost the thread that he had himself spun. For the whole point of Stevenson's 'Lantern Bearers' was to remind his readers of the 'personal poetry' almost invisibly stitched into normal persons' (our) lives, however prosaic they may appear to the eye focused 'realistically' on externals. Nor, I believe, did the author of *The Prelude* seek to set himself up as a unique sensibility among 'narrow', 'tight-lipped' neighbours. And, while James, having quoted Whitman, takes him to be revealing his difference from the average suburban ferry commuter, the poet is much more concerned to express a common delight that he shares with the 'crowd' on this twice-daily trip. Romanticism has a democratic thread and one which James himself picks up again (though he appears to bring it from outside; from the sight of the skyscraper workers) when he talks about the poetry that can live in and not just behind the lives of persons themselves incapable of articulating it in memorable words, images or tunes.

It would be tempting to rest content with thus labelling this doctrine 'individualism' and to let it lie among others on the shelf accommodating this category. To do so would be wrong. For I do not think of James as offering his young listeners individualism packaged in rhetoric and poetry. Rather, the rhetoric and poetry are internal to the individualism; and to the pluralism—the attack on 'hideous ancestral cruelties' towards the 'impenetrable' in others. (Ibid. p. 268). James's individualist vitalism expresses, after all, what can come home to us at the death of a person we know and especially of someone we love. It is the sort of individuality. of personal light, that is disclosed to a friend or loving companion—or that a schoolteacher might surprise a parent with by an observation about some manner or quality in a child scarcely appreciated. Here James is surely right to avoid the sociological reductionism of seeing our identity as constituted by our social roles. For, while James's individual is not the vacuity of 'interest' and 'rationality' that some liberals seek to pump up into the contractual structure of our ethical life, nor is his 'self' 'encumbered' in the fashion prescribed by contemporary 'communitarian' philosophy of the MacIntyre–Sandel variety ('we all approach our own circumstances as bearers of a particular social identity. I am someone's son or daughter, someone else's cousin or uncle; I am a citizen of this or that city, a member of this or that guild or profession; I belong to this clan, that tribe, this nation. Hence what is good for me has to be good for one who inhabits these roles' (MacIntyre, 1981, pp. 204–205).) Indeed James goes out of his way to follow Stevenson in hearing the 'nightingale' in inappropriate places, just as he had missed its song in the most propitious circumstances of Chautauqua—where every one was earnestly in role up to the hilt. James is seeking to communicate an 'attitude to a human soul', to remind or apprise his listeners of what that means, and to do so far more truly and effectively by the assembling of examples than by a Millian elaboration of criteria of higher pleasures. In other words, what Stevenson and Wordsworth and James himself draw attention to does not so much 'refute' as 'show up' the antithetical poverties of abstract individualism (especially in its rationalistic or economistic forms) and concrete communitarianism (especially in the statuesque *curriculum vitae* forms exemplified in the above quotation from MacIntyre). Philosophers such as Thomas Nagel (Nagel, 1986) talk about individuals' particular viewpoints. But James's lectures remind us that 'we ought, all of us, to realise each other in this intense, pathetic and important way' (James, 1917a, p. 267).

But would this mutual realisation be a realisation among equals? Now, James certainly does want to say that when our eyes are open we will recognise different levels of value—something missing at Chautauqua that is there among the North Carolina hillbillies, for example. At one stage, as we have seen, he comes up with 'virtue' and 'ideality' as the nuptial couple constituting 'significance'. Elsewhere, he talks about 'zest', 'vitality', 'secret joy', 'reverence'—indeed, he seems to succumb to the temptation to generalise from each example without always noticing that the rich array of illustrations that he gives us upsets each in turn. I suggest James's generalisations be treated as less important than the observations and insights that occasioned them. And then, among other pluralisms, we are left with a 'pluralism' which is more a matter of values disclosed to the free and friendly eye (Arnold's phrase) open to the indefinite diversity of our preoccupations and receptivities. James, it is true, does not offer much guidance here, too concerned as he is to admonish the 'practical' to notice the Stevensonian point that the practical can itself be an obscure form of the poetic. But if this had been an essay on 'multi-culturalism' I think it could have done worse than take its tenor from James' attempt to maintain, as he oversteers then over-corrects, a balance between bigotry and relativism.

Cultural Realism: the ancient philosophical background

J. D. G. EVANS

Pluralism and Aristotle

I understand Pluralism to be the doctrine that, either generally or with reference to some particular area of judgement, there is more than one basic principle. It endorses the possibility that some particular case may arise which will be adjudicated in one way if one principle is applied while another principle points otherwise and to an answer which, at least in practice, is incompatible. Thus in morality, according to pluralism there may be more than one correct answer to the question of which of the decisions available in some particular situation is the best (Kekes, 1993, esp. pp. 9–15; see also the valuable collection of essays Paul, Miller and Paul, 1994).

The fundamental values are incommensurable in their plurality; there is no single scale within which all the competing considerations can be weighed with the result that what is promoted on one side will predominate over what is preferred on the other. The same kind of thing can be said about pluralist conceptions of, for example, logic or indeed of philosophy. Divergent systems of logic will sort arguments into valid and invalid specimens in different ways. Different styles of philosophy will assess the significance of various issues and positions in different measure.

In all such cases someone who adopts a pluralist conception will say that we are not required to operate with a single set of commensurable criteria in order to reach the best conclusion. Instead we are urged to select the most appropriate among the plurality of criteria; and to the question of which ones are the most appropriate, there will likely be more than one possible answer. Value pluralists, in particular, deny that there is necessarily a single fundamental scale of values such that different options can be definitively graded in accordance with the varying degrees to which they fulfil these values.

Pluralism can be set beside both realism and relativism as a distinct available option. It stands in contrast with realism in that there is no way to settle which of two alternative actions is to be preferred. No decision procedure is available for a unique ordering of these alternatives. But it also sits in contrast with relativism in holding that there does exist an objective fact of the matter as to which actions are preferable. The relativist view, which asserts the moral facts to rest on some relevant authority rather than what is objectively the case, precisely confuses authority with truth (for further discussion see Kekes, 1993, pp. 13–14 and 31–34. Also relevant is Williams, 1974–5).

Pluralists, in the sense just sketched, sometimes invoke Aristotle as an intellectual ancestor and ally (see MacIntyre, 1988, pp. 109–111, and Sorabji, 1993, pp. 218–219). In a number of areas of philosophy Aristotle's stance can be contrasted with that of philosophers who advocate a single criterion for adjudicating between possibilities. There are several features of Aristotle's work which encourage this interpretation. While he is generally empiricist in his philosophical approach, he also allows room for an alternative transcendent position. Thus in metaphysics, the greater part of his investigation concerns individual perceptible substances —'moderate-sized specimens of dry goods', as Austin has put it (Austin, 1962, p. 8, see also Furth, 1988, pp. 50–54)[1], but room is also left for purely intelligible, unchanging objects such as God. In his analysis of human nature and life, he mainly proceeds on the assumption that the person is an essentially corporeal entity, but he also maintains that not all human life-functions require embodiment and he allows that pure reason might survive the death of the body.[2]

The same duality is to be seen in his work on ethics and politics. On the one hand, there is the empirical Aristotle who takes human nature and society as they are, in all their diversity and complexity; but on the other hand, less frequently but equally prominently, we have the visionary Aristotle who offers an ideal blueprint for all human beings and their social structures. The blueprint greatly simplifies and generalises over the details which are examined in Aristotle's other, more descriptive mode.[3]

There is twofold scope for a diagnosis of pluralism here. First, we have the general contrast between the idealistic simplifier and the realist who registers the complex facts. Secondly, if we concen-

[1] This idea is of immense—but inadequately examined—importance in contemporary ontology.

[2] These observations are intended to encapsulate the hunch that such texts as *De Anima* Γ5, *Metaphysics* Λ7–9, and *Nichomachean Ethics* K7 represent an unusual tendency in Aristotle's philosophy. Despite that, the tendency is not dissonant from its wider setting. See Evans, 1987, pp. 171–173.

[3] The attentive reader could reasonably expect a simple and single account of how to live, individually and socially, from such texts as *Nichomachean Ethics* K7–8, *Politics* B1.

trate on Aristotle's analysis in its second, more empirical manner—and this is the style which occupies most of his time and effort—we can detect pluralism in his willingness to consider a range of factors which cannot readily be accommodated within a single theoretical frame.

More specifically, but also more controversially, Aristotle's ethics of virtue has been held to accommodate a situation in which a person might be good in respect of one parameter—say, generosity in money— but not in another—say, truthfulness (This line of thought is usefully explored by Brown, 1981–2.) There is no single standard for determining whether a person or his actions are good or right; instead, rightness and wrongness are functions of which of these essentially unconnected standards is taken as salient. This seems pluralistic; and so also does the variety of distinct political systems which he commends in different parts of the Politics. In addition to the ideal state which is constructed in Books 7 and 8, we find preference being given to aristocracy, monarchy, and also the more democratic constitution which he calls simply 'constitution'. All of these different structures, from the appropriate point of view, can be defended as providing the best system for ordering social relations.

Although a case can be made along these lines for construing Aristotle as a pluralist—in matters of value and elsewhere in philosophy—I believe that it needs supplementation from another quarter. My aim in this paper is to provide such supplementation, and in doing so to contribute to the understanding both of Aristotle and of pluralism. I call my essay 'Cultural Realism' because I believe that this is the appropriate name for the theoretical position which Aristotle stakes out. I also offer it as an alternative formulation for pluralists who wish to distance themselves, more emphatically than seems to be currently possible, from relativism.

Aristotle's predecessors

At *Nicomachean Ethics* E7 (1134b35–1135a5) Aristotle says: 'Things that are just according to contract and mutual interest are like measures. The measures by which people trade in wine or corn are not everywhere the same; those at which people buy are higher, and those at which they sell are lower. In the same way the non-natural, human parts of justice are not everywhere the same; neither are the political systems. But everywhere there is naturally only one best form of justice.' I want to draw attention to the last sentence.[4] It is likely to strike us as ambiguous; it seems to embody a classic example of ambiguity of scope.

The ambiguity concerns the scope of 'everywhere', 'naturally' and 'one'. Is Aristotle saying that there is a single form of justice which is everywhere naturally the best, or is the claim rather that what is natural everywhere is that one form of justice is the best? The second claim differs from the first, of course, in not requiring that it be one and the same form of justice which is best. I shall argue that the second interpretation, which gives wider scope to 'everywhere' and narrower scope to 'one', is the correct version. But we should not dismiss the first interpretation outright on that account. As I shall try to show, the effect of the third operator—'naturally'—is to reduce the contrast between these two versions.

In the earlier part of the E7 passage Aristotle has emphasised the thoroughly conventional character of the matters which he is discussing. These are practices which are the product of human contrivance; and the reference to measures of goods is surely a reminder of Protagoras's famous relativistic dictum that man is the measure of all things. The remark about what is 'naturally' best at the end of the passage is meant to remind us of the contrast between nature and convention and the debate between realists and relativists which was built on that contrast.

Let me briefly recapitulate the debate. The phenomenon of cultural relativity was first noticed by pre-philosophical geographers and anthropologists in Greece. They observed, first, that human habits were liable to differ in various parts of the world known to them, and secondly that this difference of practice was accompanied by differences in the ways in which such habits were valued (see Guthrie, 1969, pp. 55–63, 164–175, and Ehrenberg, 1968, pp. 329–330).

The intellectual movement from relativity to relativism is philosophical. It was, in the first place, the work of the Sophists; and their ideas provided a background against which Socrates and Plato strongly reacted. The point at issue may be put as follows. Does the existence of different values provide the end or the beginning of discussion? Should we note—or even, welcome and nurture—the diversity of views and values which are actually found between different groups of people? Or should we regard

[4] The interpretation of the second sentence is uncertain. Aristotle is clearly making a point about the conventional and variable character of economic measures; and I believe that he does so by way of an anti-commercial joke.

such diversity as a matter for regret, if it is real, but perhaps also seek to show that it is not real but rather an illusion? Is there—and ought there to be—one culture or many?

The problems here are both theoretical and practical. We want to obtain a more secure grasp of how to analyse the relation between people and the objective world. At the same time we need to establish effective attitudes—and, as necessary, policies—to regulate the ways in which divergent views should be received and should influence the outcome of events.

We may take Protagoras's defense of his profession as representative of sophistic thought about culture.[5] In Plato's Protagoras (318e5–9a2, 328a7–b5) his position is presented in the following words: 'The subject of study is good decision-making—of his own affairs in order to manage his own household as well as possible, and of the affairs of the city in order that he may be as effective as possible at public action and speaking' (318e5–19a2). 'It is the same as regards virtue and all such other matters. If anyone of us is slightly ahead of the rest at being able to help us progress towards virtue, this should be welcomed. I consider myself to be such a person—to be ahead of the rest at helping someone to become fine and good, so that I am worth the fee which I charge' (328a7–b5).

Protagoras here urges how important it is to recognise the variety and complexity of values. People live in a cultural context; and this context should be understood by the politician who seeks to manage people. Protagoras is required to justify his claim to be able to teach civic virtue. His reply is to emphasise the social nature of virtue. As a prerequisite for survival in a society we must both understand and possess virtue to a significant degree. The role of the teacher is to enhance this degree beyond the average norm, rather than to introduce a change of kind into his pupil.

Socrates is deeply opposed to this line of reasoning. His objections focus on the notion of knowledge.[6] Suppose that someone claims to possess some skill for the exercise of his own interest; he

[5] A fuller discussion than is possible here would need to comment explicitly on the somewhat different positions advanced by such figures as Callicles in the *Gorgias* and Thrasymachus in *Republic* 1. But I believe that all the positions against which Socrates reacts share the significant leading feature of underestimating the power of rational enquiry to explore questions concerning value.

[6] The considerations canvassed here seem to me to tell decisively against the influential view that Socrates had a specialised concept of knowledge as something certain and infallible. See Vlastos, 1994, pp. 39–66, and Reeves, 1989, pp. 43–45. If that idea were right, the central role assigned to knowledge in testing claims about value would be untenable.

can then be challenged as to how he is to know what is in his own interest. Any claim about values—about what is good or bad—which fails to incorporate the notion of knowledge, leaves out what is most important. We may put Socrates's question in the following crisp form. Protagoras can teach a person how to do the right thing. But is doing the right thing, the right thing to do? That question cannot even be formulated, let alone receive the affirmative answer it would need, while we remain within the limits of the sophists' science of values. Some sophists appealed to the possession of power as the criterion of what qualifies as knowledge of value. But Socrates will press the question, how do we know that this is the correct criterion?

The Socratic challenge to cultural relativism was developed by the mature Plato into a transcendental metaphysics of mind and meaning. Knowledge of unchanging reality was elevated over opinion about mutable particulars; and knowledge of values was raised to the chief position in philosophical science.[7] Socrates challenged the sophists to show how their values were grounded in knowledge. Plato interpreted this requirement as pointing to the idea that value is the fundamental element in the structure of knowledge. Hence the Form of the Good is the key to the proposal that in order to know anything, you have to know everything.

Plato believed that his monistic theory of value was immune from relativistic objection based on the contrast between nature and convention. The sophists' theories were dependent on a preference for one of these poles over the other; but Plato counters by denying that there is an important polarity here at all. In Plato's ideal society, as in those of the sophists whom Socrates opposes, control and power are exercised by experts. The society which they fashion is, to this extent, a product of contrivance and convention. But the difference is that in his scheme the qualification for expertise is itself controlled by the fidelity with which the contrivance reflects the natural order (*Laws* 888e–890e; *Phaedrus* 270, with its emphasis on the relevance of natural science to artistic skill, is also pertinent). For the sophists, on the other hand, there is scope for the expert to make his own addition to whatever is supplied by nature.

I shall return to these Platonic developments, which have done so much to determine the shape of the subsequent debate between realism and relativism. But first we need to scrutinise more critically the nature of the disagreement between Socrates and the

[7] This is the message of *Republic* 5–7, see esp. 505a, 531–532. The posthumous reports of Plato's lecture on *The Good* indicate that he did not abandon this ideal of knowledge. See Cherniss, 1962, pp.1–3.

sophists, and consider where the philosophical merit lies. In particular, is Socrates justified in his use of the appeal to knowledge, in order to contest the sophists' value relativism?

Consider an apparently analogous case, one which Socrates himself frequently cites. This is the case of medicine and health. It is possible to recommend rules and practices within the context of the assumption that health is a good to be pursued and that medicine is a skill that tends to deliver this good. There might be rival systems, so that different skills would be valued depending on which kind of health they could provide. For example, we could have health achieved through surgery or through homoeopathic methods; and in the face of that distinction in the results, the skills which could deliver them would be differently valued. But whether the simpler or the more complex situation obtains, Socrates can raise the question of why we should value health at all?

The demand behind this Socratic question should be resisted. We have to insist that such a question can only be confronted within some context of values. Otherwise it is hard to see how we could possibly get any purchase on the question. Nothing could serve as a premise for an argument which issued in a conclusion, either way, about the value of health; for the Socratic question would be used to call into question the premises of anyone who sought to mount an argument of this form. Such considerations indicate that the question does not have the rational justification which at first it appears to.

Socratic dialectic is a disciplined and effective way of scrutinising ill-founded claims to expertise, including expertise about values. But Plato came to be aware that the method needed a framework of theory in order to be able to effect positive intellectual advance. Without this, Socratic questioning could achieve no more than the unmasking of inconsistencies; and while this would have the effect of exposing falsehood, it would not put us on the track of truth. Accordingly he devised the metaphysical structure of Forms, with the chief value-concept—the Good—occupying the fundamental position in the system.

Plato's own conception of human nature is notable for the way in which it ignores the social and cultural dimension of human life. As a striking example, consider the famous challenge from Glaucon and Adeimantus to prove that the just life is intrinsically preferable to the unjust one even in the absence of associated rewards including the recognition of its just character (*Republic* 367b–e; see Kirwan, 1965). We can all appreciate the sense in the suggestion that a gap could, in certain circumstances, be opened up between a person's true character and the external circumstances of his life. But it is an unacceptable exaggeration of this possibility, if we maintain that generally and in principle the nature of a person's character has nothing to do with the social surroundings of his life—surroundings which include the reception which society accords to his character. There is an ineliminable social dimension to being a person of a particular moral kind (Williams, 1976; Nussbaum, 1986, pp. 18–21).

Plato's strategy in value enquiry thus comes into question. He makes value reside in essences which are independent of social context. The lesson should be that the person who seeks expertise in living well cannot ignore the social or cultural dimension of human life.

Aristotle's theory

In a number of key respects Aristotle signals his disagreement with Plato's method of analysing human value. He maintains that value cannot coherently be abstracted from the context of human nature; and in his analysis of the operations of the rational person, he emphasises the importance of action, as opposed to the pure exercise of thought. It is a consequence of this change of focus that Aristotle is more aware of the limitation of general rules in guiding conduct, and more alert to the special character of the particular case, than are most other moral philosophers (*Nichomachean Ethics* A3, 1094b14–22; B2, 1104a1–10).

These features of Aristotle's philosophical style are generally well known. Despite this there has been a failure to integrate these insights with those aspects of Aristotle's thought which suggest a more absolutist conception of value. I have argued elsewhere that his general theory should be seen as steering a middle course between extreme realism and extreme relativism (Wisdom, 1965, pp. 148–149; Evans, 1977, pp. 53–68). There is a correct conception of value that transcends the variations between different people and groups; but it is a mistake to infer from this apparent convergence that the differences between the people and groups are not essential to the very notion of such a value.

A notably concrete example of this phenomenon is provided by the concept of Wealth. On the one hand, we have the idea of wealth as something which is possessed or attainable by some people, perhaps, but not necessarily by everyone; indeed it may be the case in some societies that wealth in this sense is possessed by nobody. 'Wealth', in this sense, means roughly 'great wealth'. But this analysis points the way to a second sense in which the word designates that amount of money or possessions which is realisable by each more particular group or even individual person. Thus we speak of so-and-so's wealth, and thereby refer to possessions which may fall far short of wealth in the first sense. The general concept of Wealth needs to accommodate both these features of the world. That is why it is correct to speak both of absolute and relative wealth or poverty, even though these contrasts can easily be dismissed as absurd.

Other concepts which yield insights under this kind of treatment are humour and taste. Some things are (simply) amusing, while others are amusing only to a particular sense of humour. Some people's taste is such that only they have it, whereas other have taste *tout court*: poor taste both is and is not taste, as Kant also recognised (Kant, 1978, sec. 56; see Evans, 1994). In all these cases it would be a mistake to see the issue as a choice between a relativistic and an absolutist construal of the concepts. Instead both aspects need to be kept under consideration; and skill comes in deciding which kind of construal is more appropriate in the particular circumstances.

Aristotle systematically recognises that the central concepts of moral and practical value have this dual form. This is the idea that underpins his habit of emphasising the importance of the differences between the people who are involved in a moral transaction. Such transactions include giving practical advice and lecturing on or writing a book on ethics. When he speaks of progress in ethics, he distinguishes between things that are good simply and things that are good for someone, and offers the following advice about how they should be valued: 'People pray for things that are simply good and pursue them; but they should not. Instead they should pray that what is simply good is good for them too, but they should choose what is good for them' (*Nichomachean Ethics* E1, 1129b3–6).

Here we are given an injunction to have regard to the personal differences among those who pursue the good, even though what they are pursuing exists in a form which makes personal differences irrelevant. Some things are simply good; and this is so without reference to the people involved, not even the people who are affected by these particular items. Yet despite the unqualified goodness of these things, it is wrong for certain people to opt for them.

Aristotle makes notable allusion to the earlier debate about the roles of nature and convention in determining human values. Characteristically, in his own analysis of the nature of justice, he allows a role for both of these strands from earlier thought. There are certain practices which derive their rightness or wrongness from the nature of things; others, by contrast, require a law to impose the particular value on them. He notes that some thinkers saw a conflict between these two ideas about the sources of value, but maintains that this diagnosis depends on a basic error (ibid. E7, 1134b24–33).

The error is to suppose that nature is invariant and immutable. If that view is taken, the variations in human institutions seem to stand in dramatic contrast to the rigid permanence of nature. But the view of nature is wrong. The realm of nature in which humans live and act, is itself dynamic. So the variability which is introduced by the factor of legal institutions does not affect the fundamental facts about values.

So law—or convention—is a natural element in the sphere of human value. If this sounds like an ad hoc squaring of the Sophists' circle, what follows should not. The man-made part of a culture's system of values contains both the written laws and the products of equity (epieikeia). Equity is, of course, for Aristotle a disposition of human character; and as such it is defined by reference to the appropriate type of person—the equitable person. Such a person is marked by his ability to supply the correct insights into the particular case which are missed by the written law (ibid. E10, 1137b11–19). It is inevitable that the law will need such supplementation if there is to be justice. This is because the law is necessarily general; yet what it pronounces upon is a particular case.

The emphasis here on exceptions to the general rule is a recurring theme in Aristotle's ethical theory. It is prominent in the introduction to the work, when he distinguishes the unscientific character of practical philosophy from the simple precision of the sciences; this difference arises from the greater complexity of the material which practical thought has to handle. In the same vein he notes the special nature of the intellectual skill which is needed for practical decision-making. This skill is different from the various intellectual virtues —wisdom, scientific knowledge—which are manifested in the grasp of the unchanging truths of nature. Practical sense—phronesis—shows itself in sensitivity to the particular circumstances which can provide the grounds for exceptions to general rules.

Equitable judgement, then, is a necessary supplement to the generality of the written law; its function is to guarantee that when that law is applied, we do not achieve injustice rather than justice. But there is a corollary to this emphasis on the variability of the particular case. This is that the generalisations of the conventional law also have their part to play in establishing and maintaining justice. Aristotle can so easily be congratulated on his attention to the particular, that we lose sight of what is equally important, his respect for the general.[8]

The conventional law is no impediment to justice but instead one of its principal instruments. With this thought Aristotle tries to lay to rest the old conflict between nature and convention. The things in the world which form the subject-matter of judgements about value are themselves variable. We may speak about their nature, but we should not be misled by this talk into supposing that this nature is determinate. On the other hand, the value which is embedded in the law is not an arbitrary matter, and this for two reasons. First, it is possible to grade parts of any given system of law by reference to their success in establishing the justice of nature; there are better and worse possibilities, and in each culture there is one that is best. Secondly, the general law will tolerate supplementation by the judgements of equity. This extra factor enables it to escape rigidity, as it must do if it is to cope in a just way with complex facts.

With these provisions Aristotle makes the cultural environment of law and equity a crucial surrounding for the realisation of value. But the value which can thus be realised, is as natural as any culture-independent form that Plato might propose.

Cultural Realism

I want finally to explain how Aristotle's theory is indeed a form of pluralism, to which I give the name of 'cultural realism'. In the earlier Greek debate about the relative significance of nature and convention, the options explored were a form of cultural relativism, on the one hand, and on the other, a form of realism which devalued the significance of culture. By contrast Aristotle's account combines a recognition of the importance of cultural variation, with a commitment to the significance of what is natural. Part of his insight is into the variability which naturally characterises human affairs; and part of it consists in a refusal to accept the relativist idea that convention can ultimately determine what should be done.

[8] Although Aristotle distinguishes practical and theoretical rationality, he also marks very extensive similarities between the two. A good example is the account of the practical syllogism, *De Motu Animalium* 7, 701a8–25. So there is no reason not to apply the ideas of Metaphysics M10, 1086b32–7, *Posterior Analytics* A24, about the importance of generalisation, to practical reason as well.

'Cultural relativism' has an easy ring of familiarity, while 'cultural realism' may seem something of an oxymoron. This is because we assume too readily that if we refer to cultural variation to explain differences in values, the elements in the resulting plurality of values are incommensurable. This is indeed a key thesis of contemporary pluralists, and it seems hard to reconcile with value realism. One might say: if the cultures are real, the values are not (see also Kekes, 1993, pp. 127–132).

But Aristotle's theory is a realism which embraces both cultures and values. There are objective facts about how decisions affecting individuals and societies should be taken; these matters can be ordered better or worse (for examples of such grading in Aristotle see *Nichomachean Ethics* H6, *Politics* Δ2, 1289a38–b5). An essential element in the real values thus construed is the cultural context. How a person ought to act—really, and not just as an imposition of external authority—is a function of the values which prevail in the local culture, among other factors. Therefore cultural facts form part of the realism; and cultural realism is not the oxymoron which at first it appears to be.

The particular idiom in which Aristotle's predecessors posed the issue of the significance of culture as a feature of the world, was the contrast between convention and nature. We have examined the stages through which debate about that contrast proceeded. Aristotle resolves the earlier theoretical conflicts over nature and convention, by reconciling these two elements in the sphere of social value. Laws are conventional and variable. But their application must be supplemented by judgement of the equitable person; and there is no cultural relativity in the nature of this person's disposition.

In the light of this theory we are better placed to understand the words of *Nicomachean Ethics* E7 (1134b35–1135a5): 'Everywhere there is naturally only one best form of justice'. These words do indeed express a pluralist interpretation of the nature of justice, but one with a particular character. Everywhere justice has some definite nature, without it being necessary that this nature be everywhere the same. When it is correctly interpreted, this formulation allows for cultural differences in the conception and interpretation of justice; but it does not require that it should be subject to such relativity. The charge of ambiguity against his formulation in E7 fails once we understand the thesis of cultural realism.

The relativity which can characterise wealth or humour does not exclude the possibility of absolute, unqualified wealth or humour. For the same reason the real values which reside in the plurality of cultures are compatible with the existence of universal and culture-transcendent values. These latter values do not take precedence over the former kind. But they are available; and there will be circumstances in which they should be preferred. I shall briefly consider two difficulties which might be raised against Aristotle's position, since this will help us to appreciate the philosophical significance of cultural realism.

First, we must reflect on Aristotle's directive that, given the scope for a distinction between what is simply good and what is good for oneself, one should pursue the latter. He appears to be saying that a person who recognises some action as good, should yet not do it. This sounds incompatible with the kind of realism which I want to attribute to Aristotle. For how can he both characterise something as absolutely good and direct us not to pursue it?

I construct Aristotle's reply as follows. There is a requirement upon agents to pursue the good which is relative to their local culture. This requirement is itself absolute and not conditional on the nature of the cultural environment. Socratic questioning and possible rejection of the entire cultural context is not an available option. However the fact that absolute, culture-neutral values exist, provides an escape option for circumstances where the values of the local culture are unacceptable. Nonetheless that would be an exceptional situation, albeit one that is theoretically possible. Cultural realism does not easily dispense one from the obligation to accord serious moral recognition to the varieties of culture.

Secondly, the emphasis on the importance of cultural variation may encourage acceptance of relativism. Is this not precisely the effect of the requirement, which we have just emphasised, to respect the local culture? That reaction leads straight to cultural relativism and is a mistaken understanding of Aristotle's account. Cultural realism is to be sharply distinguished from a 'when in Rome' theory. It is a mark of relativism to elevate all cultures to equal moral status; and this is a feature which Aristotle's theory eschews. The distinction between what is good simply and what is good for someone is an analytic one which may be otiose in practice. In particular it is redundant where the person is already good. Nor does anything in Aristotle's account commit him to a 'convergence' conception of cultural pluralism, according to which distinct cultures must be expected to fall away in favour of some universal system. That can be postulated as an ideal, but only by someone who accepts the obligation to pursue the locally determined values.

In this paper I have tried to rescue for philosophical inspection a feature of Aristotle's theory of value which can easily be missed.

As with most other aspects of his philosophy, it is necessary to understand Aristotle's account against the intellectual background from which it dialectically emerges. Cultural realism can be seen as a version of cultural pluralism or as a refinement of it or even as a corrective to it. I believe that it is something of all of these; but whether or to what extent that is true, will obviously depend on the particular pluralist stance which is one's point of reference. Be that as it may, I offer the contribution of Aristotle to the subject of our debate.[9]

[9] Earlier versions of this paper were given to audiences at Notre Dame University, the University of Toledo (Ohio), the Chinese Academy of Social Sciences in Shanghai, Hebei University in Baoding (PR China), Janos Pannonius University in Pécs (Hungary) and Uludağ University in Bursa (Turkey), during 1990-2. A more remote ancestor was a reply to Garrett Barden at the Irish Philosophical Club in November 1979. I also benefited from discussions at the Royal Institute of Philosophy conference, and I am particularly indebted to Alasdair MacIntyre, Eric Snider, Dajian Xu, György Andrássy and Sevgi Iyi.

Religion And Pluralism

TERRY O'KEEFFE

The fact of a religiously plural world is one that is readily acknowledged by believers and non-believers alike. For religious believers, however, this fact poses a set of problems. Religions, at least most of the world's great religions, seem to present conflicting visions of the truth and competing accounts of the way to salvation. Faced with differing accounts of God in Judaism, Buddhism, Islam or Hinduism, what, for example can the Christian claim for the truth of Christian beliefs about God? John Hick, reflecting on the phenomenological similarity of worship in some of the great religious traditions, asks 'whether people in church, synagogue, mosque, gurdwara and temple are worshipping different Gods or are worshipping the same God?' (Hick and Hebblethwaite, 1980, p. 177). He rejects two possible answers to this question: that there exist many Gods, or that one religion, for example Christianity, worships the true God while all other religions worship false gods, which exist only in their imaginations. His favoured response is one that underpins his recent attempts to establish an account of religious pluralism, with which to oppose claims of religious absolutism and exclusivism:

> (T)here is but one God, who is maker and lord of all; that in his infinite fullness and richness of being he exceeds all our human attempts to grasp Him in thought; and that the devout in the various great world religions are in fact worshipping that one God, but through different, overlapping concepts or mental images of him. (Ibid. p. 178)

It is now customary to distinguish within Christian thinking three main approaches to other religions. Alan Race in *Christians and Religious Pluralism* (1983) adopts the headings Exclusivism, Inclusivism and Pluralism. Exclusivism asserts that only Christianity possesses the truth and that there can be no truth or salvation outside it. It depends on the belief that the Christian revelation is true and final and that no other revelation is possible. Inclusivism, on the other hand, suggests that other great world religions like Islam, Hinduism or Buddhism can offer important spiritual insights and visions of holiness but that these are not alternatives to the Christian vision. They are included in

Christianity and must be regarded as partial and incomplete articulations of the truth which is completely found within Christianity. On the inclusive view, as with exclusivism, only Christianity is truly salvific.

There is a third approach which is the pluralist view. In opposition to the absolutist claims of exclusivism or inclusivism, a pluralist version claims that the truth-content of faith can have a variety of legitimate articulations. So, for example, Gavin D'Costa argues that 'other religions are equally salvific paths to God and Christianity's claim that it is the only path … or the fulfilment of other paths … should be rejected for good theological and phenomenological grounds' (1986, p. 22). This view need not be construed as religious relativism—the claim that no religious belief is absolutely true—or as a claim that conflicting or contradictory beliefs about God can all be true. It seems to rest on an assumption that there are some underlying and fundamental religious truths which are presented in a variety of cultural forms in various religious belief systems. Thus, for example, we might think that the attempt of Rudolf Otto in *The Idea of the Holy* to describe what he calls 'numinous experience, beliefs and feelings' and a 'definitely numinous state of mind' as lying at the heart of all religious systems, from the most primitive to the most theologically sophisticated (1958, pp. 7, 18), could be seen as an attempt to articulate the basis of such religious pluralism. (It should be noted that Otto was not a pluralist in the terms of this definition, for he believed that Christianity was the culmination and fulfilment of all partial experiences of the numinous.)

If this view of religious pluralism is to escape the charge of religious eclecticism, it must seek to avoid two main difficulties. One is that the identification of some 'religious foundation', present in all religions from the most simple to the most complex, from the most primitive to the most sophisticated, has proved extremely difficult. Despite, for example, Otto's identification of this with the *mysterium tremendum et fascinans*, with all its objective trappings in his descriptions, his account succeeds best when he speaks of it as a psychological state. He asserts that 'the "numen" must be experienced as something present … (t)here must be felt a something numinous, something bearing the character of a "numen" to which the mind turns spontaneously' (ibid. p. 11). Yet this 'objectivity' is seen to be resting on the dubious foundations of a rewritten Kant when he speaks of 'the Holy' as an *a priori* category (cf. ibid. p. 136f). Another religious thinker, Paul Tillich has little more success in attempting to establish 'ultimate concern' as a universal religious element, claimed to be present in all persons (in that all are said to have an ultimate concern) and capable of being identified in a variety of cultural expressions (Tillich, 1955, 1963, 1957).

Arnold Toynbee, for example, presented such a pluralism as the basis for tolerance between different religions.

> I think that it is possible for us, while holding that our own convictions are true and right, to recognise that, in some measure, all the higher religions are also revelations of what is true and right. They also come from God, and each presents some facet of God's truth. (Toynbee, 1953, p. 111)

John Hick has done most to develop this notion of religious pluralism in opposition to the absolutist claims of any religion, including Christianity. He argues that each of the great world religions presents genuine although different encounters with the divine. They embody 'different perceptions and conceptions of, and correspondingly different responses to, the Real or the Ultimate from within the major variant cultural ways of being human' (1985, p. 47). Hick is anxious to combine both the truth-claim and the salvation-claim which he identifies in every great religion. The great religious traditions are thus also to be regarded as 'alternative soteriological "spaces" within which, or "ways" along which, men and women can find salvation/liberation fulfilment' (ibid.).

It is easier to accept this in terms of the soteriological claims of religious traditions than the truth claims. After all, we can imagine a number of different accounts of salvation which, although competing and even mutually exclusive, are not necessarily of a sort which demands that we say one is true and the others false. Indeed we might say that differing cultural environments could be expected to produce differing accounts of a salvific way of life.

It is more difficult to accept in terms of conflicting truth-claims of the various religious traditions. If we assume that each of the great religions does indeed make truth claims in their credal statements, and that in at least some cases these claims are in direct opposition to the claims made by other religions (as, for example monotheistic against dualistic accounts of God, or trinitarian as opposed to non-trinitarian beliefs), then the problem of competing truth claims will not be solved simply by reference to 'genuine although different encounters with the divine'. Hick, like Otto, has recourse to Kant. He identifies two basic religious concepts, the concept of Deity, i.e. the Real as personal, and the concept of Absolute, i.e. the Real as non-personal. We do not ever encounter either Deity in general or the Absolute in general in religious experience. 'In Kantian language, each general concept is schematised, or made concrete ... For there are different concrete ways of being human and of participating in human history, and within these different ways the presence of the divine Reality is experienced in characteristically different ways' (ibid. p. 41).

The notion that religious traditions are to regarded as phenomenal and that there is a divine noumenon, unknowable in itself, is used by Hick to undermine any absolutist or exclusivist claims by any concrete religion. He presents it as the philosophical underpinning of a religious pluralism. But it is a pluralism which calls for a radical re-examination of the traditional truth claims made by Christianity. The Christian claim to exclusive truth rests in great part on its claim that God's revelation in the person of Christ is absolutely true because of the fact of the Incarnation—that Christ is indeed God as well as man. Hick accepts that religious pluralism as he has defined it requires a setting aside of this doctrine, or at least a redefinition of it as a myth rather than an ontological reality as in traditional doctrine from the time of the Council of Chalcedon. This redefinition—he calls it a 'Copernican revolution' for understanding religion—allows Hick to claim that 'the religious universe centres upon the divine Reality; and Christianity is seen as one of a number of worlds of faith which circle around and reflect that Reality' (ibid. p. 53).

Problems arise from this 'Kantian' shift. One involves a major reinterpretation of the central doctrine of the Incarnation and therefore of the central core of beliefs which identifies the Christian as opposed to any non-Christian religious tradition. 'We are no longer speaking of an intersection of the divine and the human which only occurs in one unique case, but of an intersection which occurs, in many different ways and degrees, in all human openness and response to the divine initiative' (ibid. p. 63). All religious traditions are thus on an equal footing, offering more or less adequate responses to and articulations of the divine noumenon. But they cannot be thought of as making truth claims as traditionally understood, nor can a doctrine be said to be true or false, correct or incorrect. Indeed, the Kantian appeal suggests a move to an account of religious traditions which stresses their human and cultural origins and an agnosticism about the ultimate validity of the religious drive. It could be seen as moving in the direction of religious relativism rather than religious pluralism.

Hick sees his account of religious pluralism as undermining the absolute and exclusive claim made by a number of religious traditions. In some religions, this claim to truth rests on the belief that they possess written texts which are the inspired word of God. The Roman Catholic theologian, Hans Küng, wrote that 'the boundary between the true and the false, even as Christians see it, no longer seems simply between Christianity and other religions but, as least in part, *within* each of the religions' (1986, p. xviii). The appeal to written texts as proof of the truth of certain beliefs adds a further dimension to the discussion of pluralism.

Recently, the Chief Rabbi, Dr Jonathan Sacks, shocked many liberal religious thinkers by a strong attack on the Masorti movement within Judaism. Among the reasons for his attack was that the Masorti movement, founded by a former Chief Rabbi, Louis Jacobi, disputes the divine authorship of the whole of the Torah—the first five books of what Christians call the Old Testament. Dr Sacks's attack drew condemnation from a Masorti Rabbi from the New North London Synagogue, Rabbi Jonathan Wittenberg:

> One doesn't want an environment in which only one form of thought is acceptable. One has to be firm in insisting that there is a place in Jewish life for many currents of thought. (*The Tablet*, 1995, p. 94)

What seems to be at stake in such a dispute is the view that there is a set of religious beliefs which can be claimed to be true because they are contained in a written text, such as the Torah, whose author can be said to be God. This thesis, which Rabbi Sacks called the 'Torah min haShamayim'—the Law from Heaven—rests on a view of revelation which involves the belief that God so inspired the author (or authors) of the text that the words can be said to be God's as well as the author's. So, whether a believer holds to a strict view of the unique Mosaic authorship of these books, or is prepared, on good exegetical grounds, to accept that a variety of subsequent writers and editors have incorporated traditions, some dating from the time of Moses, into the final texts, this view of inspiration commits the believer to the view that these texts are the word of God, they are normative for religious belief, and that what the texts tell us is *true*. What Rabbi Sacks was rejecting was the view that not every statement in the Torah is true, that it can and perhaps does contain errors and that the believer must discern within the texts in question those parts which are genuinely revealed truth or inspired truth, and the view that there may not be only one truth but a plurality of views acceptable within a religious tradition.

These somewhat esoteric disputes within Judaism raise key questions about religion and pluralism. They are raised in a particular form when the religions in question claim to possess absolute truth because of the presence of written texts inspired by God. Thus those (monotheistic) religions like Judaism, Islam and

Christianity—the religions of the Book, as they are sometimes called—all exhibit a similar set of characteristics and raise a similar set of problems for pluralism.

These religions are clear that their claim to absolute truth rests on the claim to possess texts which can be said to be 'God's word'. All must rely on some theory of divine inspiration to uphold this claim. This may be a 'dictation' theory of inspiration, such that some Orthodox Jews believe that the Torah was dictated by God to Moses. For many Muslim scholars, the Koran in its form, content, words and language (Arabic) has its source exclusively in God, with Muhammad merely a conduit. Therefore it can be asserted that 'when the Koran is recited, the voice is that of the reciter but the speech is God's' (Arberry, 1957, p. 26). And some christians hold a similar understanding of inspiration. Or the theory of inspiration may be a more sophisticated one which permits the attribution of the text to God while at the same time accepting that the language, form and style is that of a human author.

It may be useful first to distinguish the notion of inspiration from that of revelation. The notion of revealed truth is primarily that of truths which are revealed by God and which could not otherwise be known to human reason. Thus, within traditional Christianity, the doctrines of the Trinity or the Incarnation are properly speaking revealed truths. Inspiration, on the other hand, refers to the belief that the sacred scriptures recognised by the religion are written under the inspiration of God. It is accepted that these scriptures contain a variety of information, of which revealed truths in the strict sense might be a very small part. Thus they may contain moral teaching, factual information, historical judgments, etc. Two strong conclusions, however, follow from a belief in inspiration : that everything contained in a genuine passage of scripture is the word of God, and that everything contained in a genuine passage of scripture is infallibly true. It is this sort of belief which lies behind Rabbi Sacks's attack on the Masorti, and on denunciations of heterodoxy within particular religions.

The following is a definition of inspiration which is a standard Roman Catholic interpretation of the doctrine:

> Inspiration is that supernatural action of God on the sacred writers in accordance with which He so moved and impelled them to write and so assisted them when writing, that the things which He ordered, and those only, they first rightly understood, then willed faithfully to write down, and finally expressed in apt words and with infallible truth ... All the books which the

> Church receives as sacred and canonical are written wholly and entirely, with all their parts, at the dictation of the Holy Spirit; and so far is it from being possible that any error can coexist with inspiration, that inspiration not only is essentially incompatible with error, but excludes and rejects it as absolutely and necessarily as it is impossible that God Himself, the Supreme Truth, can utter that which is not true. (Van Noort, 1961, p. 70)

These words (of Pope Leo XIII) give rise to a number of problematic issues. There is first of all the decision to accept some works as canonical—part of the received canon of sacred writings—and therefore inspired. Both the Jewish canon of Old Testament writings, and the New Testament canon have writings which at one time or another have been contested, not necessarily only because of their content but also because of doubts about their authorship or authenticity. There are no 'internal criteria' within the text. Secondly there is the question of what the terms 'moved', 'impelled' and 'assisted' mean with respect to the authors of inspired scripture. Do they imply a 'dictation' theory of inspiration or do they permit a separate, human role in authorship? And if texts can now be regarded as inerrant—free of any error—does this inerrancy include not merely doctrinal matters but also historical and even 'scientific' issues? For a religious believer who accepts the notion of the inerrancy of certain texts, could such texts be thought of as providing definitive answers to historical or archaeological questions about the Israelite conquest of Canaan, say, or scientific questions about the origin of human life on the planet?

It is at this point that philosophers of religion need to pay attention to three moves which are made in sophisticated religions if they are to understand correctly what is being claimed as true in a particular religious discourse.

The first is what might be called the heresy move. Those religions which claim absolute truth based on inspired writings are bound to have internal disputes about the meaning and extent of doctrinal statements. Often credal statements are drawn up to exclude certain types of error by declaring that this way of speaking about God rather than that is correct. For example, in the formation of the early Christian Church, disputes with considerable theological implications were decided by adopting a particular word. The Council of Ephesus in 431 opposed the Nestorian heresy by declaring that the word *Theotokos* (God-bearing) was correctly used of Mary (rather than the Nestorian restriction to *Christotokos*). Or the Council of Nicea in 325 which adopted the term *Homo-ousias*—of the same substance or consubstantial—as correctly describing Christ, to oppose the Arian heresy. These are, however, theological moves which interpret the inerrant scriptures, articulating orthodox and anathematising heterodox interpretations.

The second move is adopt a much more sophisticated attitude towards the writings themselves. Instead of simply accepting the texts as a given, as the *Torah min ha Shamayim* of Rabbi Sacks, sophisticated exegetical discussion takes place to establish not merely the texts themselves but the purpose and meaning of the texts. So, for example, if we take the Book of Genesis, and in particular the creation account, it is common to identify three distinct sources and accounts which have been interwoven into a single narrative: the J account, which is the most primitive and uses the name Yahweh for God; the E account, where the term Elohim is used for God, and the P account, a later narrative expressing the concerns of the priestly element within Israel, fascinated by the symbolism of numbers and tracing the details of the law and Jewish worship to antiquity. Knowing this about the book, then, gives us a very different account of the way to read it. As one commentator says, 'whoever … thinks that the author's primary intention in writing his book was to tell history is inevitably going to arrive at some very wrong conclusions about the meaning of Genesis' (Vawter, 1957, p. 20). And therefore some wrong conclusions about what is and is not true and free from error in the book.

A third move is to insist that what is inspired and therefore inerrant is not the actual text or the actual words but rather what was *intended* by the author or authors as the meaning of the words and the work itself. This becomes crucial in establishing what sort of literary form a writer was using, when they wrote a book like Job. If Job was meant as historical, the argument runs, then it is true history because it is inspired. If, however,it was meant as an allegorical story, written quite late in the Jewish period but using an early and primitive folktale as the framework within which to create a sophisticated debate on the problem of omnipotence and human suffering, then that is what is true about the book of Job.

All this can make it extremely difficult for the believer and for the philosopher of religion seeking to determine what the truth claim is. An example from the New Testament is that scholars have identified as a type of literary device used by Semitic writers the *midrash*, roughly a story which appears to be a factual or historical account but is in fact not designed as history at all but is rather meant to convey a particular moral or religious message. But what tells us whether the story of the Three Wise Men and the

Star, in Matthew's Gospel, is meant as historical fact or as a midrashic story designed to underline the universal scope of the Incarnation? And if some seemingly historical or factual parts of the scriptures can be interpreted in this way, why not all or most of the traditional historical claims of Christianity?

Such theological complexities illustrate two points about pluralism and religious truth within individual religious traditions. One is that by the very nature of those religions which appeal to a written record as the inspired and inerrant word of God, there will be statements and doctrines claimed as true and other claimed as false. There will be orthodoxy and heresy. Another is that, unless the religious tradition has an accepted source of definitive interpretation of the texts, or unless an extremely simplistic theory of the self-evident meaning of the texts is adopted, the scope for disagreement is enormous.

There is one interesting idea, put forward by Augustine, in the *Confessions*, that there can be a plurality of meanings of the texts, all of them true.

> When someone says, '(the author of the Pentateuch) meant what I think he meant' and another, 'No, it is rather my interpretation which catches his meaning', I think I can say with all reverence, 'Why cannot you both be right, if the meanings you propose are true?' And if someone should propose a third or fourth meaning, or even if someone should find an altogether different truth in these words, why may he not be believed to have discerned all of these meanings, he through whom one and the same God accommodated the sacred words to the understanding of many, who would find therein true albeit divergent meanings? (Augustine, 1961, p. 257).

In general, however, Augustine's acceptance of pluralism, in one sense of the term, was never accommodated in mainstream Christian thinking. Nor, given the way Augustine himself attacks heretical opinions and uses scripture to prove his points, should we think of him as providing much scope for pluralism in this passage.

So far, the emphasis has been on a set of rather theological and exegetical issues. Philosophers of religion should be centrally interested in examining religious statements, seeking to establish the truth or otherwise of the religious claims made. They should be interested in establishing the truth or otherwise of such claims as that there is a supreme being, that God acts in the world, that human persons are immortal, and so on. This is best done by careful analysis of individual belief statements or doctrines, seeking to understand them in the context of the belief system in question. We should be suspicious therefore of any all-embracing accounts of the meaning of religious assertions which would make unnecessary the detailed understanding and analysis of the beliefs and in particular would ignore the wide variety of types of religious statements which go to make up the religious belief system in question.

There is on the one hand the type of sweeping test of meaningfulness proposed for religious statements by positivism and its successors. One—although only one—of the weaknesses of this approach was that it assimilated all religious beliefs to a single type of statement and then proposed a simple test of meaningfulness for them. John Passmore once remarked of this attempt to eliminate religious statements from the language that it is surely unreasonable to stipulate that some words and sentences have no right to be in the language. As he put it, 'they take part in sentences and win a place in dictionaries, nevertheless they have not satisfied the minimal entrance requirement for being intelligible expressions' (Passmore, 1961, p. 83).

Two other standard moves have recently been made within philosophy of religion. One is the neo-Wittgensteinian move, of philosophers like D. Z. Phillips or Norman Malcolm, which would seek to insulate against philosophical criticism any of the credal statements of religion on the grounds that the criteria of intelligibility and truth of religious assertions are internal to religion and cannot be criticised from outside that 'language game'. In other words, within what is known as Wittgensteinian Fideism, the claim is that, since the criteria of intelligibility of religious statements are internal to religion, in a real sense only believers can understand the meaning of the religious beliefs in question. Ninian Smart remarks:

> It is true that we must have some fairly extensive experience of religion and religious activities in order to have a rough comprehension of the point of religious utterances ... But it follows neither that one should believe in some creed at the time of philosophising in order to give a reasonably accurate account of what the creed amounts to nor that such belief would necessarily help the philosopher. For often the strength of conviction will make philosophy appear trivial, or more dangerously it will tempt one into substituting apologetics for analysis. (Smart, 1958, p. 17)

The second standard move is that of redefining the content of the religious statements in question. It has been tempting for some philosophers to substitute for the religious assertion some quite different type of statement. So R.B. Braithwaite's well-known analysis of religious assertions as covert expressions of an intention to act in accordance with a certain system of moral principles governing 'inner life' as well as external behaviour relegates the expressions of religious doctrines to a set of stories which the believer entertains but which are not in any sense truth claims (Braithwaite, 1971). The more contemporary move of some liberation theologians is to lay the stress on behaviour rather than doctrine so that the defining characteristic of the Christian, is correct behaviour—'orthopraxis'—rather that correct belief—orthodoxy.

The consequence of asserting non-pluralist absolutism, doctrinal certitude and therefore salvific efficacy can be difficult to face. The firm doctrinal statement that '*extra ecclesiam nulla salus*—outside the Church there is no salvation'—if interpreted literally, may be taken to assert that all those failing to adhere to the Catholic faith are thereby damned. The Council of Florence (1438–1445) was adamant that this was the case.

> No-one remaining outside the Catholic Church, not just pagans, but also Jews or heretics or schismatics, can become partakers of eternal life; but they will go to the everlasting fire which was prepared for the devil and his angels, unless before the end of life they are joined to the Church. (quoted in Hick and Hebblethwaite, 1980, p. 178)

In fact, the pressure of tolerance, ecumenism and sheer common sense has led theologians to moderate and change such claims. Thus, there have been attempts to redefine those who can be considered to belong to the Church. This ranges from differentiating those who hold *explicit* Catholic faith from those who can be regarded as *implicit* believers, to the belief that, although only those baptised can be saved, there is such an event as 'Baptism by desire' available to those who, although living a good life by their own lights, are not in a position to receive the Christian message. There have been efforts to differentiate a manifest from a latent Church and, in Karl Rahner's famous suggestion, to identify 'anonymous Christians'. As John Hick comments of this suggestion, 'we have to say that devout and godly non-Christians are really, in some metaphysical sense, Christians or Christians-to-be without knowing it' (ibid. p. 178).

In arguing that philosophy of religion must take seriously the truth claims embedded in religious assertions and beliefs, the understanding of inspiration and the complexities of reading correctly texts claimed by believers to be inerrant because inspired must be considered. It becomes a difficult task for the philosopher of religion to know what type of truth claim is being made by the religious person: whether the particular Christian belief, for example, in the Resurrection, commits the believer to some factual or historical beliefs, or whether it is best interpreted as containing no such empirical-type claim, as John Hick asserts. Even within a single religious tradition, there is a plurality of voices. What is the common thread running through Christian statements about God such as 'we must conclude that there is a prime Mover and this all call God' (Aquinas, 1952, p. 57), 'God is being-itself and ... nothing else can be said about God as God which is not symbolic' (Tillich, 1951, p. 239) and 'God is the sum of all our values, representing to us their ideal unity, their claim upon us and their creative power' (Cupitt, 1984, p. 269)? And if we were to include in this list the concept of God addressed by 'ordinary' or perhaps non- theologically sophisticated believers in their petitionary prayers for health or protection from some evil, we would certainly add to that plurality of voices.

Philosophy of religion must show sensitivity to the context of faith assertions and to the possibly multiple theological nuances in interpretation. The central place claimed by many religions for their particular truth-claims, allied to the attempt to substantiate such claims by reference to written, inspired texts, makes religious pluralism difficult to sustain. This need not necessarily lead to intolerance unless it is held that error has no rights and that it must be not merely anathematised but persecuted. For religious believers, particularly those from traditions in which the claim to absolute truth is standardly made, the possibility of *different* interpretations of an inspired text and therefore different and equally *sustainable* articulations of fundamental doctrine ought to give pause to those religious believers who oppose those who differ in beliefs and thereby reject pluralism in the name of infallibility.

A Single True Morality? The Challenge of Relativism

HARRY BUNTING

Ethical objectivists[1] hold that there is one and only one correct system of moral beliefs. From such a standpoint it follows that conflicting basic moral principles cannot both be true and that the only moral principles which are binding on rational human agents are those described by the single true morality. However sincerely they may be held, all other moral principles are incorrect. Objectivism is an influential tradition, covering most of the rationalist and naturalist standpoints which have dominated nineteenth and twentieth century moral philosophy: there is widespread agreement amongst relativists themselves that objectivism is firmly rooted in common sense.[2]

Moral relativism is an important alternative to this view. Relativists challenge objectivism by drawing attention to the extent of moral diversity between different cultures; to the variation in morals within a given society at different historical epochs; and to the existence of a remarkable degree of moral disagreement within cultures at a single period of time. In the light of such diversity relativists argue that the objectivists' belief in the existence of a single true morality is a product of human ethno-centrism and, invoking Protagoras, suggest the more modest thesis that the moral opinions 'of each and every one are right' (Theaetetus 162a, Plato 1961). Traditional moral relativism therefore, normally involves the theses that different societies hold incompatible basic moral principles, that each of these incompatible principles is in some sense correct, that morality has its foundations in varying human affective dispositions and that, as a consequence, there is no single true morality. The flourishing of relativism which modern moral philosophy has witnessed (Arrington, 1983, 1989; Foot, 1982; Harman, 1975, 1977, 1978a, 1978b; Margolis, 1988; Williams, 1974–5; Wong, 1984) has been largely associated with two developments in the understanding of rela-

[1] I use the term 'objectivism' rather than 'universalism' since the existence of principles applicable to all rational human agents is consistent with these principles not being recognised by some agents.

[2] An exception is Gilbert Harman who holds that relativism is a common-sense view. See Harman, 1975, 1977, 1978a, 1978b.

tivism: a new understanding of—or perhaps a renewal of interest in—the role of truth for relativism and a redefining of the relationship between relativism and the emotions. It is around these themes that the present discussion will revolve.

Twentieth century interest in relativism can be traced to the impressive, though greatly neglected, empirical and philosophical work of the Finnish writer, Edward Westermarck (Westermarck, 1906–8, 1932). Westermarck's relativism centred around the two themes—the role of truth and of the emotions—which I have identified as being central to modern relativism and if the details of his account are unsatisfactory he nonetheless foreshadowed the direction in which successive defenders of relativism have looked and signalled the difficulties which modern relativist theories have confronted. Westermarck's significance is sometimes obscured by the tendency of some commentators to view him as a defender of that form of naive subjectivism which holds that moral terms describe the approval and disapproval of the person making the judgment or as a defender of that equally naive relativism which holds that all moral judgments are relative to the person who makes them. As recent scholarship has shown (Nielsen, 1972, 1982; Mackie, 1977; Stroup, 1981, 1982, 1985). Westermarck held neither of these theories. The central purpose of his moral theory was to undermine the various forms of objectivism, both naturalist and rationalist, which dominated late nineteenth century ethics and to put in their place a descriptive-explanatory relativism which denied the relevance of truth to morality and stressed the role of the emotions in the moral life. In attempting this ambitious project he demonstrated that the theoretical interest of relativism extends far beyond naive subjectivism and relativism and sketched contours within which much recent relativist thought has operated.

Westermarck criticised objectivist normative ethics as being 'the fruit of an illegitimate union between the theoretical search for truth and the practical need to erect norms for human conduct' ('Normative and Psychologische Ethik', Westermarck Archives, Abo Akademi, Finland, quoted in Stroup (1985)). Although it is clear that the first two chapters of *Ethical Relativity* are designed to demolish objectivism the exact position which Westermarck took with regard to the possibility of moral truth is not entirely clear: at times he seemed to argue that questions of truth and falsity simply do not arise in connection with moral issues, at other times he holds that moral judgments have truth values but that all moral judgments are false. What he does make clear, however, in a way that looks back to Smith and Hume and looks forward to

Mackie, is his belief in the centrality to morality of the retributive emotions. The sentiments of gratitude and resentment give rise to impartial and disinterested moral concepts and it is the emergence of these moral concepts which causes us to attribute to actions and characters qualities which they do not in fact possess. The objectivisation involved in this process, the persistent yet misguided human tendency to treat subjective dispositions as if they were the objective properties of actions, is responsible for the tendency which we have to attribute to objects moral properties which do not exist.

The most impressive feature of Westermarck's work is the way in which it combines philosophical, anthropological and psychological insights into a descriptive-explanatory account of morality; its least satisfactory aspect is the inconclusiveness of the arguments that Westermarck advanced for his basic philosophical positions. Difficulties of exposition and argumentation affect both his treatment of the truth of moral judgments and the role of the emotions in the moral life. Consider first the issue of whether or not truth-values apply to moral judgments.

Throughout his writings Westermarck oscillates between what are now referred to as 'error theory' and 'irrealism'; between the view that all moral judgments are false and the very different, and incompatible view that truth and falsity are not applicable to moral judgments. Neither his own work nor the work of sympathetic commentators yield a single coherent position on this fundamental point. Both views face formidable obstacles (see the discussion in Harrison, 1982). The first view is at variance with unreflective moral discourse. In non-philosophical moments a person who believes that cruelty is wrong would happily agree that the statement '"cruelty is wrong" is true' accurately describes her position on the morality of cruelty. Why, then, is falsity applicable to moral judgments but truth is not? Everyday moral discourse provides no hint as to why the one is appropriate and the other is not. Secondly, we support some moral judgments with reasons and reject other moral judgments with reasons; and these reasons, if conclusive, would naturally be construed as reasons for the truth and falsity of the moral judgments in question. However, although the reasons against a judgment can be reasons for its falsity the reasons for a moral judgment can not be construed as reasons for its truth. This also seems counter-intuitive. Thirdly, moral judgments can contradict each other. '"Cruelty is wrong" is true' would naturally be viewed as contradicting the judgment '"cruelty is wrong" is false' but this appearance of contradiction must be misleading if, *ex hypothesi*, moral judgments cannot be true. On this construal moral judgments cannot contradict each other. It may be replied that these arguments merely reiterate common sense convictions which it is the job of philosophy to challenge. But if we are to set aside such deep-seated features of human thought at the bidding of a philosophical theory we are entitled to ask what the theory is and which arguments require us to accept it. Neither Westermarck nor contemporary defenders of 'error theory' have provided any such arguments.

It may be more charitable, therefore, to interpret Westermarck as holding the second view, namely that truth and falsity do not apply to moral judgments. This is an intelligible view, but it is at variance with the way in which we think and talk about moral issues and requires a philosophical defence which Westermarck nowhere provides. In place of arguments, what he does provide is a descriptive-explanatory account of the role of the emotions in moral life, and it is here, perhaps, that the core of his argument is to be found. Unfortunately, Westermarck's account of the emotional foundations of morality is as ambiguous as his account of moral truth. In what sense do the retributive emotions of indignation and approval cause moral judgments to be made? Is there a causal relationship between morality and the emotions? Does a stronger, necessary connection obtain? Textual evidence suggestive of each of these positions can be found.[3] Undoubtedly contingent associations exist between morality and the emotions but it is not clear that a causal link has ever been established. However, these unclarities do not go to the root of the problem. Even if a constant association or a universal causal connection were established between morality and the emotions, this in itself would not be sufficient to undermine objectivism and secure Westermarck's relativism. To take the most obvious example, the utilitarian belief that there is an intimate connection between morality and affective dispositions does not in any way undermine the possibility of moral truth. The provision of a descriptive explanatory account of morality does not refute objectivism in any obvious way.

It seems then that neither the account of moral truth nor the account of the moral emotions gives adequate reason to accept Westermarck's relativism. His claim, in the opening pages of *The Origins and Development of the Moral Ideas* (1906–8, p. 60), that 'moral concepts are ultimately based on emotions either of indignation or approval' has not been clarified sufficiently to enable it to do the work required of it. As Nielsen, a sympathetic commen-

[3] K. Nielsen, for example, lists twelve different interpretations which may be placed on Westermarck's views. See Nielsen (1982) pp. 126.

tator has argued, 'his (Westermarck's) account is just too indeterminate, too imprecise, and too subject to various readings to carry the day for ethical skepticism.' (Nielsen, 1982, p. 128)

That there are philosophical weaknesses in Westermarck's work should not, however, obscure his contribution to the modern rehabilitation of moral relativism. He restated a bold relativism at the end of a century when objectivism had been in the ascendancy and, even if it cannot be claimed that his work shaped later developments, his account certainly foreshadowed the shape that twentieth century defences of relativism would take. Whether modern developments in the field of truth and the emotions have made good the deficiencies in Westermarck's account we may now begin to assess.

Truth is a particularly difficult concept for relativists because it seems that it is, at one and the same time, both essential to their theory and fatal to it. The case for saying that it is essential to it is easily appreciated. Firstly, relativism must in at least some sense be viewed as true by its defenders: their arguments being designed to establish just that. Secondly, moral relativism differs from cultural relativism in that it goes beyond the claim that different societies hold different basic moral principles: moral relativists hold that incompatible basic moral principles are both, in some sense or other, correct. This feature of moral relativism is sometimes disguised by the terminology in which it is presented. Thus it is common to read, for example, that the moral norms of a community are the only valid basis for moral appraisal, that different societies are subject to different moral constraints, that human custom determines what is right and wrong, that a plurality of adequate moral systems apply to human conduct. Although expressed in a number of different ways, what these formulations have in common is their endorsement of the differing and incompatible moral systems. Truth, therefore is essential to relativism.

Paradoxically, as the Platonic critique of relativism makes clear, truth also threatens to generate fatal incoherencies in a relativist theory. Socrates argues that an assertion of the truth of relativism involves assenting to contradictory moral principles, involves claiming for the relativist principle a status which it claims to be impossible, involves undermining that very notion of rightness which relativism itself must use. The force of these arguments has been widely recognised throughout the history of ethics and the arguments have been given numerous contemporary restatements. They are controversial, however, because they construe relativism as being constituted by what is now commonly referred to as 'vulgar relativism', and it is to restore the integrity of relativism that modern 'sophisticated' versions of the theory have been constructed. What is interesting about the 'sophisticated' relativist account of truth is that it recognises the importance of truth to relativism, it avoids Socratic charges of incoherence and it avoids Westermarck's view that all moral judgments are false.

A central theme in modern defences of relativism is that Protagorean relativism has never been given a fair hearing; relativism has been especially weakened, it is argued, by grafting onto it an absolutist theory of truth. According to Socrates, Protagoras held that 'my perception is true for me' (*Theaetetus* 160c, Plato, 1961) and 'what seems true to anyone is true for him to whom it seems so' (ibid. 170a). But when it comes to examining the view Socrates conveniently forgot the hyphenated conception of truth and talked of truth simpliciter, thinking of the predicate as complete, like 'round' or 'red'. A thorough-going relativist, however, takes 'true' and 'false' to be incomplete and to require reference to a person or culture. If, in this spirit, we assert that 'P' is true and false when expressed in two cultures S_i and S_{ii} our assertion is not incoherent, just as the claim that a person is big is consistent with the claim that he is small when a comparison is being made with two people of different size. 'True' and 'false' may be contradictories, but 'true-in-S_i' and 'false-in-S_{ii}' are not contradictories. Relativism, therefore, is not incoherent. Protagoras' germinal idea was that there is no such thing as truth, only truth-in-S_i; there is no such thing as rightness, only rightness-for-S; indeed, there is no such thing as reality, only reality-for-S.

Moral relativists such as Philippa Foot and Robert Arrington are attracted to this line of argument. According to Arrington, 'The whole point of the relativist position is that we cannot assert that a moral judgment is true simpliciter, we can only assert that a judgment is true for a particular person or social group' (1983, p. 228). Foot, discussing the relativity which she discerns in judgments of taste, writes,

> if we are talking of the views of another society we shall speak of what is true by their standards and by our standards, without the slightest thought that our standards are 'correct.' If the ancient Mexicans admired the looks of someone whose head had been flattened, a proposition not about this admiration may have been true as spoken by them, though it is false as spoken by us. (Foot, 1982, p. 155)

Whilst many relativists appeal to relative truth, the concept rarely receives the elucidation that it requires. What is meant by saying that a statement is true relative to some culture or belief-system?

Is it any different from saying that the belief in question is true? Does it mean no more than that the statement in question is believed?

One philosopher who views relative truth as of fundamental importance to epistemology and who has sought to provide an account of its meaning, is Jack Meiland. He develops (1977, p. 571) a distinction between 'absolute truth' which involves a two-term relation between statements and states of affairs, and relative truth which involves a three-term correspondence relation between statements, states of affairs and a third term which is either persons, world-views or cultural situations: it is correspondence-to facts from the point of view of the person or society.

The presence of the hyphens in 'true-for-W' distinguishes relative truth from absolute truth, and Meiland continues:

> Thus one can no more reasonably ask what 'true' means in the expression 'true-for-W' than one can ask what 'cat' means in the word 'cattle'. True-for-W denotes a special three-term relation which does not include the two-term relation of absolute truth as a distinct part. (Ibid. p. 574)

Critics of relativism have dismissed Meiland's analysis of relative truth. Harvey Siegel (1987), for example, points out that the analogy with 'cat' and 'cattle' does nothing to help explain the meaning of relative truth. The word 'cattle' is made up of the letters c/a/t/t/l/e; 'cat' is no more independently meaningful than are 'att' or 'ttle'. 'True-for-W' on the other hand, is made up of the hyphenisation of distinct concepts, each of which is independently meaningful. Wholly sceptical conclusions are drawn from this: relative truth is meaningless and reduces on analysis either to mere belief or to absolute truth. Siegel is right to point to the inadequacies of Meiland's attempted elucidations but his scepticism about relative truth is premature. Indeed, it is not clear that he has properly understood Meiland's intentions. What Meiland is arguing in the (admittedly strange) passage quoted above is that relative truth is a primitive term and that it is not reducible to or analysable in terms of anything else. The concept of relative truth may fail for other reasons but it does not fail because it is unanalysable in terms of other things.

An alternative, though ultimately no more successful approach to the nature of relative truth is contained in an article by F. C. White (1986). White takes 'true' and 'false' to be incomplete and argues that 'P is true' in society S_i and 'P is false' in society S_{ii} involves no incoherence. The explanation is that P means quite different things in the two contexts. It is the error of thinking that they are univocal which generates the charge of incoherence. White illustrates his account by reference to alternative geometries. How can we reconcile the fact that a statement such as 'the sum of the angles of a triangle are equal to two right angles' is true in one geometry with the fact that it is false in another geometry? White argues that when stated in terms of relative truth the appearance of contradiction is removed: the presence of hyphens means that two distinct and consistent propositions are being asserted. Hence relativism, interpreted in terms of relative truth, does not involve assent to contradictory propositions. White says, 'When S_i is true and S_{ii} is false, different propositions are at stake' (ibid. p. 333). The use of a common expression serves simply to remind us that truth is always system-relative.

Admirably clear though this account may be there are two difficulties in connection with it. Firstly, why is a theory of relative truth needed at all? Relative truth was introduced in order to prevent relativism lapsing into incoherence, but on White's account incoherence is no longer a problem: all that is needed is for the distinct meanings of ambiguous expressions to be clearly delineated and this can be accomplished within the context of an absolute theory of truth. Secondly, if the propositions are indeed ambiguous how can the fact that both interpretations are true undermine objectivism? No doubt objectivism is in jeopardy if a single belief is true in one society and false in another, but objectivity is in no way threatened by the fact that we may say of two propositions, that both are true or that one is false and the other is true. White's account of truth fails, therefore, because it makes relative truth redundant and it transforms relativism in such a way that it no longer threatens objectivism.

The concept of relative truth can be given content which is intelligible, does not involve ambiguity, or collapse into absolute truth if we construct a minimalist account and build on it. Consider an account in which 'P is true for S_i' merely means that P is believed by society or belief-system S_i. This minimalist account can be enriched if we draw on ideas in epistemology. On a widely held theory of epistemological justification a belief is justified if it coheres within a comprehensive set of explanatory beliefs. However, in addition to asking if a belief is justified within a total belief-system S_i we can also ask if a belief coheres and is justified within a specified sub-system of beliefs S_{ii}. If a belief displays maximum coherence within such a sub-system then we may express this by saying that it is justified-in-S_{ii}. The purpose of the hyphens in this context is to indicate a qualified form of justification: the belief is justified, but it is justified only in relation to a limited class of beliefs. A similar point might be made in connection with truth. Just as issues of absolute truth can be raised in connection with a total system of beliefs so issues of relative truth can be raised in relation to specified sub-systems of belief: a belief which coheres within a comprehensive, explanatory sub-system of belief might therefore be viewed as relatively true. To say that P is true-for-S_i is to say that, judged purely in the context of the sub-system of beliefs, P is true. This is, I think, the most plausible way to construe Protagoras' conception of relative truth. It allows for continuity between absolute and relative truth, it makes an intelligible distinction between relative truth and falsity and it is significantly applicable to different societies and belief-systems. If relative truth has a role in the vocabulary of rational inquiry then its most satisfactory explanation is in this form.

As was the case with White's account, the conception of relative truth which I have described, although intelligible, nevertheless fails to undermine objectivism. The fact that relative truth can be predicated of limited sub-systems of belief is wholly consistent with the absolute truth of those beliefs which display maximum explanatory coherence within a comprehensive belief-system. The history of human thought is a long story which illustrates this point: beliefs which are considered true when viewed from a limited perspective have been transcended when placed within a wider framework of beliefs. This is no less true of moral than of scientific beliefs: the goal of rational moral inquiry must be to transcend relative truth, to build upon its partial insights, and to bring about a comprehensive and rational synthesis of our moral judgments and principles.

Truth, therefore, remains a fundamental obstacle to the development of a relativist ethic, rendering relativism incoherent if construed in absolute form, and failing to undermine objectivism if construed in relative form.

A second strand of modern relativist thought places less emphasis on truth and seeks foundations for relativism in a theory of the emotions. Its advocates constitute a very heterogeneous group of philosophers embracing non-cognitivists such as C. L Stevenson (1944, 1963) and R. M. Hare (1952, 1963) and more recent writers such as G. Harman (1975, 1977, 1978a, 1978b) and B. Williams (1974–5). In a variety of different ways, however, and especially in their rejection of any strong sense of moral truth and their acceptance of some form of internalism, the relativism inherent in their position provides a coherent expression of Westermarck's claim that an adequate relativism is properly grounded in a theory of human affective dispositions.

Internalism, the view that assent to a moral principle provides an agent with a reason to act in favour of it, has a relationship with relativism which has rarely been systematically explored. The classical expression of twentieth century internalism which is developed in the work of Stevenson and Hare explicitly repudiates relativism but these writers have sustained their positions by misrepresenting relativism and by neglecting important relativist aspects of their own theories. Both Stevenson and Hare equate relativism with the naive subjectivist view that moral predicates describe subjective states and since this view forms no part of their theory they reject the charge of relativism. However, this is an inadequate conception of relativism, and central aspects of non-cognitivist views of truth and rationality justify one in viewing them as variants of relativism. Their view of truth is a convenient point of entry into their theories.

Unlike Westermarck who, as we have seen, was equivocal concerning the possibility of moral judgments having truth values, non-cognitivists view moral judgments as being analogous to commands or expressions of approval and as being true only in the sense that calling them true expresses an appropriate form of assent. According to Hare (1963, ch.11) moral judgments are 'universal prescriptions' distinguishable from straightforward commands chiefly by virtue of the fact that assent to a moral judgment implies commanding consistently in relation to everything that is similar in morally relevant respects. Several aspects of his non-cognitivism are strongly relativist in character.

Firstly, according to Hare, no necessary connection, semantic or otherwise, links moral predicates to the properties upon which they are supervenient. Ultimately, the only connection between the cruelty or the dishonesty of an action and the wrongness of an action is the fact that the person judging cruelty and dishonesty to be wrong has chosen or decided to accept a principle involving the connection; or, at most, the part that the principle plays in the way of life that they have chosen. A person making no such connection and sharing no such way of life, would be guilty of no rational error. Secondly, Hare's account of morality contains an elaborate theory of justification which allows for moral argument and rational criticism. An important part of that account is that accepting a moral principle entails acting on it in appropriate circumstances. If this is taken along with the universalisability of moral judgments we get the view that a person only assents to a moral principle if he is willing to play his part in the situation even if he were in the position of one of the other parties affected. Thus if I hold that racial discrimination is justified I must prefer that I be discriminated against if I belonged to an appropriate racial group; if I am a committed Nazi I must consent to my being exterminated if I were a Jew. Provided, however, that he is consistent in the moral principles to which he express allegiance the 'fanatic', at the deepest level, is no less rational than a person who adopts an ethic of equal respect for persons. An acceptance of internalism entails that incompatible conceptions of the nature of moral properties and incompatible ways of life are equally rational.

Gilbert Harman shares none of the non-cognitivists' reservations concerning describing himself as a relativist. In a number of articles (Harman, 1975, 1977, 1978a, 1978b) Harman defends a form of internalism whose relativism turns on the motivational attitudes of moral agents. Unlike legal requirements which are binding whether a person finds them acceptable or not, moral requirements are binding only if a person finds them acceptable. One is subject to a moral requirement only if one has a compelling reason to act in accordance with it. Thus if a person says that a second person ought to perform action A, then the first person implies that the second person has motivating attitudes towards doing A which the first person endorses. Hence it would not make sense to say 'You ought not to do that' to Hitler in connection with his treatment of the Jews or to a member of Murder Incorporated planning the execution of a rival gang leader. Morality is founded on agreement and in such cases the relevant agreement in motivational attitudes is not present. Harman's theory is relativist because he holds that, by virtue of different motivation, two agents may be subject to different moral requirements, and that this difference is not accountable for by reference to some more fundamental requirement which applies to both agents.

In spite of the great philosophical subtlety and ingenuity with which these internalist systems are constructed, it is remarkable how very small are the aspects of moral experience for which they provide explanations and how extensive are the aspects of moral experience which are at variance with them. Non-cognitivists commonly pay attention to action-guiding aspects of our use of moral language, to the fact that 'ought' statements typically answer the question 'what shall I do?', and to the oddity involved in assenting to moral judgments and not acting in accordance with them. They ignore the fact that the same considerations apply to many other types of judgments whose objectivity is not in question. They also ignore the alternative explanations which are available for the distinctive linguistic features to which they refer. For example, the inappropriateness of the judgment 'You ought not to do that' uttered to Harman's Nazi, to bloodthirsty Martians or to a member of Murder Incorporated is easily recognised, but an explanation seems more plausible on grounds quite different to those offered by Harman. If the creatures in question are not capable of human communication, if they are corrupted by evil, or if they are indifferent to moral considerations then we have explanations for the forms of linguistic oddness which internalists highlight which are quite consistent with a thorough-going objectivism. Harman's 'inappropriate' remarks are indeed odd, but the explanation is to be found in their weakness: is it conceivable that we would challenge evil of this magnitude with a remark as mild as this!

Equally important are the large areas of moral experience which defy the type of analysis which internalists propose. Central to internalism is the desire to affirm the existence of a link between assenting to a moral principle and acting on it and the main weakness of the theory has been that the link is forged so tightly that important areas of human experience—moral cynicism, deliberate wrongdoing and intentionally immoral advice—are rendered unintelligible.

The strength of relativism has traditionally been seen to lie in its capacity to provide an explanation of moral diversity which does justice to the integrity of contrasting moral traditions. Westermarck was concerned to describe and analyse the significance of moral diversity, but his attitude to it was ambiguous and he frequently stressed that it was not the prevalence of moral diversity which convinced him of the truth of relativism. He recognised that, far from displaying chaotic diversity, moral experience is constrained by the basic regularities of human emotional experience.

Further, he recognised that diversity can be explained in ways that are consistent with objectivism; that values may manifest themselves in very different ways in different contexts. Thus moral diversity may reflect variation in derivative and not in basic principles and may establish only the existence of different institutional expressions of universal principles.

Recognising the universal elements in human experience, Westermarck justified his relativism, therefore, by an appeal to the role of the emotions in moral life; a role which, he argued, was fundamental, and undermines any belief in objective moral truth. But having detailed the ways, consistent with objectivism, in which diversity can be explained he, along with other contemporary relativists, should have realised that the intimate connections which exist between morality and the emotions can also be readily accommodated by objectivists. That this point is overlooked is due in large part to a failure to distinguish between the thesis that morality is relational and the quite distinct thesis that morality is relative. Harman's theory provides a classic example of how this confusion can occur. As we have seen, Harman bases his relativism on the claim that morality is relative to agreement. This, however, is not sufficient to establish the truth of moral relativism, because agreements can be relativist or universal in character, depending on whether they are binding on all rational beings or apply only to a designated cultural group of humans. One can adopt a relational account of morality without embracing relativism. Westermarck, likewise, may have been correct to remind us of the importance of the relations which hold between morality and the emotions but is wrong in inferring from this the truth of moral relativism. Once again we see how a theory which purports to be relativist can fail through its central ideas reducing to ideas which are compatible with objectivism; and we see how a theory can fail to be relativist through its association with notions which cannot be reconciled with the basic facts of moral experience.

Pluralism, Realism and Truth

C. J. McKNIGHT

Recent interest in ethical pluralism derives from Isaiah Berlin's reflections on the writings of Vico and Herder and their opposition to the views of the Enlightenment. I begin with two quotations from Berlin:

> It (pluralism) is not relativism. Members of one culture can, by the force of imaginative insight, understand ... the values, the ideals, the forms of life of another culture or society, even those remote in time or space. They may find these values unacceptable, but if they open their minds sufficiently they can grasp how one might be a full human being, with whom one could communicate, and at the same time live in the light of values widely different from one's own, but which nevertheless one can see to be values, ends of life, by the realisation of which men could be fulfilled. (Berlin, 1991, p. 10)
>
> Relativism is something different: I take it to mean a doctrine according to which the judgement of a man or group, since it is the expression of a taste, or emotional attitude or outlook, is simply what it is, with no objective correlate which determines its truth or falsehood. I like mountains, you do not; I love history, he thinks it is bunkum: it all depends on one's point of view. It follows that to speak of truth or falsehood on these assumptions is literally meaningless. But the values of each culture or phase of a culture are (for Vico or Herder or their disciples) not mere psychological, but objective facts, although not therefore necessarily commensurable, either within a culture or (still less) as between cultures. (Ibid. p. 80)

From the above description it appears that pluralism makes at least the following claims. (1) There is a plurality of values which are mutually irreducible. (2) These values are objective and not simply matters of taste. (3) These values are true and (4) the values may clash, conflict with and contradict one another. (5) Relativism about values is false.

TASTE. Differences of taste are characterised as follows: 'I prefer caviare, you prefer champagne. There is nothing more to be said'. In saying that value judgements are objective Berlin wants to say that they are not like this. But there is quite a lot more to say about differences of taste before we agree with him. To begin with it does not seem true that there is literally nothing more to be said, no place for reasons and arguments; so that the discussion must end immediately. I can surely point to features of caviare which you may not have noticed or may have forgotten about which are what make me prefer it. Perhaps you have only tried inferior brands or your long residence in Russia gave you a surfeit of the stuff then but you might enjoy it if you tried it now. Equally you can try to persuade me of the merits of champagne; perhaps I should try a drier version or try it at breakfast mixed with marmalade (highly recommended this!).

In the second place it is a trite observation that the quoted remarks are capable of being read in at least two ways. They may be taken as autobiographical descriptions by the speakers of their preferences. Since the speakers are different, providing their utterances are sincere, they are not self-deceived etc., both claims may well be true. But on this reading there is no disagreement let alone clash or conflict. We have simply two correct descriptions of differing tastes.

But there is obviously a sense in which the speakers do disagree. The disagreement is brought out by treating their utterances not as descriptions of themselves but as claims about champagne and caviare. There is now a place for disagreement since they have the same subject matter. In a similar vein two speakers one of whom says 'I believe that cows eat grass' and the other 'I believe that cows do not eat grass' may simply be giving descriptions of their current mental states in which case both may be true but by the same token there is no conflict or disagreement. Taken another way they are both making (tentative) claims about the same thing—the feeding habits of cows. These beliefs do indeed conflict and are incompatible, simply because they cannot both be true. Reverting to caviare and champagne, our speakers might express their difference in the form of value judgements, one saying 'champagne is better than caviare' the other 'caviare is better than champagne'. In some sense they are now disagreeing; in some sense they are saying incompatible things. In what sense we must consider soon.

Before doing this however we need to notice that whereas in the example of the two beliefs we had not only disagreement but also conflict in the case of preferences, though the people involved disagree about the relative merits of caviare and champagne we do not yet seem to have a case of conflict. The reason is that the beliefs were in conflict because they cannot both be true. That is what conflict is for beliefs; it is conflict about truth values. Preferences, however are not naturally viewed as candidates for truth and falsity. What would lead us to say that the preferences of the two speakers were in conflict? Surely there being something about the situation which meant that both preferences could not be simultaneously satisfied. If there is plenty of caviare and champagne to go around there need be no conflict. But if for example we are dining at Le Tour d'Argent and have money enough for either champagne or caviare but not both, then our preferences may fairly be said to conflict. Our preferences are incompatible and in conflict not because of anything to do with truth but because owing to other facts (contingent facts in this example) of the situation they cannot both be satisfied. Where preferences are concerned conflict and incompatibility are not truth conflict and truth incompatibility but conflict and incompatibility of satisfaction.

Pace Berlin, then, there is a sense in which judgements of taste can be held to be both incompatible and objective (they are about the things judged rather than the judgers). Berlin of course is not interested in trivial things like caviare and champagne. When he talks about values he is talking about different answers to big questions like 'how should one live one's life?' 'which goods are absolute goods?' and so on. But he does little if anything to show that answers to these questions are different in kind to answers to 'is champagne better than caviare?' And we saw how easy it is to express differences of taste in terms of differing value judgements ('champagne is better than caviare', etc.)

RELATIVISM. Berlin equates subjectivism with relativism. He is right I think to do this, though far from clear how pluralism is supposed to differ from them. Relativism imprisons a person (or a culture or a group within a culture) in their own values and their own beliefs and thereby misrepresents those values and beliefs. It does so by replacing 'true' by 'true for me' and 'good' e.g. by 'good for me'. Thus what appear to be objective claims about something in the world turn out to be really claims about the speaker. 'It is raining' said by me becomes 'it is raining is true for me' which is a misleading way of saying 'I believe it is raining' 'It is not raining' said by you on the same occasion becomes in my mouth 'it is false for you that its raining' which again boils down to 'you do not believe that it is raining'. But in removing 'true' (non-relative) from our language and replacing it by 'true for' (relative) we have left ourselves unable to say how the speakers disagree with one another. Their claims and the beliefs underlying them can only be in conflict if they are incompatible in terms of truth non-relativistically understood. Equally the content of those claims and beliefs can only be properly represented by using a non-relativist notion of truth. What the first speaker is claiming is something about the state of the weather not about his own belief-set. This claim can only be made using a belief-transcendent concept of truth. It is that same claim about the weather which is being denied by the second speaker and he can only do this by making use of the same belief transcendent concept of truth which rescues him from imprisonment in his own belief set.

The same goes for relativism about values. If 'good' and 'bad' are replaced by 'good for me', 'bad for you', etc., our earlier differences about the relative value of champagne and caviare cannot be represented as disagreements since my remark that caviare is better than champagne is treated as a description (true no doubt) of my value system and yours that champagne is better than caviare a description (no doubt equally true) of your system. As long as we remain prisoners of our value systems those systems cannot conflict. To allow for such conflicts we need system-transcendent notions of 'good', 'bad', etc. We need these equally to represent our original claims properly in the first place. My remark was intended not as the system relative claim that caviare is better for me but the transcendent one that caviare is better simpliciter. So was yours about champagne. The same will remain true where the disagreements are of the sort which mainly interest Berlin and his forerunners; namely value disagreements between different societies. The ancient Greek who says that the best life is that of the Homeric hero is not claiming it as the best life for ancient Greeks but as the best life simpliciter. So too is the Christian missionary who advocates a life of humility and forbearance. He is advocating it not as the best life for missionaries, but as the best life simpliciter.

TRUTH. Berlin is right then when he says that we must reject relativism if we are to make sense of conflicts between values and of conflicts between beliefs and also if we are to represent properly the values and the beliefs which are in conflict. Given that relativism and subjectivism come to the same thing, he is right too in thinking that we need an objectivist account of beliefs and values of some sort. In the case of beliefs it is clear enough that we shall need an account which involves the notion of truth. What we have already noticed in the examination of tastes is that it is less clear that the objectivity required for disagreement and conflict need always be truth-involving.

For much of the time Berlin writes as though it must. The peculiar insight of pluralism which distinguishes it from monism is not that people have conflicting values. A monist can acknowledge that and simply say that because they conflict some at least of those values must be mistaken. What the pluralist claims is that there are conflicting and incompatible values all of which are true. The first passage quoted above tells us that pluralism is not the same as relativism and claims that we can understand the values of alien cultures even though we find those values unacceptable. The second passage repeats the claim that pluralism and relativism are distinct and adds the statement that fully rational people may seek different ends.

In calling alien values 'true values' Berlin's pluralists are making the following claims; (1) other cultures have values which conflict with ours but we understand those cultures and those values. (2) Understanding does not involve agreement. We can criticise and reject alien values while at the same time understanding them and sympathising with them. (3) Fully rational beings can have quite different and conflicting values.

Suppose we assess these claims, reading 'beliefs' instead of 'values' and 'true beliefs' for 'true values'. (1) Becomes the claim that other cultures may have beliefs (and indeed true beliefs) which conflict with ours, but which we can nevertheless understand. There need be nothing particularly problematic about the claim that we understand those beliefs, but if we add the word 'true' there is an immediate problem. If their beliefs are true and they conflict with ours then our beliefs must be false. If we are rational then in such a situation we must change our own beliefs. The same does not appear to hold for values as conceived by the pluralist. We can admit that the alien values are true and that they conflict with ours without being in any way forced to revise our own. If so the kind of truth involved for values and the kind of conflicts that arise between values must be very different from those that arise with beliefs. (2) Maintains that understanding alien beliefs does not commit us to agreement with them. This is perfectly correct since we may understand the beliefs and think them false. But where values are concerned, pluralists apparently want to hold that this applies to values which we take to be true as well. Indeed, Berlin says surprisingly little about false values; the alternatives offered are usually truth or unintelligibility. For beliefs, however, the corresponding claim that understanding a true alien belief does not commit us to agreeing with it is quite unacceptable. To accept a belief as true is to agree with that belief. (3) Too is quite problematical as far as beliefs are concerned. On one plausible realist account of truth at least, true beliefs are those on which all fully rational believers would converge. For pluralists there is no single set of values on which the value judgements of all fully rational evaluators would converge. The moral seems again to be that when pluralists talk of true values the sort of truth they are talking about is very different from that involved in belief.

The upshot of these observations seems to be that, though pluralists may be right in their negative claims that relativism and subjectivism are unacceptable, their positive accounts of truth and conflict show how different these notions are when applied to values rather than beliefs. Indeed pluralism as Berlin sometimes states it looks highly paradoxical. This is brought out when he describes the Enlightenment position (here referred to as 'the old view') to which pluralism is opposed. 'The old view', he writes, 'rested upon at least three central presuppositions; first, that all questions of value were answerable objectively ... second, that the universal truths were in principle accessible to human beings ... third it was assumed that true values could not conflict with each other' (ibid. p. 183). It is not clear which of these Berlin's pluralist rejects. It cannot be the first, because pluralism affirms the objectivity of values. There is no hint that pluralists disbelieve the second. It looks therefore as if it must be the third presupposition which they reject. This is confirmed by what comes later 'This can be put in another way. All questions have their answers. The answer must take the form of a true statement of fact. No truth can contradict any other truth—that is a simple and undoubtedly valid rule of logic. ... From this it logically follows that since all truths are compatible with one another or perhaps even entail one another it must be possible to deduce the perfect pattern of life compounded of all the true answers to all the agonising questions and this pattern men should seek to realise' (ibid. p. 184). It now looks as though pluralists have to deny the 'undoubtedly valid rule of logic' that no truth can contradict another and that all truths are compatible with one another; but what can such a denial mean? In particular what do they mean by 'contradict' and 'compatible'? What the Enlightenment spokesmen say about truth and compatibility seem to be platitudes and it is these same platitudes which pluralists seem to deny.

What account are we to give, then, of value judgements in order to make sense of the pluralist claim that there can be conflicting values without recourse to relativism or subjectivism? To what other types of discourse might we turn for enlightenment?

One obvious candidate is imperatives. Imperatives can conflict and can be inconsistent. Inconsistent imperatives such as 'shut the door' and 'do not shut the door' are such that there is no possible situation in which they can both be obeyed. They can conflict in a particular situation if it is impossible in that situation to obey them both. So 'give a lecture at 3 p.m.' and 'catch a train at 3.45' are in conflict if lectures have to last a full hour and the station is 20 minutes away by car. Here we have objectivity since the actions commanded are at least as objective as the propositions which form the content of beliefs. What we do not have is truth; imperatives are not candidates for truth or falsity. Since relativism and subjectivism are claims about what sort of truth belongs to judgements of a particular type, where truth is inapplicable questions of relativism and subjectivism cannot arise. What we need to do is to revise our notions of conflict and inconsistency. When we were talking about beliefs we defined them by reference to truth and falsity. Where imperatives are concerned we need to replace 'true' and 'false' by something like 'obeyed' and 'not obeyed', or 'satisfied' and 'not satisfied'. But in doing so we are changing the concepts. Though we can continue to use 'conflict' and 'inconsistent' for both they are different concepts and we must not lose sight of that.

Another type of discourse at which we might look is the expression of desires. Desires, like imperatives, can be inconsistent and can conflict. My desire to eat this apple is inconsistent with my desire not to eat it as it is with your desire to eat the same apple. They are inconsistent because there is no possible way in which they can both be satisfied. Equally my desire to park my car conflicts with your (or indeed my own) desire to park you motor cycle if there is only one parking space; otherwise they will not conflict. For desires as for imperatives there is no question of truth or falsity; conflict and inconsistency must be defined by reference to satisfaction and non-satisfaction or some such concepts. Here again we have objectivity in that what is desired is as objective as anything could be and again because there is no question of truth neither is there any question of relativism.

Do these points about different notions of conflict and consistency throw any light on the conflicts and inconsistency between values emphasised by pluralists? Here we are on Bernard Williams's territory. Williams in 'Ethical Consistency' (Williams, 1973, ch. 11) wants to point up analogies between ethical judgements and expressions of desire and disanalogies with beliefs. These centre around the notions of consistency and inconsistency.

Where beliefs are concerned consistency is an absolute requirement. This is because inconsistency shows that at least one and perhaps both of the inconsistent beliefs is false; and it is the function of beliefs to aim at truth. The discovery that a particular belief is false must, if we are rational, lead to its rejection. Inconsistency in beliefs shows not just that there is something wrong with the beliefs but also that there is something wrong with the believer. A fully rational believer, like R. M. Hare's archangel perhaps (Hare, 1981, ch. 6), would have no false beliefs let alone any inconsistent ones. If we are forced to abandon a belief because it is false there can be no reason for regret or for any sense of loss. We might regret having to abandon a pet theory or a favourite belief, but once we are convinced that the theory and the belief concerned are false such regret would be irrational. There can moreover be no question for a fully rational believer of dilemmas about what to believe. Such dilemmas can only be the result of ignorance or faulty reasoning, hence of incomplete rationality. We must hold, if we are realists, that in each situation there is a true belief and for each question there is a true answer on which the beliefs of all fully rational believers must converge.

Things are quite different, according to Williams, when we come to desires. In the first place there is not necessarily anything wrong with inconsistent desires or with the person who has them. If desires are inconsistent I cannot, it is true, satisfy them both but it does not follow that if I choose to satisfy one rather than the other I must on pain of irrationality abandon the other. I might try to get rid of the unsatisfied desire but it is not an absolute requirement of rationality that I do so. The unsatisfied desire may remain and I may persist in the hope that I might satisfy it at some later time. If I eventually decide to abandon it I may do so with regret and it is by no means clear that such regret must be irrational. A real loss has occurred and it is quite rational to regret that loss. There can, in addition, be genuine dilemmas where desires are involved. If I have inconsistent desires of which I can satisfy at most one there need be no uniquely rational way of resolving the problem. This may be because the desires are equally strong or because, there being no neutral standard for comparing them, they are incommensurable. And there is no reason to suppose that further information might resolve the dilemma. In such cases there need be no uniquely correct answer; there need, in other words, be no fact of the matter.

These differences arise because whereas beliefs are directed at truth and, if we are realists, truth is single, desires are directed rather towards action and choice. The 'direction of fit' is different. If beliefs fail to fit the world and are thus false it is the beliefs which are at fault. If desires fail to fit by being unsatisfied it may be the world which is at fault rather than the desires.

Some of the things pluralists say about values parallel what has just been said about desires. When values conflict there may be nothing wrong with the values or the valuers. It may be the world that is at fault. Again where values conflict in a particular situation there may be no single answer to the question of what the best outcome might be. This may be because the values, though comparable, are equally balanced or it may be because the values are incommensurable, there being no neutral or independent standard against which to measure them. Liberty and equality, for example, may be values which conflict in a given situation; liberty can only be achieved at the expense of equality and vice versa. Sometimes the answer may be obvious; perhaps all rational valuers must agree that it would be wrong to trade off a large diminution of liberty in the interests of a minuscule increase in equality and the other way round as well. But there will inevitably be cases where the correct trade off is not obvious and where equally rational people will disagree about the correct choice. There need be no particular reason to think that this is a result of defective rationality or that the problem would vanish as a result of further information or ratiocination. With values as with desires we experience dilemmas. Like Hare's Oxford colleague we may face conflicting obligations (Hare, 1981, p. 27). We ought to go for a picnic tomorrow because we have promised to do so and the family will be disappointed if we do not but at the last moment an Australian friend turns up who wants to be shown the colleges, tomorrow being the only day when this is possible. Considerations of friendship tell us that we ought to spend the day with him while family obligations require us to go on the picnic and we cannot do both. Neither of these obligations is obviously more pressing than the other and it seems that equally rational people might make opposite choices about what to do. It is implausible to suppose that further information or further thought about the situation would necessarily show that one choice was right and the other wrong. We may also experience regret when we make a choice, even when we think we have made the right choice, that we were unable to do the other thing as well. If on a particular occasion we choose liberty in preference to equality we may feel regret that something of value has been lost. If we eventually opt for obliging our friend we may well regret that we could not also carry out our family obligation. That obligation does not disappear as a result of not being honoured and something is lost by us not honouring it, even if we are convinced that we chose rightly. The feeling of regret and the feeling that we should try to make restitution in some way are not irrational in the way that it is irrational to regret the loss of a false belief. The conflicts, dilemmas, losses and regrets to which pluralists draw attention do not seem to involve belief and truth; they seem rather to involve actions, choices, fulfilment and non-fulfilment. Homeric values conflict with ours because we cannot live in the light of both of them. Again my obligation to my friend conflicts with the obligation to my family not because of considerations of truth but because circumstances are such that I cannot fulfil them both. What is lost is not some false belief, it is not indeed a belief at all; it is rather the ability to carry out an obligation which I could have met had I not given precedence to the other one.

We are not realists about desires in the sense that we do not ascribe truth and falsity to them. In 'Ethical Consistency' and 'Consistency and Realism' (Williams, 1973, chs. 11 and 12) Williams suggests that the similarities between ethical judgements and expressions of desire emphasised by pluralists should persuade us to see them too as something other than assertions to be assessed for truth and falsity and consequently abandon ethical realism. The question we must now ask is whether the analogies are conclusive or whether they can be accommodated within a realist view which treats ethical judgements as assertions which state beliefs which can be assessed just like any others for truth and falsity.

One way of bringing about the reconciliation is suggested by Walter Sinnott-Armstrong in his book *Moral Dilemmas* (1988). His strategy is to distinguish what he calls 'truth-inconsistency' which is what we have been discussing in relation to beliefs from 'act-inconsistency' which is what we have highlighted in non-assertoric discourse. The novel suggestion is that at least for the type of moral judgement typically involved in dilemmas and expressed by 'ought' and 'ought not' both types of inconsistency are applicable. 'I ought to do *x*' and 'I ought not to do *x*' may both be true though they cannot both be acted on and are thus act-inconsistent. Act-inconsistency would reduce the truth inconsistency if we accept 'ought' implies 'can' together with the principle of agglomeration which says that '*x* ought to do *p*' and '*x* ought to do *q*' imply '*x* ought to do both *p* and *q*'. The reasoning is as follows: from '*x* ought to do *p*' and '*x* ought to do not *p*' agglomeration gives us '*x* ought to do *p* and not *p*'; 'ought' implies 'can' takes us from this to the truth inconsistent '*x* can do *p* and not *p*'. The claim that 'ought' and 'ought not' are truth-consistent thus depends crucially on the denial of one or both of these principles. If Sinnott-Armstrong is right we can coherently affirm both the existence of moral dilemmas to which pluralists draw attention and that 'ought' judgements can be treated in realist fashion as beliefs apt, like any other belief, to be assessed for truth and falsity.

This strategy has a price, however. To treat moral beliefs in this realist fashion is to view moral theory as a search for a correct description of moral reality and is tantamount to deciding that its practical aspects are merely accidental. The denial of agglomeration and 'ought' implies 'can' reinforces this decision.

It should be clear that moral theory viewed in this way as a search for realist truth leaves no room for pluralism. Where judgements are genuinely truth-incompatible, they cannot both provide true descriptions of moral reality. In the case of conflicting 'oughts' which feature in dilemmas, both can be true because the conflict is not a truth conflict but here again there is no space for pluralism about truth. We might of course encourage the development of a plurality of theories on the grounds that truth, though single, is by no means always easy to discover and conflicting theories may have an equal chance of being right or may both contain elements which are true. Thus Popper, whose account of science is as realist as one could wish, favours the proliferation of theories without being at all committed to pluralism about truth. We can agree with Mark Platts when he says first that 'it is indeed a consequence of the kind of moral realism considered here that, in some sense, everybody SHOULD have the same moral beliefs' and second that 'what we might overlook are features OF THE WORLD, not fictions of our own imagination. Moral pluralism is desirable not for liberal-cum-aesthetic reasons but for EPISTEMIC ones' (Platts, 1979). And we should add 'and not for theoretical reasons'. We should add also the observation that even the epistemic reasons apply only when the truth is difficult or complicated; in the case of obvious truths and obvious falsehoods there will be no need for toleration of a plurality of views at all.

Suppose we decide, however, that the practical aspect of ethical judgements is not an accidental feature but an integral part of them being the sort of judgements they are. What effect will this have on our attitudes to realism and to pluralism? Williams has consistently argued that we should distinguish the moral 'ought' from the 'ought' of practical deliberation which is designed to answer the question 'what ought I to do simpliciter?' or perhaps better 'what am I to do?' rather than 'what morally ought I to do?' (Williams, 1973 and, for example, Williams, 1985). The questions are not the same because it makes sense to answer the former but not the latter 'you ought to forget about morality this time and concentrate on your career'. Even if the answer to both questions turns out to be the same the second answer is not a mere repetition of the first. The practical 'ought' seems moreover to have different properties from the moral one. In this case 'ought' is not compatible with 'ought not', agglomeration and 'ought' implies 'can' do seem to apply and the practical question does not admit of more than one answer.

So far so good; but things are more complicated, I think, than Williams allows. There does seem to be a sense of 'ought' in which one can ask even in dilemmatic cases 'what really ought I to do morally speaking?' which resembles the practical 'ought' in allowing of only one answer and in permitting 'ought' implies 'can' and agglomeration but still differs from it in that even when the final moral question is answered the practical question remains open. And it makes perfect sense to answer them differently; 'clearly your moral duty is to do missionary work in Africa, but what you really ought to do is sign up for a Business Administration course'.

The point to which Williams is drawing attention is that even when morality delivers a single answer to the practical question that answer may conflict with non-moral answers to the same question. There need be no single answer to that question on which all fully rational thinkers must converge. Someone who is, in Williams's phrase, 'morally motivated' may answer it in one way and someone else, equally rational but differently motivated can give an incompatible answer. This suggests that when it comes to assessing answers to the final practical question there is no place for realist truth (a suggestion borne out by the fact that often the question can be answered equally well by an imperative). The considerations about conflicts, dilemmas and incommensurability highlighted by pluralists suggest that the same may be true of the final moral question 'what, morally speaking, ought I really to do?'. In cases of conflict equally rational people may arrive at different answers and there is no guarantee that further information or further ratiocination would lead to convergence. If that is right, ethical realism is undermined by the fact that some ethical questions as least will lack a determinate answer.

Moral judgements face in different directions. On the one hand they resemble ordinary assertions enough for it to be plausible to treat them as expressions of beliefs which aim for truth and are subject to the normal constraints of consistency and rationality which govern assertions. On the other hand they are expected to be action guiding and to feature in practical reasoning for which the constraints of consistency and rationality, as Williams pointed out, appear to be different. Whatever doubts we may have about the details of his arguments he is surely right to highlight these differences and to trace them to areas of discourse where truth is the target and those where it is not. Insofar as we conceive ethics realistically as the search for the correct description of moral reality, pluralism will have no more (and no less) of a place than it has in any similar search. Most plausibly this will amount to the toleration of a number of theories on the grounds that, though at best one can be correct, there may be elements of truth in them all. And such toleration will extend only to areas where truth is thought to be difficult to come by. The Enlightenment platitude that every truth is compatible with every other is indeed a platitude and the apparent denial of it by Berlin's pluralists is absurd. What they may have been pointing at, however, in a confused way is something that could still be correct; namely that different values, ways of life and obligations will almost certainly conflict in practice. Ways of life have to be lived, values realised and obligations met, whether they be those of different societies, of different people within a single society or even those of a single individual. But these are practical conflicts and practical disharmonies and as such are not truth-involving. Pluralism comes into its own when ethical discourse is seen as addressing practical questions; but that is the point at which realism becomes inappropriate. Pluralism and realism make uneasy bedfellows.

Value-Pluralism

JOHN SKORUPSKI

I. Introductory

A view with some considerable influence in current moral and political philosophy holds that there is a plurality of values, all of them fundamental and authoritative and yet, in some genuinely disconcerting way, *in conflict*. I shall call it 'value-pluralism'.

It is a philosophical thesis. It does more than record the fact that choice often involves conflicts, moral and other, and that choosing can be a difficult and sometimes even an appalling thing to do. That experience any serious ethics must acknowledge. It is basic, but it is not a surprise, philosophically or otherwise; whereas the claim of the value-pluralist is meant to be philosophically surprising and significant. Further, value-pluralism is to be distinguished from what Mill, Moore and Rawls call 'intuitionism' in ethics: the view that there is no single ethical standard to which all principles of conduct must conform, but a number of ethical principles all equally fundamental.[1] 'Ethical pluralism' would be a good term for this view; it is a philosophical thesis, and certainly not uncontroversial—but value-pluralism is meant to go beyond it. The question is how. There are two main suggestions. One is that, at least in some cases in which fundamental values conflict, there is no rationally determinable answer to the question which should take precedence. The conflict is *inarbitrable*. Another is that in some such cases one does wrong whatever one does, Wrong doing is *inescapable*. Both suggestions take value-pluralism beyond simple ethical pluralism—this paper considers both of them.[2]

[1] Mill (1969, p. 206): 'the intuitive school'; Moore (1903, p. x): 'the common doctrine, which has generally been called by that name'; Rawls (1972, p. 34). The term 'intuitionism' is often used to refer not just to the thesis that fundamental ethical principles are irreducibly plural, but to that conjoined with the further view that these plural principles are known by rational or a priori 'intuition'. In section III I refer to this conjoint view as 'rational intuitionism'.

[2] One or both of them can be found in some measure in the writings, for example, of Isaiah Berlin, Alasdair MacIntyre, Bernard Williams, Charles Taylor. John Gray has recently emphasised this side of Isaiah Berlin's thought (Gray, 1993, 1995). Unfortunately space precludes discussion of these writers, or of Gray's account of the relations between value-pluralism and the politics of liberalism (an interesting issue in its own right).

Some terminology is required. I will call propositions about reasons—which may be reasons to believe, do, or feel—*normative* propositions. *Epistemic* normative propositions are propositions about reasons to believe; they concern the relation *the fact that p gives N reason to believe that q*. For example, the fact that black clouds are coming up over the horizon gives me reason to believe that it's going to rain. *Practical* normative propositions are about the relation *the fact that p gives N reason to ø*. The fact that a car is coming gives you reason to get out of the way. *Evaluative* normative propositions, are about what there is reason to feel—the relevant relation here is *the fact that p gives N reason to F*. Example: the fact that Emma broke the record gives her reason to feel proud. I will for brevity call true normative propositions *norms* and evaluative normative propositions, true or false, 'evaluations'. And I include propositions which are not explicitly about reasons, but from which propositions about reasons are analytically deducible, in the normative class.

The value-pluralism we are to consider is not a form of subjectivism. (This point is emphasised, for example, in Gray, 1993.) It grants the 'objectivity' of practical and evaluative norms. What does this involve? There is a familiar sense in which a person's *judgement* can be more or less objective: it is objective to the extent that it is free of personal bias, prejudice and the like. My judgement of how well my daughter plays the piano may in that sense be less objective than the examiner's. But what do we mean when we ask about the objectivity or otherwise of normative *propositions*?

Firstly, it is a question of whether they are genuinely that—propositions. A proposition is a judgeable and therefore truth-evaluable content. Here my use of the word 'true' is intended to be non-committal on issues of ontology. A philosopher who wishes to stress the difference between propositions about facts and propositions about reasons, and to reject a realist ontology with respect to propositions about reasons, might want to reserve 'true' and 'false' for factual propositions, and use some other terms, such as 'correct' or 'valid' for normative propositions. I sympathise with this approach—however the relevant point about it for present purposes is that it still maintains the view that normative propositions are judgeable contents, evaluable for correctness or validity. Since this discussion will not need to go far into questions about the ontology of norms I will, simply for convenience, use the term 'true' broadly (i.e. to cover both 'factual truth' and 'normative validity', should that be the preferred fundamental terminology).

A good name for the view that normative claims are genuine

judgements is 'cognitivism'. *Objectivism* is worth distinguishing from it only because it can usefully label a position which is stronger. It holds not only that normative claims are genuine judgements, but that some normative propositions are true—there are norms. In contrast scepticism about norms holds that we cannot know whether there are norms (whether any normative proposition is true); nihilism holds that we do indeed make normative judgements but that there are no norms. (Any wide-scope negation of a normative proposition is true, or neither true nor false.)

Relativism, finally, as I understand it here, is a variety of objectivism, one which holds that the truth-predicate is a relational term with a place reserved for a term denoting a community, form of life, theoretical framework, tradition etc. If relativism is the correct view for a given class of propositions then propositions in that class will not be simply *true*. They will be true-relative-to-*k*, where *k* denotes a community, form of life, theoretical framework or tradition. So relativism about normative propositions is the view that there are indeed norms—true normative propositions—but that truth in their case is a relation to some such parameter. Value-pluralism may or may not be a form of relativism; the question will be considered in section V.

II. Relativities of Situation

Reasons for action and feeling can have a relativity which is in no way connected with relativism as I have just defined it.

It concerns the relational character of reasons themselves. Consider: I have reason to look after my children, you have reason to look after yours. This reason is relative to the agent in the sense that it supervenes on a relation between the children and the agent. What gives *x* reason to look after *y* is that *y* is *x*'s child. Such reasons for action are often called 'agent-relative'. Not all practical reasons are agent-relative—some are 'agent-neutral'. For example, everyone has reason, where possible, to come to the aid of a person in distress, irrespective of that person's relation to them.

A parallel distinction can be made for reasons to feel. Seeing an old photograph of the house from which her family was expelled will very probably be a moving experience for my grandmother. There is every reason for her to be moved. But there is not necessarily reason for someone unconnected with the family to be moved. For him, quite understandably, it might be just an old photograph. Again, dumb-Polack jokes are quite reasonably irritating to Poles. There's reason for Poles to be irritated—but there is not the same reason for non-Poles to be. The latter may reasonably disapprove of insensitive jokes in general, but feeling disapproval is not the same as feeling offended or irritated.

In each case what makes it reasonable or intelligible for the person to have the reaction, of nostalgic sentiment, or irritation, towards the object is a relation it has to the person. These are, as it were, *patient-relative* evaluations ('agent' and 'patient' corresponds to 'action' and 'passion').[3] But as in the case of practical norms there are also patient-neutral evaluations. Most importantly, aesthetic and moral evaluations, which concern what there is reason to admire or to blame, are patient-neutral.

To say that is to make something like the Kantian claim that aesthetic and moral evaluations are universally legislative. The claim is stronger than saying that they are 'universalisable' in the usual sense. For a relative practical or evaluative norm can also be universalisable in that sense. Everyone has reason to look after their own children. Anyone who sees a photograph of a house associated with a very significant part of their past life has reason to be moved. People who find themselves, or a group to which they belong and with which they identify, the butt of denigrating or belittling humour have reason to be annoyed or irritated. To say that aesthetic and moral evaluations legislate universally is to say that they are not patient-relative: they assert that there is reason for anyone, not just those persons who stand in a certain relation to the object, to admire or blame it. (A patient-neutral moral evaluation may concern an agent-relative practical maxim: for example that it's blameworthy to give preference to one's relatives in making appointments.)

One obvious source of these relativities, practical and evaluative, is the diversity of people's histories and social relations. Agent-relative reasons for action, including agent-relative duties and obligations, arise from one's social status or office, previous commitments, accumulated emotional ties—from our concrete historical and social position in the world. I have these reasons for action because I am a parent or guardian, or the treasurer of the club; or I have agent-relative practical reasons which arise from patient-relative evaluations—because I have reason to feel grateful to you for past kindness I have reason to go out of my way to help you in a present predicament.

Another important source of relativity has to do with the diversity not of our positions but of our natures. I will refer to both of

[3] I discuss a definition of agent-relativity in Skorupski, 1995. Patient-relativity can be defined along parallel lines.

these as aspects of our *situation*. We are 'situated' in determinate, though mutable, positions and characters. What is desirable for you, what there is reason for you to desire, is patient-relative. If wealth will make you happy that's a reason for you to desire it. It's not a reason for *me* to desire wealth— the relevant question in my case is whether wealth would make *me* happy. Unlike judgements about the admirable and blameworthy, judgements about the desirable are not patient-neutral. If a person's good is characterised in terms of what there is reason for that person to desire, judgements about a person's good—what is good for that person, will be patient-relative in this obvious way. And what there is reason to desire varies with one's nature. Wealth will make you happy but not me. The general form of the underlying judgement is: If *y* will make *x* G then there is reason for *x* to desire *y*. So a further question arises: is there just one such property G. or a number of them? 'Is happy' may be used formally, to mean 'has a property which there is reason for him or her to desire that he or she should have'. But if it is used more concretely, the question will arise whether it is the only property that can stand in for G. What about knowing, or being free? And if we allow the possibility of a concrete plurality of categorial ends, as one might call them, is the list the same for all kinds of persons? Or even for all kinds of human beings? Perhaps the underlying form should be 'If *y* will make *x* G and *x* is the kind of being for whom it matters to have G then there is reason for *x* to desire *y*.' That would build, so to speak, a double layer of patient-relativity into judgements about a person's good.

A similar diversity arises with what ideals I should pursue; despite the patient-neutrality of the admirable. There is reason to admire profound musical sensibility or great physical courage and endurance but it does not follow that these are ideals that I should seek to cultivate in myself. I may not have the talents to do so or I may have different capacities whose realisation will make my life fuller. Ends and ideals may be categorical but the degree to which different people should steer by them may differ.

III. Inescapable Blame?

These relativities, arising from diversity of situation, are a main source of the diversity of obligations and commitments—within a culture and across cultures. They give substance to 'ethical life'. But do they give any basis to value-pluralism? Nothing in our sketch of their logic so far provides it. Value-pluralism involved the thesis that some conflicts of values are *inarbitrable*, or that in some conflicts of value wrong doing is *inescapable*. Let us first consider the second of these ideas, the idea that there are conflicts in which whatever one does one does wrong.

The moral dilemmas most likely to produce a sense of the inescapability of wrong-doing seem to be conflicts between agent-relative obligations, or between agent-relative and agent-neutral obligations. A conflict between duty to family and duty to country or state would be an example of the former; a choice between saving the life of a relative or friend and saving the lives of strangers would be an example of the latter. Less dramatically. but perhaps closer to experience, there is the case of choosing a school for one's child, where many parents have felt a tension between what they see as the relative obligations of family and the neutral considerations of justice. Of course there can be equally difficult choices which involve agent-neutral considerations on both sides, such as whether to give in to hostage-takers. But I suspect that these dilemmas, equally difficult, nevertheless do not conjure up the thought of inescapable self-blame as the others do.

The most natural representation of this thought about fated, inescapable blame is a world-picture in which one is subject to separate laws, coming from distinct but severally authoritative sovereigns, all of them legitimately armed with punishments for transgression: these gods and those, the edicts of the gods and the necessary law of the state. I am only saying 'the most natural'—I can see nothing positively incoherent in the idea of a single source of legitimation which sanctions laws capable of throwing the agent into inescapably wrong doing. But it seems to me to lack any plausible, self-sustaining *rationale*. The very legitimacy of the source is vitiated if it dooms agents to unavoidable blame. If therefore we think of morality as an integral, unitary system—as I believe we do—it becomes hard to understand the possibility that moral blame might be inescapable. Is it not anachronistic to conceive a plurality of ethical sovereigns? I think (to be blunt) that it is. But the world-picture that goes with that way of thinking depicts something psychologically real. Though our idea of the moral is the idea of an integral and unitary sovereign source of law, its *content* comes from disjoint sources—the blame-feeling, which has its own spontaneous natural objects, and ethical notions coming from pure practical reason.[4]

A purely rational intuitionism cannot explain the feeling that one transgresses whatever one does, let alone endorse it, because it fails to take account of this plurality of sources. The irreducible

[4] In the paragraphs which follow I draw on a view of morality, practical reason and blame outlined in Skorupski, 1993.

and potentially conflicting obligations it envisages still fall into a system of morality with a *single* source—reason. But if we recognise that morality has sources both in the emotions (those which lie at the spontaneous core of blame) and in reason, then we do at least have materials for *explaining* the feeling. That does not mean that we can *endorse* it. It is an internal norm of the blame-feeling itself that to blame the unavoidable is unreasonable. So a sovereign which sanctions punishment of the unavoidable must lose legitimacy. And hence we cannot seriously endorse the idea of the inescapability of blame—punishability—unless we seriously believe in the existence of a plurality of separate sovereigns, issuing potentially conflicting laws. But to acknowledge that morality has sources both in various clusters of spontaneous moral feeling and in practical reason falls short of claiming that those sources are separately *sovereign*. What could it mean to say they are? One does not have to be a rationalist to acknowledge that in conflicts between them reason is supreme. For saying that spontaneous moral feeling, or tradition, can come into conflict with practical reason is just a vivid way of saying that there can be good reason to override spontaneous moral feeling, or tradition. Or that there can be good reason to give preference to a less strongly felt cluster of obligations over one that is more strongly felt.

That leads us back to the other value-pluralist claim, that there can be conflicts which are rationally inarbitrable—conflicts in which there simply is no good reason to give preference to one side over the other.

We need to distinguish here the claim that there are conflicts of choice which no rational *decision-procedure* or *criterion* can decide from the much stronger claim that there are conflicts which are rationally inarbitrable. Value-pluralism has to say something more than that in some conflicts 'there is no overarching standard whereby their claims are rationally arbitrable' (Gray, 1993, p. 291). A dedicated hedonistic utilitarian, who believes that there is an 'overarching standard' in the sense that the only ultimate ethical value is happiness, could still agree with that. For he might well hold—if he was realistic he would hold—that this thesis about ultimate ethical value provides, in many concrete cases, no decision-procedure or criterion of choice. On the other hand, a rational intuitionist would agree that there is no overarching standard. But he would not agree that that implies that conflicts are rationally inarbitrable. He would rightly point out that reason can be a matter of exercising judgement rather than applying decision-procedures or overarching standards or criteria.

A second obvious point is that both the rational intuitionist and the utilitarian can agree that there may be rationally inarbitrable choices. Where there is more than one best action, choosing between them is rationally inarbitrable. There is no right answer to the question, what ought I to do?—but there is no conflict either. It really is a matter of choice—perhaps indeed very distressing choice; but certainly no blame attaches to whatever choice one makes. What then is the value-pluralist saying? Apparently he envisages *strong dilemmas*, as I will call them, in which there is a plurality of justified but incompatible answers as to which course of action I uniquely ought to pursue. The answers are rationally inarbitrable: this must mean that there is adequate reason to accept each one of them, and no adequate reason to accept just one of them over the others. The situation differs from that in which there is simply a short list of optimal things to do. But what difference to moral life does this abstractly framed distinction, between strong dilemmas and choices between optimal actions, actually make? The only possible answer is that in the strong dilemma one incurs legitimate blame whatever one does. And the only way to give genuine substance as against bare logical coherence to the idea of inescapable blame (I have suggested) is to appeal to the anachronistic world-picture of separate and ultimate ethical sovereigns.

IV. Objectivity and Ideal Convergence

In the previous section we were considering the idea that a single ethical tradition might generate strong dilemmas: there might be situations in which it gave incompatible, justified and rationally inarbitrable answers as to what one ought to do, so that blame was unavoidable. But in political theory value-pluralism is often advanced in a somewhat different context: as a response to the historical existence of *different* ethical traditions. There are familiar cases of ethical choice in which these different ethical traditions each produce unitary answers as to what one ought to do—but the several answers they produce conflict. The value-pluralist response is that the conflicting answers may *all* be correct. In this context the idea of inescapable blame is not usually mentioned; presumably the different ethical traditions give incompatible correct answers as to what is blameworthy as well as giving incompatible correct answers as to what one ought to do.

This is certainly the important form of value-pluralism in current political and cultural debate, rather than that discussed in the previous section. But does this form of value-pluralism differ from relativism? Before addressing the question we need to delve further into the philosophy of judgement and assertion.

To judge is judge the content of one's judgement true. This observation uses the notion of truth broadly (section I). Truth in the broad sense may be partially characterised as a property F such that for any judgement or assertion, J, if it is shown that there is no adequate ground to hold that J has F, reason (as against etiquette, discretion or whatever) requires withdrawal of J. This characterisation appeals to the notion of rational justification for belief. It is partial because being rationally justified is itself a property of beliefs and assertions which satisfies it. But truth is not rational justification. A judgement may be true but not rationally justified, or rationally justified but not true. The two notions are distinct. In the domain of belief, however, both are required. Whereas an action or a feeling may be assessable as rationally justified or not, neither is assessable as true or not. But it is inherent to the notion of judgement that a judgement is assessable in both these ways.

Now value-pluralism holds that there can be true, incompatible but rationally inarbitrable normative judgements. Do the points just made about judgement rule that possibility out? Not straightforwardly. Suppose the value-pluralist holds that there are cases in which it is true that one ought to do X and that one ought not to do X, or that one ought to do X and one ought to do Y, where doing X is incompatible with doing Y. These normative judgements are not contradictory (without further assumptions) but they are in conflict. The value-pluralist holds that they may all be rationally justified, and that there may be no question of using rational judgement to determine what one 'really' ought to do. This is all consistent with the points about judgement.

Of course if 'ought' connects with blame in the normal way then in these cases whatever the agent does incurs blame. He either fails to do what he ought to do or he does what he ought not to do. If one is influenced by the considerations about blame and avoidability aired in the previous section one will not accept the possibility of such cases. But now we must consider another kind of thought, which remains even if such cases are ruled out. It is that one person or tradition may *justifiably* come to the conclusion that (it is true that) one ought to do X and another person or tradition may *justifiably* come to the conclusion that (it is true that) one ought not to do X (or indeed that it's not the case that one ought to do X)—and that the conflict between their views may not be rationally arbitrable. I now want to propose that this thought should be dismissed too.

I have argued elsewhere (Skorupski, 1985–86) that to judge is to engage in what I will call *the convergence commitment*. When I judge, I *wager*, so to speak, that inquirers who scrutinised the relevant evidence and argument available to them would converge on my judgement—unless I could fault their judgement or their evidence. Faulting an inquirer's *judgement* would involve showing some relevant internal weakness or inadequacy in his judging propensity on the subject in question, sufficient to justify me in discounting the judgement. That can include weaknesses of taste or sensibility, and distortions produced by special pleading or wishful thinking etc.—not just faults of logic. Faulting the inquirer's *evidence* would involve showing that the information input into his judging process is faulty or restricted in such a way as to vitiate his assertion on the subject in question—that is, in such a way as to justify me in discounting it, even if I can find no fault in his judgement. The critical standards for fault-finding are those which normally apply. Thus the commitment is that if relevant data (where data are relevant at all) went on being collected, and reasoning rescrutinised, inquirers who did not fall out of consideration through demonstrable faults of evidence or judgement would stably converge on agreement with the judgement.

When I speak of a 'wager' I mean that we are not called upon to give grounds for expecting this convergence, over and above our grounds for the judgement itself. Rather, the existence of the commitment shows itself negatively. If I come, in one way or another, to have reason to doubt that my judgement would attract convergence, I thereby come to have reason to withdraw it. When those grounds for doubt become strong enough, they force withdrawal.

What case can be made for this claim? The first relevant point has already been made:

(1) To judge that p is to judge that it is true that p.

The second is this:

(2) It is irrational to judge that: it is true that p but one has no sufficient reason to judge that it is true that p.

There is of course no self-contradiction in the proposition 'It is true that p but I have no sufficient reason to judge that it is true that p.' Indeed it can be true. But to judge it to be so would be irrational. I cannot rationally judge that p while also judging that I have insufficient reason to judge that p.

Now this only shows that if I judge that p I am rationally *committed* (by (1) and (2)) to holding that I have sufficient reason to judge that it is true that p—even though the proposition that p of course does not *entail* the proposition that I have sufficient reason to judge that it is true that *p*. It does not on its own show that if I judge that *p* I must hold that *anyone* who holds that there is insufficient reason to judge that *p* is faulty either in judgement or in evidence. But consider now the following principle

> (3) If *p* then any evidence that justifies a thinker in judging that there is insufficient reason to judge that *p* is either also insufficient to decide whether or not it is the case that *p* or else is misleading inasmuch as it warrants the thinker in denying that *p*.

Suppose the evidence available to a thinker other than myself is insufficient to decide whether or not it is the case that *p*, and that I judge that *p*. By (1) and (2) I am committed to judging that I have sufficient reason, and thus (in cases where evidence is required) sufficient evidence, to judge that *p*, and so I am committed to judging that thinker is faulty in evidence (because he doesn't have enough). Suppose on the other hand that the evidence available to that thinker justifies him in believing that it is not the case that *p*. Then by (3) I must judge that that evidence is misleading—partial or distorted in some way—and so once again I must judge that the thinker is faulty in evidence—or I must conclude that it is my own evidence which is insufficient and withdraw the judgement that *p*. Suppose, finally, that the evidence available to a thinker justifies him in believing that *p* but that he refuses to accept that *p* (he doesn't just fail to consider the question whether *p*). Then that thinker is faulty in judgement. So given (1), (2) and (3) if I judge that *p* then I am committed to judging that any thinker who refuses to judge that *p* is faulty in evidence or judgement.

It is the *judgement* that incurs the commitment—not the judgement's *content* that entails it. I am not defining truth itself in terms of convergence. There are—of course—factual assertions which would in fact be correct if made, but on which convergence could not occur because sufficient relevant evidence could not be collected. But just because evidence for them is not available, they could not be *justified*, even though they would be correct. It is also true that whenever we accept a judgement—however good our evidence and reasoning for it—the possibility always remains open that we are wrong in doing so and hence wrong also in thinking that impeccable inquirers would converge to stable agreement on it. The convergence commitment is compatible with as radical a form of defeasibility as one likes.

There is however a fundamental asymmetry between normative and factual judgements. In the case of a factual proposition there is the simple possibility that there may not be enough evidence to pass a verdict, however long and expensive the inquiry. The point arises from the very idea of a single world *within* which the knowing subject is situated (and mobile) and in which it interacts epistemically with other objects within it. It is a necessary consequence of this idea, which relates knowing act and fact known as patient and agent within the world, that for any knowing subject there must be truths which that subject is not, and given the limitations determined by its particular epistemic powers, *could not be*, justified in asserting. Such a world cannot be fully transparent to such a knower. There must be such limitations on the epistemic interactions possible for any particular knower in the world, even if there are no limitations which must apply on all.

In the case of normative propositions no such point applies. The metaphysics of the normative domain provides no basis for the idea of fundamental norm which we could never be justified in recognising as true.[5] Corresponding to this distinction between normative and factual propositions there corresponds a distinction in their epistemology. It's the distinction between what one might call the epistemology of spontaneity and the epistemology of correspondence. My grounds for asserting a normative proposition turn in the first instance on what I'm spontaneously inclined to think, do or feel. They are correctable by further reflection and discussion. This correctability by reflection and discussion, of which the convergence commitment is one aspect, underwrites the distinction between what seems to me to be true and what is true: it allows one to treat normative claims as genuine judgements. In the case of factual propositions the same conditions of objectivity apply; but whether I am justified in asserting the proposition turns on whether I am appropriately linked to what it asserts to be the case. Grounds for holding that I am not so linked are grounds for holding that I am not justified in asserting the proposition. Such a notion of breakdown of evidential linkage simply does not apply in the case of fundamental norms.

Now let's return to the suggestion that one person may justifiably come to the conclusion that one ought to do X and another person may justifiably come to the conclusion that one ought not to do X (or that it's not the case that one ought to do X) but that the conflict between their views may not be rationally arbitrable, even though both conclusions cannot simultaneously be true. The suggestion is ruled out by the thesis which has just been argued

[5] A normative proposition deduced from decidable normative premises together with some undecidable factual proposition would of course also be undecidable. By 'fundamental norm' I mean 'normative proposition knowable independently of deduction from any factual proposition'.

for: that judgement incurs the convergence commitment. If both judgements cannot be true then at least one of the judgers has to be faulty in evidence or judgement.[6]

V. Value-pluralism as Relativism

If the arguments of the preceding section are right then the value-pluralism we were there considering has to turn into relativism—that is, into the view that apparently conflicting moral judgements may be true relative to different parameters, for example, ethical traditions. If one takes that view of moral judgements then, firstly, arguments from the avoidability of blame do not apply. For attribution of blame will also be valid only relative to the parameter in question, and so as long as that parameter is held constant, it will not be the case that blame is unavoidable. There may be choices where whatever one does is blameworthy according to some ethical tradition or other, but this is irrelevant. Secondly, the point that a convergence commitment is incurred by any judgement is not in itself inconsistent with relativism. If a judgement is only true relative to some parameter k then the commitment is that reasoners not faulty in evidence or judgement would agree that it is true relative to k.

But does anything makes relativism plausible for *fundamental normative*, as against factual, propositions? This may seem a surprising question to raise. Is it not particularly with respect to the normative that relativism has proved tempting? Nevertheless, in the case of factual propositions there is a forceful and familiar kind of relativism which says that they can be true only relative to some

[6] Thus the thesis that judgement incurs the convergence commitment differs from a view recently argued by Wright (1992, 1996). He holds that a concept of truth as representation or 'fit' carries with it the convergence commitment: to judge true in that sense is to incur the commitment. But he holds that the concept of truth applicable to ethical judgements does not involve the notion of representation. The concept of truth which is applicable there, he suggests, allows that a person may, without irrationality, judge that an ethical proposition p is true while *also* judging that convergence of fault-free thinkers (thinkers who suffer from no 'cognitive shortcoming') cannot be expected to occur on that judgement. I agree that ethical truth involves no notion of 'fit' to a domain of reality. But if what has been said here is right that is irrelevant. *No* notion of *truth* allows a person to judge a proposition true without incurring the convergence commitment, because the convergence commitment arises quite generally from the *rationality* of judgement rather than any particular notion of *truth*.

theoretical framework. The standard argument for it is the supposed underdetermination of theory by data. On that thesis, there is more than one optimal overall theory, judged by *all* accessible data and *all* epistemic norms. Assuming that to be so, the relativist about factual propositions argues that the notions of truth—and of correspondence—make sense only intra-theoretically. Relative to a theoretical framework, you can ask which propositions in it are true, correspond to the facts; but you cannot ask which theoretical framework is true or corresponds to the facts.

Whether or not this relativism is finally tenable, there is at any rate an opening for it, provided by the underdetermination thesis, an opening which has no parallel in the case of the normative. For while factual judgements may be underdetermined with respect to all data and epistemic norms, there is nothing with respect to which *fundamental* normative judgements themselves are underdetermined. The parallel, rather, is this. Fundamental practical and evaluative norms, together with the 'data' of the circumstances in which we find ourselves. may underdetermine our non-fundamental, applied practical and evaluative judgements. So more than one morality may be optimal by those fundamental norms, just as more than one overall theory (according to the underdetermination thesis) may be optimal by our fundamental epistemic norms. And if more than one moral framework is indeed optimal relative to fundamental practical and evaluative norms then (the relativist may argue) a moral judgement may be true relative to one optimal moral framework and not true relative to another. But that is not relativism about fundamental as against applied norms—in fact we have made sense of it only on the assumption that there are non-relative fundamental norms.

As well as the possibility that those fundamental norms may leave space for more than one optimal application in the same circumstances, there is the more obvious possibility that in *varying* circumstances they may optimise different moralities. The repertoire of virtues optimal among hunter-gatherers or marauders may not be the same as that which is optimal in technically advanced industrial societies. Let us call these possibilities, that different moralities may be optimal in different circumstances, and that more than one morality may be optimal in the same circumstances, the *relativities of circumstance* (as against the relativities of situation discussed in section II).

The relativities of circumstance may seem to give more support to a kind of value-pluralism than do the relativities of situation. They highlight two things. The first is the historicity of moral schemes. That is hardly new. If value-pluralism boils down to this, it is a doctrine which would have been widely accepted in the nineteenth century. The other, slightly less familiar point, concerns the scope for indeterminacy in moral argument. There may be much in concrete moral discussion which is underdetermined by any plausible set of fundamental norms. Justice, for example, may dictate impartiality. And justice is plausibly a fundamental norm. But it may well be underdetermined by those fundamental norms what exactly impartiality requires. However, one should not on this basis leap too quickly to a view of justice which relativises it to ethical traditions. If the question is indeed underdetermined, then by the argument of this section it is also indeterminate. It is not that in these circumstances there is more than one right theory of justice—there isn't one at all. There is only a shortlist of principles compatible with impartiality, among which no objective ranking can be sustained. By what magic, then, would it become determinate, 'relative to an ethical tradition', that a particular principle of justice on this shortlist is the one that is correct—as against just being the one that is received in the tradition?

It may be that there is an answer to this question—at least in the particular case of justice—which has to do with the artificiality of principles of justice and the holism of traditions. At any rate, it is in this direction that the prospects of elucidating a politically germane kind of value-pluralism seem to me to lie.

Moral Philosophy and its Anti-pluralist Bias

BHIKHU PAREKH

It is an obvious fact of history that human beings have always entertained and continue to entertain different conceptions of the good and lead very different lives both individually and collectively. This raises two questions. First, why do ways of life differ? And second, how should we respond to their differences? The first is an explanatory, and the second a normative question, and the two are closely related. The first question has been answered differently by different writers, of which I shall mention three by way of illustration.

First, for some writers such as Montesquieu and Holbach, whom I shall call naturalists, differences between ways of life arise out of differences in climate, geographical conditions, history and temperament of the people concerned. Just as different vegetations grow in different places, different societies throw up different ways of life depending on their natural and historical contexts.

Secondly, some writers such as Herder and Shelley, whom I shall call romantics, argue that differences owe their origins to the fact that as free, creative and imaginative beings, human beings think differently, value different goals, experiment with new ideas and ideals, strive after new forms of social organisation, and evolve ways of life best suited to their self-understanding and needs. The differences are not accidental products of external factors and contingent in character, but deeply rooted in man's creative nature.

Thirdly, for some writers such as those discussed in this paper, whom I shall call rationalists, differences in ways of life arise because different groups of human beings are unequally endowed or are at different stages of intellectual and moral development. If they had all been equal in their intellectual and moral capacities or were equally enlightened, they would think more or less alike, arrive at common values and ideals, and evolve identical ways of life. Since that is not the case, the differences in their ways of life are only to be expected.

Each answer has important normative implications. For naturalists the plurality of ways of life is an inescapable fact of life in just the same way that differences in human shapes, sizes and pigmentation are, and is to be neither regretted nor celebrated. The naturalists take a largely positivist view of difference, and do not see it as a value or build a justificatory theory around it. Although they accept plurality, they are not pluralists.

For romantics the diversity of ways of life expresses, exemplifies and sustains human creativity, is a tribute to the ingenuity and resourcefulness of the human spirit, and a matter for celebration. As such it is to be greatly welcomed and encouraged. Since the romantics value plurality and consider its disappearance and even diminution a loss, they may properly be called pluralists.

Rationalists take a wholly different view of plurality. Subsuming goodness under truth, they argue that like truth the good is singular in nature. Even as the same proposition cannot be true in one place and false in another, the same thing cannot be good in one society and bad in another. Only one way of life is the best for human beings, and those falling short of it are to that extent defective and inferior. Those rationalists who trace the plurality of ways of life to unequal human abilities argue that the plurality, although regrettable, must be accepted as an inescapable fact of life. Those who trace it to unequal levels of intellectual and moral development argue that the plurality can and should be eliminated or at least substantially reduced by suitably guiding those at the lower rings of the human hierarchy into the best way of life. In either case rationalists regard one way of life as the best, use it to judge others, consider plurality to be a form of moral falsehood, and regret it. For convenience I shall call them moral monists.

These three, and several other responses to the plurality of the ways of life that I have not mentioned, have had their eloquent spokesman in the Western tradition of moral and political philosophy. In this paper I intend to argue that of these, moral monism has commanded the allegiance of some of the most eminent philosophers, and that this has resulted in a deep anti-pluralist bias in Western thought.[1] In the first section I trace the presence of this bias in influential philosophers, in the second I draw out its consequences, and in the third I show how it derives its plausibility and can be countered.

I

The Sophists were struck by the fact that different societies were organised around different conceptions of the good life and followed different customs and practices. Although each society

[1] The tendency is, of course, not confined to Western philosophy, and is to be found in almost all non-western systems of thought. I am concerned only with the former.

understandably considered its way of life to be the best, the Sophists thought that there was no objective basis for such a judgement. Conceptions of the good life were entirely conventional in nature, and not amenable to rational arbitration and hierarchical gradation. For the Sophists differences between societies were a brute fact of life and neither to be resented nor celebrated.

The Sophist view had obvious weaknesses. First, it bordered on relativism with all its attendant difficulties. Secondly, while appreciating the differences between societies, it ignored those within them, and tended to assume that each society was internally homogeneous and rested on a uniformly shared view of the good life. Thirdly, the Sophists offered no coherent explanation of the differences, and either left them unexplained or attributed them to such factors as variations in social structures, customs and the history and self-understandings of the people concerned. Since they considered the differences accidental, they denied them an ontological status. Fourthly, the Sophists stressed the fact but not the value of differences. They treated each society as morally self-contained, and did not ask if they complemented and could learn from each other and whether and why it was wrong to suppress their differences by means of intellectual or military conquest.

Plato brilliantly exposed many of the weaknesses of the Sophist thought. He attacked not the Sophist failure to explain and appreciate the significance of differences but their tendency to give them even such limited importance as they did, and developed an alternative and basically monistic view of the good life. Building on the ontological distinction between *nomos* and *physis* and the related epistemological distinction between *doxa* and *episteme*, he argued that human beings had an unchanging essence or nature and that the good life ought to be based on it. The human soul had a tripartite structure, consisting of reason, spirit and desires. Desires, which men shared in common with the animals, were inherently unruly and chaotic and needed the directive and regulative control of reason, a faculty that men shared in common with god. The spirit or courage too had an irrational impulse and needed the guidance of reason. Since reason was the sole source of order, reproduced in the human soul the harmony of the cosmos, and was divine in nature, it was the highest human faculty. Reason was both theoretical and practice in nature, and the former, being free of the constraints of time and space, was higher. Plato therefore concluded that the highest form of life was one in which the rationally disciplined soul led a life of contemplation. Such a life realised all the good and all the important virtues that human life ought to realise, and was in that sense perfect. Since Plato regarded theoretical and practical reason as aspects of a single faculty, and the latter as implementing the conclusions of the former, he had no doubt that those possessing the former in the highest degree also possessed the latter in an equally large measure.

Although all human beings shared a common nature and possessed all three faculties, Plato argued that they did so in different degrees and were unequally equipped to lead the highest form of life. Depending on which of the three elements was dominant in them, different human beings found their happiness in different forms of life. Although these forms of life were good *for* them and indeed the only possible form of life available to them, their *objective* moral worth could be rationally determined and hierarchically graded. For Plato a just polity institutionalised the hierarchy, and vested political authority in the suitably trained men of reason or philosophers. He thought that since non-philosophers possessed enough reason to see the rationality of the hierarchy of ways of life including the philosopher's rule, they could be expected to accept it with good grace. However they might not, and therefore a blend of the 'noble lie' and coercion was deemed necessary.

Although Aristotle's moral and political thought differed from Plato's in significant respects, he shared many of Plato's basic assumptions. All human beings shared a common nature which, while partaking of the animal and the divine nature, also had several distinctive features of its own. Reason was the highest faculty, was both theoretical and practical in nature, and the former was uniquely divine. For Aristotle the life of contemplation satisfied man's highest faculty and offered the purest, noninstrumental and abiding pleasure. However since men were not disembodied reason, he seems to have thought that they needed to combine it with a balanced life of virtue under the guidance of practical wisdom (Ross, 1923, pp. 232–234; MacIntyre, 1981, pp. 137–153; Taylor, 1955, pp. 98–100). In such a life the highest forms of human excellence were realised and nothing of value was lost (Aristotle, 1984, *Nichomachean Ethics*, X.7). Since the impulse towards perfection constituted the *telos* of human nature, Aristotle thought that all human beings naturally strove towards the highest life as he described it. However they varied in their intellectual and moral capacities and led lives that fell short of it in varying degrees. Unlike Plato who made the structure of the human soul the basis of the *polis* and fused the personal and collective life, Aristotle rightly separated the two. He too thought that perfect men should ideally rule the *polis*, but he realised not only that such men were extremely rare but also that political institutions should correspond to and be designed in the light of the prevailing social structures including their dominant class divisions. While arguing for one best way of personal life, he was more open than Plato about the best form of political life. A qualified political pluralist, Aristotle nevertheless remained a moral monist (Hampshire, 1989, pp. 17–35).

Christianity represented a very different world of ideas and sensibilities, but retained a strong monistic orientation. For Christian philosophers humankind constituted a single species and shared a common nature. Being made in the image of God, all human beings had an inbuilt love of God and a desire to please Him by obeying His will. However as a result of the original sin incurred by them in the course of exercising their God-given capacity for free will, they also had an in-built tendency towards evil. Thanks to God's mercy, humankind was reconciled to Him through Jesus, who atoned for man's sinfulness, offered true moral and religious knowledge, and created the possibilities of human redemption. For Augustine, Aquinas and other Christian writers not the natural reason but true faith, which fulfilled and guided it, was the highest human faculty, and the highest form of life consisted in accepting the moral and religious doctrines of the Christian scriptures as authoritatively interpreted by the Catholic church (Gilson, 1961, pp. 143–184). Christianity was the only true religion, the Catholic church was its only authorised spokesman, and there was no salvation outside the Church. Protestants challenged the traditional importance of the Catholic Church, but shared its view that only the religiously grounded way of life was truly good and that Christianity was the only true religion. All non-Christian ways of life were devoid of true goodness, and Christians not only had nothing to learn from them but found them corrupting. Since all human beings were made in the image of God, they were naturally endowed with moral knowledge which they could discover with the help of their natural reason. However the natural reason was liable to error and lacked an adequate power to motivate. And hence, although some kind of good life could be lived on the basis of the natural reason alone, it was inherently precarious and devoid of spiritual depth and energy. Only the Christians stood any chance of leading a truly good life, not fully of course because of the original sin but to a considerable degree and even they could do so only if their faith was free of theological errors. Not surprisingly Christian writers took a dim view of non-Christian views of life, were particularly harsh on the Jews for rejecting the divine guidance they were the first to receive, and thought it their supreme duty to spread the Christian ways of life. (Augustine,

1957, vol. 2, pp. 258, 265; Deane, 1963, pp. 72, 206–220; Aquinas, 1952, vol. 2, pp. 432–440; Aquinas, 1955, pp. 15–50).[2]

While Christianity cannot avoid being dogmatic, at least to some extent, without losing its religious identity, one would expect classical liberalism to be far more open to moral and cultural pluralism. After all it arose as a reaction against the Catholic orthodoxy and sectarian wars, and prized freedom of individual belief and dissent. The picture however is more complex. Liberalism grew up within a milieu suffused with centuries of Christianity, and could hardly avoid imbibing its ethos and ways of looking at the world. In many respects it was structured by Christianity and was often its secularised version. Almost all classical liberals were Christians, and even those who were not largely rejected its theology but neither its basic morality nor its central categories. Although an atheist, Jeremy Bentham deeply admired Jesus's ethics and called him the 'first utilitarian'; the agnostic J. S. Mill thought that Jesus's teachings summed up the basic principles of his brand of altruistic utilitarianism; and while rejecting much of Christian theology, Tocqueville could not see how a liberal society could be built on any other foundation than Christianity, the 'only religion of free men' as he called it. Since almost all liberals aimed to retain some aspects of Christianity, they reinterpreted it along liberal lines and brought in within the limits of liberal reason. Locke's suggestively entitled *The Reasonableness of Christianity* was an excellent early example of scores of works with similar titles in all of which the 'natural reason' was defined in distinctly liberal terms. Just as liberal writers liberalised Christianity, they Christianised liberalism, and took over some of its central beliefs, myths, imagery and idioms. The liberal civilising mission was a secular version of its Christian original, which is why liberalism and Christianity were able to operate in a tandem and the expression 'spreading civilisation *and* Christianity' among the colonies aroused no anxiety on either side.

Although, unlike their Greek and Christian predecessors, liberal writers were sceptical about the possibility of a single and rationally demonstrable substantive vision of the good life, they were convinced that it was possible to arrive at rationally demonstrable or at least rationally defensible substantive moral principles which all visions of the good can be legitimately required to satisfy. These

[2] The writings of many Christian writers are deeply informed by the spirit of universal *caritas*. In criticising them I am only concerned to show how the ideas of even the noblest thinkers, when these are grounded in a monistic vision, lead to one-sided judgements on and even intolerance of other ways of life.

principles did not specify only the moral minimum that all ways of life should conform to, but constituted the foundations on which the latter were to be built and by which their complex moral structures were to be judged. Not surprisingly these principles were basically liberal in nature with the result that, although liberalism claimed to be neutral between different conceptions of the good, in actual fact it set itself up as a norm and dismissed non-liberal conceptions as defective, inferior and unworthy of human beings.

Broadly speaking the classical liberals argued that individuals were the basic units of moral and political life. Unlike the animal, they were endowed with reason, were capable of freedom and self-determination, and possessed dignity. If they were not to forfeit their dignity and the moral inviolability that went with it, they should formulate and follow their own purposes, determine their beliefs and opinions themselves, choose and plan their own ways of life, and in general be the authors of their own destiny. Being rational they should also seek to understand the world including themselves, and cultivate the arts, sciences, culture and other forms of self-knowledge. They should also conquer nature, exploit the earth's resources to the fullest, produce material abundance, and lead a life of leisure and comfort. And since all this is only possible in an orderly and law-governed society, they should create a civil society based on equal respect for individual rights. All this is encapsulated in the liberal conception of 'civilised' life or civilisation, only the 'civilised' life being worthy of human beings for the liberals. Although the classical liberals did not generally prescribe what kind of life individuals should live, almost all of them were convinced that a good life must be self-chosen, autonomous, self-critical, based on continuing choices, self-conscious, orientated towards self-knowledge, active and energetic, averse to wasting natural and human resources including human talents, free of dogmas and superstitions, largely concerned with worldly though not necessarily material concerns, and based on equal respect for others' interests. Although some liberals were sympathetic to and even admired the religious way of life, they thought it marginal and parasitic and worthy of respect only if it met their test of 'reasonableness'. Not surprisingly liberal writers took a dim view of ways of life that were traditional, communal, deeply religious, hierarchical, not given to self-knowledge, averse to constant self-criticism, or contemptuous of worldly interests and achievements. Since these ways of life did not respect human dignity (J.S. Mill), betrayed man's vocation (Kant), stifled all that was distinctively human (Locke), ignored the inherent strivings of human nature (Constant and Tocqueville) etc., they did not measure up to man's unique status and could be peacefully and in some cases forcibly dismantled in the long term interests of those involved. Liberal attitudes to nonliberal ways of life within their own countries and outside Europe bear witness to this.

The tendency not to prescribe a substantive vision of the good life and yet to do so by means of apparently formal principles is to be found in almost all liberal writers from Hobbes onwards, albeit more pronounced in some than in others. John Rawls's insistence on the priority of the right over the good is the most recent example of this. He says that individuals may entertain whatever conception of the good they prefer so long as these conform to certain general principles of right. Since these principles embody a liberal conception of the good, Rawls says in effect that all 'reasonable' conceptions of the good should be little more than variations on the liberal (Rawls, 1993, pp. 173–211). His reasonable pluralism is pluralism within the limits of liberalism, and excludes a wide variety of ways of life while claiming to remain neutral. In him as in many other liberal writers, liberalism is both a specific vision of the good life and the arbiter of all others, both a moral currency and the measure of all others, both a player and an umpire, and is open to the charge at best of circularity and at worst of bad faith.

I shall take three of the greatest liberal philosophers to illustrate the point. On the basis of his conception of the minimum conditions that the good life should satisfy, Locke argued that the American Indians were savages and led lives unworthy of human beings. They were lazy, had minimal wants, and lacked rational discipline and a sense of individuality. They roamed freely over the land, did not enclose it, and lacked the institution of private property, the *sine qua non* of progress. They had no arts, sciences, culture and true or 'reasonable' religion either. And although they called themselves nations, they lacked the familiar features of the European state. Since the Indians had no sense of private property, 'their' land was really empty, free, vacant, and could be taken over without their consent. And since their society was not organised as a state, it enjoyed no immunity from outside interference. The English were not only at liberty, but had a duty, to take over the 'surplus' Indian land, force them to live closer together, teach them commerce, and in general to undermine their way of life. God had given man land on condition that he should exploit it to the full, and He had given him reason in the expectation that he would lead a law-governed civil life and develop science and technology. Since the Indians did neither, they were in breach of God's commands and stood in need of discipline and education.

English colonisation was indispensable to their transition to civilisation, and hence fully justified (Parekh, 1995).

Like Locke, J. S. Mill divided human societies or ways of life into two. In the civilised European societies human beings were in the 'maturity of their faculties' and had 'attained the capacity of being guided to their own improvement by conviction or persuasion'. By contrast non-European societies were all 'backward', and their members were in a state of 'nonage' or 'infancy'. Mill did not think much of Africa, a 'continent without a history'. And although he thought that India, China and 'the whole East' had begun well, he was convinced that they had been 'stationary for thousands of years'. Since backward societies lacked the capacity for self-regeneration, Mill argued that they needed to be civilised by outsiders. He dismissed the likely objection that all societies including the backward were attached to their ways of life, that their well-being was closely bound up with these, and that they should be free to change them at their own pace. Like Locke, Mill argued that the right to the integrity of one's way of life only belonged to those capable of making a good use of it; as for the rest it was 'either a certain evil or at best a questionable good'. For Mill, as for Locke, backward individuals had equal moral claims to the protection of their *rights and interests*, but not to the inviolability of let alone a basic respect for their *ways of life* (Parekh, 1994).

When Herder challenged the current liberal distinction between civilised and uncivilised societies and attacked liberals for despising the latter, Kant wrote a scathing reply. Mocking Herder's admiration for the happy and carefree inhabitants of Tahiti, Kant rejoined: (Kant, 1991, pp. 219–220 italics added).

> But what if the true end of providence were not this *shadowy image of happiness* which each individual creates for himself, but the ever continuing and growing activity and culture which are thereby set in motion, and whose *highest possible expression* can only be the product of a political constitution based on concepts of human right, and consequently an achievement of human beings themselves? Thus, we read on page 206 that 'each human individual has the measure of his happiness within him', and that he does not yield in the enjoyment of this happiness to any of those who come after him; but as far as *the value of their existence itself* is concerned - i.e. the reason why they are there in the first place, as distinct from the conditions in which they exist - it is in this alone that a wise intention might be discernible within the whole. Does the author really mean that, if the happy inhabitants of Tahiti, never visited by more civilised nations, were

> destined to live in their peaceful indolence for thousands of centuries, it would be possible to give a satisfactory answer to the questions of *why they should exist at all*, and of whether it would not have been *just as good if this island had been occupied by happy sheep and cattle as by happy human beings* who *merely* enjoy themselves?

For Kant as for Locke and Mill, only the industrious, rational, energetic, morally disciplined and purposive life was worthy of human beings. Since the Tahitians failed to live up to the demands of their human vocation as defined by the 'true end of providence', as discovered by Kant, they were no better than 'sheep and cattle', making Kant wonder if they had a right to 'exist at all'. In less restrained hands Kant's argument could easily lead to murderous consequences.[3]

Like many a classical liberal, the Marxists, the romantics and the Conservatives too had considerable difficulty coming to terms with cultural plurality. For Marx a truly human society was one in which human beings, at last freed of ethnic, cultural, national, religious and other ties, enjoyed unmediated unity with their species and led a life of full self-expression. Not surprisingly he found non-modern, ethnic, communal, traditional and religious ways of life rebarbative, had no room for them in his ideal society, and justified European colonialism as an evil but necessary step towards a culturally homogeneous world (Marx, 1979, vol. 12, p. 132). Even such romantic writers as Herder who celebrated differences *between* societies did not appreciate those *within* each of them. Indeed the very ground on which they celebrated the former often made them blind or hostile to the latter. Like Vico, Herder argued that since each society had a distinct and unassimilable genius or spirit which shaped the personality of all its members, it had both a right and a duty to preserve it, and hence to disallow all internal plurality that conflicted with its cultural integrity. In this respect Vico was no more hospitable to a plurality of ways of life *within* a society. Although Conservative writers have generally been more sensitive to regional, local and institutional differences, their insistence on social hierarchy, religion, organic unity of society, and a shared substantive conception of the good as the basis of social solidarity prevented them from accommodating the claims of cultural

[3] Although I concentrate on liberal attitudes to non-European societies, their attitudes to non-liberal ways of life within their own societies were often just as dismissive. The prolonged, painful, and often violent process by which liberalism came to be inscribed in the very structure of the modern European state offers ample evidence of this.

pluralism, as is evident in the writings of Joseph de Maistre, Coleridge, Burke and Roger Scruton. Even Montesquieu, more sensitive than most to cultural diversity, thought that each society was and needed to be culturally homogeneous and based on a single ethos, and that different ways of life could be judged and even perhaps graded in terms of such universal principles as political 'liberty' and 'natural' principles of justice. Indeed it is difficult to think of more than a handful of major thinkers who appreciated the *full* force of human uniqueness and cultural pluralism, admitted that different ways of life, although not equally good, were at least equally legitimate, and sought to construct a social and political order on that basis. And even they tended to smuggle in an allegedly universal substantive conception of the good to help them overcome the awkward problems posed by cultural pluralism.

II

In the previous section I argued that several eminent philosophers took a monistic view of the good life, and that directly or indirectly they insisted that only one way of life was the highest or truly good and worthy of human beings. Indeed the belief that there is only one true God, one true religion, only one true custodian of it, only one set of true doctrines, only one highest faculty, one best way to acquire true knowledge, only one truly just polity, etc. appears again and again in western thought, and philosophers who cannot show this seem to think that they have not been sufficiently rigorous or probing. Moral monism is open to several objections. First, it implies that one has discovered the final truth about how human beings ought to live, an inherently implausible and unacceptably arrogant claim to make for any human being. Even if the privileged way of life is revealed by God, it is humanly mediated and necessarily liable to errors of interpretation, translation and execution. And since other religions make similar claims, one cannot substantiate one's own without becoming either dogmatic or circular.

Second, the view that one way of life is the best and represents the highest good is logically untenable. Human capacities conflict for at least three reasons, namely inherently, because of the limitations of the human condition, and because of the constraints of social life: the first because they often call for different and contradictory skills, attitudes and dispositions, so that the realisation of some of them renders the realisation of others difficult if not impossible; the second because human energies and resources are necessarily limited so that no one can develop all her capacities; and the third because every social order has a specific structure and militates against the combination of specific capacities and values. Since human capacities conflict, the good they are capable of cultivating also conflicts. Like the human capacities, values too conflict for similar reasons. Justice and mercy, respect and pity, equality and excellence, love and impartiality, moral duties to humankind and to one's kith and kin, moral claims of contemplative life and of the dying wife, and so on often point in different directions and are not easily reconciled. In short every way of life, however good it might be, entails a loss. And since it is difficult to say which of these values are higher both in the abstract and in specific contexts, the talk of a way of life representing the highest good is unintelligible.

To suggest that different ways of life can be hierarchically graded is to presuppose that a way of life can be reduced to a single value or principle, that all such values or principles can in turn be reduced to and measured in terms of a single master value or principle, and that the good can be defined and determined independently of the kinds of agents involved. This is a wholly mistaken way of conceptualising a way of life (Berlin, 1969; Parekh, 1982, pp. 28–47). No way of life can be based on one value alone. It necessarily integrates and balances different values, and cannot be reduced to one of them. Even if *per impossible* it could be, the different values represented by different ways of life are too disparate and distinct to be translated in a common language, let alone measured on a single scale. Furthermore since no way of life can be abstracted from the capacities, dispositions and aspirations of its human bearer, it can never be judged good or bad in the abstract. It can, of course, be criticised and even compared with others in specific respects, but they cannot be graded and ranked.

Since human capacities, values, virtues and ideals conflict, no way of life can exhaust the full range of human possibilities. Each is necessarily partial and selective, and represents a valuable but limited vision of the good. Cultural pluralism is therefore a necessary condition of the human search for freedom and critical self-understanding. Human beings lack a master Archimidean standpoint from which to look at themselves and their cultures, but they do have available to them several mini-Archimidean standpoints in the form of a plurality ways of life and thought. They can use each to view the others from the outside and to tease out their similarities and differences. And they can also use their knowledge of them to uncover the full range of human capacities and achievements We need access to other cultures not so much because it increases our range of 'options', for cultures are not options, as because it helps us appreciate the uniqueness as well as the strengths and limitations of our own, extends our sympathies, deepens our self-knowledge, and enables us to enrich our way of life by borrowing whatever is attractive in others and can be integrated into our own. Cultural diversity both expresses human finitude and offers a moderate release from it. In so doing it encourages such worthwhile intellectual and moral qualities as humility, modesty, self-knowledge, objectivity and self-transcendence. It is therefore a necessary condition and component of human well-being and growth, a vital constituent of any satisfactory conception of the good life, and deserves to be given an *equal* moral status with such basic values as liberty, equality and justice.

Third, moral monism views differences as deviations, as expressions of moral pathology. It is striking, and indicative of their intellectual discomfiture, that Plato, Aristotle, Augustine, Aquinas, J. S. Mill, and others offer no coherent explanations of why ways of life differ, and tend to blame some allegedly natural deficiencies in their adherents, their social structures, or both. For Plato and Aristotle, all non-Greeks are barbarians. For Augustine and Aquinas, non-Christians, who are all classified as unbelievers, lead inferior lives, and within Christianity those departing from the official doctrines of the Catholic church are all heretics leading unacceptable ways of life. For liberals all non-liberal ways of life are irrational, tribal, obscurantist. For Marxists, all religious, traditional, and class-based ways of life are inhuman and worthy of destruction.

Since moral monism is solipsist and cannot see any good outside its favoured way of life, it is inherently inhospitable to differences and breeds a spirit of intolerance. When confronted with other ways of life, it either avoids all but minimum contacts with them or seeks to eliminate them by peaceful or violent means. Plato and Aristotle favoured the first approach because they considered the barbarians naturally defective and incapable of education. Christians and liberals favoured the second approach because they thought both that they had a duty to spread the divinely revealed truths, and that the latter were within the moral reach of all. Both Christian and liberal civilising missions rest on identical assumptions. Since moral monism implies that one way of life is either already perfect or has all the necessary resources to effect such improvements as it needs, it forecloses the possibility of a dialogue with other cultures and deprives the preferred way of life of the opportunity for self-transcendence, critical self-consciousness and self-regeneration.

Fourth, moral monism runs the constant danger of grossly misunderstanding other ways of life. Since one's approach to them is primarily judgemental, there is little desire to understand them. And to the extent that one seeks to understand them, one's focus is on explaining why they are similar to or different from one's own way of life. Such a biased frame of reference and the consequently skewed angle of vision necessarily leads to distortion, especially in the case of ways of life that are judged inferior. Since they are inferior, they are not considered worthy of the efforts required by a sympathetic and patient exploration of their complex inner structures. And since they generally cannot talk back or since one has closed one's ears to their murmurs of protest, one is rarely compelled to reconsider the theoretical apparatus one brings to the study of them. The standard Christian accounts of non-Christian religions and the liberal accounts of non-liberal ways of life provide ample evidence of this.[4]

III

I have argued that the tendency towards moral monism has deep roots in Western thought and that it is both incoherent and has unfortunate consequences. If we are to counter it, we should uncover and reassess the central assumptions from which it derives its plausibility and even the aura of self-evidence. Moral monism rests on the following assumptions.

(I) The uniformity of human nature.[5] All human beings have a common nature or essence consisting of specific capacities, drives

[4] Although moral monism is intolerant of other ways of life, it has at least the great virtue of being concerned about the well-being of the entire mankind. Pluralism might be more tolerant, but it could also imply rejection of or indifference to outsiders. For example, many Hindu thinkers argue that their religion is 'superior' to Christianity and Islam because it cherishes plural paths to salvation and does not believe in conversion. While some Hindus genuinely accord equal respect to other ways of life, others reject conversion because they consider outsiders impure, or are totally unconcerned about them, or are afraid of weakening their caste system. The latter kind of tolerance is morally no better than aggressive monism.

[5] I use the term human nature not in the standard mechanical or teleological sense but in the purely formal sense of what is distinctive to human beings and defines their species identity. In this limited sense, in which nature is equated not with essence or being but with identity, the concept dominates the thoughts of even such writers as Kant who defined human identity in non-natural and noumenal terms, Marx who defined it in historical terms, Sartre who denied that man had a nature, and the critics of the naturalistic fallacy.

and dispositions. This does not mean that they do not differ in important respects or that two human beings are ever exactly alike, but rather that differences define their particularity or uniqueness not their humanity; that is, that they make them the kind of persons they are and do not affect their humanity, which consists only in the features they share with others. Differences, further, are not autonomous, and only represent so many different ways of expressing or combining the features human beings share in common. Some men pursue wealth, others women, fame or learning. Although the objects of their desires are different, they are all driven by the 'same' basic desire for greed, power, pleasure, status, recognition or pride. Like human desires human capacities manifest themselves differently, but they too have basically the 'same' nature, structure and mode of operation. Reason, the allegedly highest human faculty, is the 'same' in all human beings and functions in an 'identical' manner.

(II) The moral and ontological primacy of similarities over differences. Since only what human beings share in common constitutes their humanity, their similarities are far more important than their differences. Differences define their particularity not their universality, are derived from their shared similarities, and do not affect let alone form part of their humanity. All human beings are human in exactly the same way, not each in his or her own different way.

(III) The socially transcendental character of human nature. Human nature inheres in human beings as their natural endowment. Although it can be developed only in society, the latter does not add new elements to or reconstitute it in a novel manner. Human beings are therefore basically the 'same' in different times and places, and their cultures or ways of life make at best only a minor difference.

(IV) Knowability of human nature. For some writers human nature is relatively simple and consists of readily specifiable capacities and desires. Other think it complex and elusive, but argue that its innermost structure can in principle be discovered by sustained philosophical, theological or scientific investigation.

(V) Human nature as the basis of the good life or, what comes to the same thing, the unity of good and truth. The good life is determined in the light of the central truths about human nature, not only because 'ought' implies 'can' but also because the content of the 'ought' must correspond to and grow out of the specificity of its intended human subjects. Since human nature consists of several different capacities and desires, we need to specify which of them should form the basis of the good. The usual procedure is to elucidate the *differentia specifica* of the human species, and to identify capacities or dispositions that are unique to it. This cannot be done without contrasting human beings with non-human beings, which is why the Greek and Christian philosophers neatly placed human beings between God and animals or between divinity and nature in their three-dimensional view of the universe, and the two-dimensional secular liberals contrasted humans with animals. In each case the writers concerned identified a specific capacity as distinctively human, be it theoretical intellect, love of God, faith or reason, and made it the basis of their conceptions of the good life.

Given these assumptions, we are well on the way to moral monism. (I) implies that the good is the same for all human beings. (II) implies that human differences ultimately do not matter, and that at best they determine *how much* good is realised by different human beings and in *what form* but neither its nature nor its content. (III) implies that the good is invariant and unaffected by cultural differences. Cultures are seen as so many different and ultimately contingent expressions of the universally common human nature, and devoid of an independent role in shaping it. (IV) implies that it is within our power to discover the true and full nature of man, and (V) that the good is objective in nature and can be determined independently of what specific human beings happen to think and desire. Taken together, these and related implications encourage a manner of thinking in which one cannot see the point of, and feels profoundly uneasy with, cultural plurality. Since human beings are identically constituted, since their obvious differences are trivial and inconsequential, and since their ultimate good consists in living up to the truth of their common nature, they should all 'naturally' live alike. The unnatural fact that they do not becomes a source of much bafflement and anguish, and leads to either despair or rage.

The five basic assumptions are flawed in varying degrees. Since I cannot criticise them in detail in this short paper, a few words should suffice. As for (I), human beings do share much in common, including several capacities and desires, common natural and social conditions of existence, and common experiences. However they are also cultural beings who, in the course of exercising their shared capacities, satisfying their shared desires, and responding to their common conditions and experiences against the background of their different historical and geographical environment, evolve distinct ways of life or cultures. Different cultures define common humanity in their own different ways, give it a distinct tone and structure, and reconstitute it in novel ways. Human similarities therefore undergo important and deep changes, even as human differences are permeated by and cannot be disengaged from shared similarities. The two interpenetrate and do not occupy separate and unrelated realms. They are both *equally* important in constituting our humanity, and neither can be treated as ontologically secondary or derivative. It is therefore wrong to draw an untenable contrast between universality and particularity, and to define human nature in terms of the former alone. Abstract universalism and its conceptual twin relativism, which stress respectively only the similarities and differences, are both false.

(II) is wrong because by concentrating on Man at the expense of men, it fails to appreciate the interpenetration of universality and particularity, the important role of both in constituting the distinctive humanity of each human being, and the inescapable fact that all men and women are human in their own unique ways. Since human beings are free, self-determining and creative, as all philosophers rightly insist, they *cannot* be human in an identical manner, and 'belong' to their species in the same way that vegetables do to theirs. To insist that human beings are free, etc. and also that they are human in an identical manner is to be guilty of self-contradiction. (III) fails to appreciate both the cultural embeddedness of human beings and the complex ways in which each culture mediates and particularises the shared humanity. (IV) treats human nature as if it were no more than a collection of specific capacities and desires, takes a simple-minded view of the nature of and modes of interaction between the latter, ignores a whole range of human capacities and desires as realised in countless ways of life, and in general offers a simplistic and distorted view of human nature. It also fails to appreciate both the importance of the human capacity for constant self-creation, and the obvious difficulties involved in human beings trying to fathom their own nature.

As for (V), it defines the good life exclusively in terms of what all human beings share in common and excludes what distinguishes them. Since the good life so defined is subject-independent or 'objective', it is good for them *qua* human beings, not *qua* unique persons, and therefore it cannot by definition represent their *whole* or even the *highest* good. Again, as we saw, most traditional views of the good life privilege specific human capacities on the basis of what they take to be the *differentia specifica* of the human species. Apart from the fact that abstracting a specific human capacity from its total context necessarily distorts it and misunderstands its relations and mode of operation, the philosophical procedure involved in identifying it is infected with circularity. Animals and humans both resemble and differ from each other in several respects, and we need a basis on which to decide *which* specific difference is distinctive to human beings. There is no obvious reason why we should stress reason alone, and that too defined in a specific manner, unless we are already committed to the view that humans should live a life of reason. We cannot define animals as non-humans without presupposing a prior conception of what it is to be human.

When we reassess and reformulate the assumptions underlying moral monism along the lines I have briefly sketched, we see that as culturally embedded beings, humans define and pursue the good life in several different ways, none perfect or the highest and none wholly misguided, and each capable of criticising and learning from the others. Culture both particularises the universal and universalises the particular, and mediates between the individuals and their shared humanity. Once we appreciate the importance of culture, we also appreciate its inescapable plurality. Thanks to the five assumptions mentioned earlier and to the concommitant tendency to think in terms of unconcretised universality, many a moral and political philosopher failed to create an adequate conceptual space for culture, and moved directly from the abstractly defined human nature to society without appreciating the vital importance of the mediating category of culture. Since culturally embedded human beings cannot escape their culture altogether, these philosophers ended up presenting the standards of their cultures as constitutive of common humanity. We stand a better chance of arriving at a genuinely universal morality consisting of *common* regulative principles and a rich *plurality* of ends and ideals if we derive it not from an abstract, difference-blind and apparently empty though really value-laden concept of human nature, but from a critical dialogue between cultures against the background of their explicitly acknowledged differences.

Coping with the Many-Coloured Dome: Pluralism and Practical Reason

KEITH GRAHAM

> The One remains, the many change and pass;
> Heaven's light forever shines, Earth's shadows fly;
> Life, like a dome of many-coloured glass,
> Stains the white radiance of Eternity,
> Until Death tramples it to fragments.
>
> (Shelley)

Pluralism and Disenchantment

At its widest, 'pluralism' signifies simply the variety of life, the teeming multitude of forms and entities, the many different properties that living beings manifest. Life is not everywhere the same but impressively differentiated, and without it eternity would be all of a piece, uniform. That is enough for life to stain the white radiance of eternity. But within the multiplicity of specifically *human* life there are not merely differences. There are tensions, oppositions, conflicts. In contemporary philosophical debate 'pluralism' then comes to signify one problematic aspect of this. Groups of people have perhaps always subscribed to very different values, and in consequence favoured very different forms of behaviour from one another, at least on a global scale. But the groups are no longer geographically separated: we live in distinct but overlapping cultures, and get in one another's way to a far greater extent than previously. Shelley's ordered image of the dome may then seem inappropriate, and it may seem unnecessary for death to trample it to fragments. Life is already fragmented, and the practical problem facing us as living creatures is to go beyond the fragments, to achieve at least a modus vivendi in the light of all our differences and incompatibilities even if not the orderliness and cohesion of a dome. Somehow, we have to live together. That is a practical problem which confronts us at every level, as members of families, neighbourhoods, departments, countries and increasingly simply as members of a world-wide human race.

A familiar story explains this predicament in term of the disenchantment of the world. The modern age is characterised by the loss of belief in a moral order in the cosmos or in nature, from which we might derive our own moral meanings. We are therefore thrown back on our own resources as human beings when it comes to making judgements about what is valuable. We can no longer simply infer what is right, and how we should be, from a set of premises about the natural order and our place in it. But then the problem is exacerbated because the loss of belief in a purposive *natural* order is accompanied by the lack, for many people, of a strong identification with any particular tradition or culture, and the loss of belief in a purposive *social* order. If we divorce moral meanings from social roles too, we are thrown back on our own resources and become the authors of those meanings in a very strong sense.[1]

Two consequences follow from our predicament, one *inter*personal and the other *intra*personal. One is that fragmentation of value is a likely result, with its attendant problems of disagreement and conflict. The other is that people are prone to rootlessness and the absence of any strongly-grounded sense of who they are and why they matter. Recognition would follow naturally from occupancy of a traditional social role, but not necessarily from a self-chosen form of identity (cf. Taylor, 1994, pp. 34–35).

We may attempt to deal with these consequences *either* by working out what political forms people can agree to, given deep differences in how they view life; *or* by harking back to, or attempting to recreate, circumstances of community where people knew who they were and why they had value. My aim is not to add to these attempts but to make a point about the process leading up to wide disagreement about practical matters. (I would comment on the first that it is much easier to work out a modus vivendi with those who accept the diagnosis of the problem in terms of reasonable disagreement. Or to put it one way, it is easier to reach a political settlement with fellow-liberals. Easier but less necessary. In the contemporary world, the practical problem for secular liberals is more commonly how to live cheek-by-jowl with people who believe that it *is* possible to read off conclusions about how we should live from premises about human beings' place in the cos-

[1] For Rawls this is an important strand in explaining the fact of reasonable disagreement. People's total experience in modern society varies enormously in the light of different offices and positions, the division of labour, the many social groups. That variation itself then importantly influences how they assess evidence and weigh values (Rawls, 1993, p. 57).

mos and who believe that nothing is gained by allowing us to decide whatever we like about the good life. I would comment on the second that it may be important not to fantasise an historical community or sense of community that never was (cf. Phillips, 1993). And, given the global nature of the problem, any idea of *creating* community must be theorised at the global level. *Local* self-protective communities à la Macintyre will not save us from a new Dark Ages but simply contribute to it by creating the darkness enjoyed by an ostrich with its head in the sand.)

For liberals there is a temptation to suppose that as long as you do what is necessary for social co-operation and don't violate anyone's rights, then for the rest you can decide what your life is like for yourself: you can create your own conception of the good. I aim to show that the constraints on rational practical deliberation are greater than this. *Interference* is notoriously and traditionally problematic, but *criticism* of some practical projects, and the conceptions of the good associated with them, is possible from a relatively detached standpoint.

I outline two formal constraints on autonomy: *the constraint of necessity* and *the constraint of precondition.* I then suggest that our *materiality* falls under each of these heads, so we have two separate reasons for paying attention to it in formulating rational practical aspirations.

The Constraint of Necessity

What I can rationally aspire to do depends on the nature of my own self and on my circumstances. I cannot simply snatch any considerations I wish to out of the air and treat them as the input into rational deliberation. For example, if I exercise my autonomy by aiming to become the world's greatest 25-year-old ballerina then my aim itself is, for more than one reason, profoundly irrational.[2]

I must, then, start from where and who I am. I cannot sensibly decide what to do until I have decided who I am. I necessarily have a (no doubt defeasible) reason to do anything which will serve my interests; so any true descriptions of me which carry an impli-

[2] I therefore reject as irrational the rational choice theory which 'just tells us to do what will best promote our aims, *whatever they are*' (Elster, 1986, p. 22; italics added). For a recent systematic attempt to establish the possibility of rational criticism of aims, see Nozick, 1993, pp. 139–151.

cation about my interests will have relevance to practical deliberation. No doubt I cannot arrive at an adequate description of who I am without building into my description a great deal of data about the various cultures, traditions and groups in which I was born and raised.

These considerations ground the communitarian idea of the encumbered self and familiar criticisms of Rawlsian theory for treating the autonomous choosing self as featureless. My concern is not with the validity of these criticisms but with how the descriptions of self affect practical reasoning. I suggest that they provide some of the input into autonomous decision-making, not a *constraint* on it (certainly not a constraint of necessity). When I reason about what to do I am an encumbered self, but I can detach myself in thought from particular encumbrances. I can ask myself 'Shall I go on allowing this description to apply to me? Do I want to be what I am in that respect?' Moreover, I can sometimes detach myself from particular encumbrances in reality. Let me give two general cases which illustrate my point. First, sometimes a description applies to me by virtue of my participation in some collective action. I am an elector, a member of the faculty committee, a soldier in a particular army or battalion. These descriptions are necessarily relevant to practical deliberation. They arise from circumstances where I am already acting, as one component in a collective actor, and therefore a question can be raised about whether to go on acting or to desist.[3] Secondly, some descriptions, in addition to or instead of carrying an implication concerning my interests in the normal way, carry what I have elsewhere called an escape-interest: an interest in ensuring that the description in question ceases to apply to me (Graham, 1986b). An escape-interest may follow automatically from a description, as would be the case with the description 'victim of racial discrimination', or it may be thought to follow plausibly from the description together with the circumstances in which it applies, as with the description 'dependant on income support'.[4]

So far I have stressed the unavoidable salience of who or what I am to my practical thinking, but observed that many descriptions

[3] They also indicate that a portion of our practical reasoning is irreducibly plural rather than singular: the question that confronts us is not 'what shall I do?' but 'what shall we do?' For further elaboration of collective practical deliberation see Graham, 1986a, pp. 108–114, Graham, 1987 and Graham, 1992, pp. 27–33.

[4] Suppose that this description applies to me, but that I receive a very favourable level of income support via the Civil List. Then the description does not carry an escape-interest automatically.

of me denote characteristics which may themselves be the subject of practical decisions. But some will not, and that finally enables me to explain the constraints of necessity. Some pertinent descriptions of me denote what I am *inescapably*. For example, my place of birth, my nationality as defined by birth, my racial origin are matters which are beyond the reach of practical decision. I may distance myself mentally from what I necessarily am, but I cannot do so in reality. Factors of that kind therefore really do place limits around my practical aspirations and my autonomy. It would be irrational of me to conceive a practical project whose realisation would involve the reversal of a constraint of necessity.

Notice four points about the constraints of necessity. First, we can if we wish distinguish between conceptual and causal necessity. Perhaps it is a conceptual necessity that I cannot make myself into a Neanderthal creature and a causal necessity that I cannot make myself into a world heavyweight boxing champion. In either case, however, it would be irrational of me to conceive a practical project that flew in the face of these truths, whatever their status.[5]

Secondly, we should distinguish between causal *impossibility*, which constitutes one kind of constraint of necessity, and causal *realisability but only at great cost* or by disturbing many other causal networks. Thus, it might not be casually impossible for me to change my shirt, my house, my country of residence, or my sex. But these different options vary enormously in the degree to which they would produce consequential changes elsewhere in my life. Within the range of causally possible projects we should therefore recognise a spectrum running from 'causally possible with relatively little disturbance' to 'causally possible but only at the cost of great disturbance'. But these differences, although they will certainly weigh with an autonomous agent, do not actually *preclude* as the constraints of necessity do. Indeed, they provide just the material for autonomous decision about how important a particular project is and whether its pursuit justifies making great changes elsewhere.

Thirdly, we should not confuse necessity with permanence (cf. Rorty, 1994, p. 154). Once we have made the distinction between what can and what cannot be changed by us, we should see that the latter may still vary, but vary in ways which are beyond our

[5] But couldn't I, say, conceive the aim of swimming the Atlantic, even though I knew it was impossible, because in that way I would succeed in swimming further than I would otherwise? My inclination is to say that my aim is to pretend to swim the Atlantic, and that aiming to pretend to do something or to fantasise doing it is not irrational in the same way as aiming to do it simpliciter if I know that I cannot.

control. A clear example of this is age. I cannot change my place of birth or my age, but the latter, unlike the former, constantly changes in a relentless and uniform way that I can do nothing about. That fact of change is something an autonomous agent will take into account but cannot alter. It is necessity rather than permanence *per se*, that places a constraint on our autonomy.

Fourthly, although constraints of necessity constrain practical reasoning, this is no ground for ignoring them. They are certainly not irrelevant to my practical projects and they may provide me with excellent reasons for trying to change what *other* people are doing. Indeed, their very inescapability may give us even more reason to attend to the form they take, because in a sense that is all we *can* do.

The Constraint of Precondition

There is a second source of constraints on autonomous aspirations. Suppose that my acting in certain ways, or being in a certain state, or having certain things, is a precondition of my doing anything else. Then although I may have no intrinsic interest in this precondition, it places constraints around my autonomous projects and it is something to which I must give my attention if those projects are to be successful. It is something I cannot rationally ignore. (That again gives us strong reasons for attending to its form: it may get in the way of those autonomous projects.) Moreover, this is a matter of some importance in the context of pluralism, and it has been argued that, if there are any universal prerequisites of this kind, then particular cultures can be assessed in a non-culture-relative way according to the extent to which they make universal provision for the satisfaction of universal prerequisites (cf. Gewirth, 1994, pp. 36–37, Kekes, 1994, p. 49).[6]

Are there any universal prerequisites of this kind? A number of theorists have thought so, and have produced varying and in some cases fairly wide lists of them. Rawls thought and thinks that his primary goods are. They are 'things that every rational man is pre-

[6] I would not endorse the way Gewirth operates such an assessment, however. He argues that freedom and well-being are such prerequisites, and that any culture must be judged according to the degree to which it provides rights to them. He acknowledges that assessment according to provision of individual rights may seem a culturally parochial criterion, but it is, more importantly, question-begging to suppose that a moral demand of a community could never trump the moral right of an individual.

sumed to want' and 'have a use whatever a person's rational plan of life' (Rawls, 1972, p. 62). He supposes that 'all citizens have a rational plan of life that requires for its fulfillment roughly the same kind of primary goods' (Rawls, 1993, p. 180 n8; cf. ibid. pp. 75–76). Kekes (1994, p. 49) argues that there are 'universally human, historically constant, and culturally invariant needs created by human nature' which stand in contrast to needs that vary with particular traditions and conceptions of the good life; and he draws up a list of candidates for the position of invariant needs falling into physiological, psychological and social categories. Gewirth (1994, p. 27) suggests that every agent must accept that they have a right to freedom and well-being, as the preconditions for any action. According to Williams (1985, pp. 56–57), a rational agent who wants to bring about anything must have a general dispositional want for freedom.

It is not as easy as might be thought to substantiate the claim that there are any universal preconditions of rational action. For one thing, there are circumstances in which suicide may be a rational project, and it is difficult to argue for much in the way of preconditions in cases of this kind[7]. It may be that the only realistic prospect in someone's life is a future of unending torment; or, as a quite different matter, they may correctly calculate that the best way of advancing some cause which means more to them than anything else is to sacrifice themselves for its furtherance. But cases of suicide are peripheral and exceptional, and it is reasonable to look for universal preconditions of rational action that at least cover the standard case of a rational agent with a continuing interest in acting in the world.

Even then, however, preconditions are not easily established and we must not be unduly influenced by local considerations. Given his specification of what a primary good is, Rawls's list, for example, is a curious and unsatisfactory combination of local and general factors. It ranges from things as general as wealth and income to something as local as free choice of occupation (Rawls, 1993, p. 181). Now, as I shall argue, on one interpretation wealth is a precondition for any rational plan; but free choice of occupation is not. For one thing, it is only in particular forms of society that people have 'occupations' where that means that they enter into relations of subordination with an employer, engage in a specific kind of work probably over an extended period, gain access to resources in consequence, and take that role as one of their prime forms of social identification.

[7] Kekes (1994, p. 50) makes a similar point.

Rawls might respond that his account of primary goods is intended to apply only to rational agents in current society, not to those in no-longer-extant societies where work did not necessarily take the form of occupation that it does now. His claim is therefore not really damaged if it is of less than universal application.

This response will not do, for two reasons. First, it ignores the fact that even in our own society there are rational agents for whom a free choice of occupation is not a precondition. I have in mind not those who cannot find one but those who do not need to: the seriously rich. At the very least he would then have to amend his claim to the claim that a free choice of *whether to have* an occupation is necessary to the pursuit of a rational plan of life. But while that is not an empty claim it is a much less interesting one. Along that line we could multiply primary goods *ad nauseam*. A free choice of whether to eat bananas or to live in Swindon is necessary to the pursuit of a rational life plan too, and many will simply choose not to. All that differs among these two cases and Rawls's case is the numbers. Secondly, the response ignores the possibility that the non-centrality of occupation may characterise not only the past but also the future. Certainly anyone who favours an unconditional distribution of basic income, or more generally wishes to break the link between employment and receipt of goods,[8] will resist the idea that choice of occupation is a precondition of rational pursuit of aims in all possible modern conditions.

In one very precise sense of a much-misused term, Rawls's claim is ideological. It involves representing what is particular as universal; or rather, representing a particular *form* of something universal as being *itself* universal. It is somewhat like arguing from the truth that we must have clothes to the falsehood that we must have tailors.[9]

But then, compounding the error with symmetry, Rawls also takes something universal and represents it as only particular. In outlining the basic liberties deducible in the original position, he includes the right to personal property, since this is necessary for a sense of personal independence and self-respect. But he calls attention to his deliberate silence on the question of access to the means of production. He explicitly excludes any right to property of that kind, in the form of either private ownership or participation in social ownership. These, he suggests, are not necessary for

[8] E.g. Van Parijs, 1995.

[9] 'Men made clothes for thousands of years, under the compulsion of the need for clothing, without a single man ever becoming a tailor' (Marx, 1976, p. 133). For the nature and the significance of a slide of this kind, see Graham, 1992, pp. 65–67.

the development of the moral powers of a sense of justice and a conception of the good, and their merits are to be decided at a later stage when much more information about a society's circumstances is available (Rawls, 1993, p. 298; cf. ibid. pp. 338–339).

Now a *choice* between private and social ownership must perhaps await a later stage. But there is as much reason to include a reference to access to the means of production in the basic liberties as there is to personal property. For the rationale for any reference to property at all is stronger than Rawls allows. We are material creatures whose material needs make themselves felt not just once or even periodically but recurrently, every day of our existence. Those needs are a constraint of precondition. Their satisfaction is not just necessary for a sense of independence or for exercising our two moral capacities but for anything else at all. Moreover, access to the means of satisfying them is not something distinct from access to the means of production. We can meet those needs on a continuing basis only through a combination of a material substrate and a means of transforming the substrate, the one being useless without the other. If there is a right to property, therefore, it is a right to the fruits of the means of production. But the fruits and the means are integrally connected: whoever owns the means and the material substrate also owns the result of joining them together. We can say, if we like, that that ought not to be so; but that simply illustrates my point that a claim about rights to personal property cannot be made without calling into question further matters to do with ownership of means of production.

I am not here concerned with whether Rawls can derive his wider conclusions from premises about primary goods. The concept of a primary good stands close to that of a constraint of precondition. If either is to function in a culturally-neutral way, the list of their instantiations must be similarly general and culturally-neutral. To say that any rational agent needs some degree of wealth is plausible; to say they need an occupation is not. It is similarly anomalous to include something as specific as choice of occupation in the list of primary goods yet to exclude something as general as a right to access to the means of production from the list of basic liberties.

The Material Constraint

My criticisms of Rawls indicate what I want to say about the importance of our materiality in practical reasoning, and by extension in any attempt to adjudicate among cultures and what they promote and exclude.

I have so far argued that there are two formal constraints on the practical aspirations of a rational autonomous agent. The first arises from any characteristic inescapably possessed by the agent in question; the second from any condition the satisfaction of which is a precondition for doing anything else. Our materiality constitutes a constraint under both headings. We are inescapably material creatures and the needs arising from this materiality place a limit on the aspirations it is rational to nurture.[10] And, with the partial exception of suicide,[11] the satisfaction of our material needs is a precondition of anything else we might want to do. To these formal claims we must add the substantive and contingent point that the satisfaction of material needs is not a peripheral or negligible part of a human life in the world as it actually is.

The centrality and importance of the material constraint now emerges. It governs not merely *permissible* conceptions of the good; nor, indeed, only things as grandiose as conceptions of the good or rational plans of life. It governs all aspirations. It does not depend on an agent's perception either of the world or of themselves: their material need-satisfaction constitutes a constraint whatever they may think, whatever culture they may belong to, and whatever their culture may *say* about it. It carries rational motivational force quite generally. You may be interested in projects far removed from any consideration of material need-satisfaction, but if it plays anything more than a peripheral role in your life (and it does), then it will be irrational of you not to pay attention to the things you must do, the relations you must enter into, the distractions from your autonomously chosen projects which material need satisfaction requires.

We need a philosophical theory of our materiality, and my aim here is to argue that claim rather than to provide the theory. The centrality and significance of our materiality can be interpreted in a number of ways, not necessarily consistent with one another, which challenge traditional philosophical categories and perspectives. There is, for example, the complaint that the individuals of traditional state of nature theory are presented as disembodied and disembedded, with serious consequences for our understanding of their situation and the problems that confront them (Benhabib, 1992, pp. 152–157). For the issue of pluralism and the politics of recognition there is the suggestion that culture, and respect for

[10] For anyone who believes we possess an immortal soul, our rational practical aspirations are limited by our materiality only *while* we are embodied. That is still a considerable constraint, however.

[11] Even for suicide some minimal material means will normally be required.

culture, may not be comprehensible in abstraction from the dynamics of political economy (Rorty, 1994, p. 155).

My own focus has been on the implications of our materiality for practical reasoning and the values arising from it. Our materiality limits the values we can reasonably hold. Even if what matters to me intrinsically is my identity as a person of a particular religion, as a parent, as a member of a particular culture, or simply as the executor of some prized, autonomously-chosen project, my existence as a material creature obtrudes, and may call for a re-prioritisation of identity.

Recall the practical problem outlined at the beginning of this discussion. How can we live together when we espouse different values? What intellectual resources are there for shifting an individual's attention beyond the horizons of what they happen to value themselves? We do differ in many significant dimensions of our life, and though we may imaginatively project ourselves into the situation of a person of another race, gender, religion, nationality, we may also fail to do so or fail to make their concerns our own. And over the area where we exercise autonomy and select goals and projects, there is the endemic likelihood of difference and separation. Why should someone whose passion is train-spotting concern themselves over another's passion for early music, or vice versa? In these respects we may imaginatively project ourselves into someone else's position, but it will always remain other in reality.

Our materiality, by contrast, is a condition we all share. Potentially, therefore, it provides a bridge from one agent, and one culture, to another. However, the potential may not be fulfilled, and the question of how this relates to commonality and individuality is more complex. Our materiality dictates that we must all be consumers, individually, interpersonally and collectively (since the satisfaction of some material needs is of its nature interpersonal or collective). And, given that we don't live in a Garden of Eden, we must collectively be producers too: our material needs go unmet unless we are. But individually we need not be. I can be the beneficiary of the productive efforts of others: exploitation or parasitism, in that sense, is a possibility for a human life.[12] Where it occurs, our materiality will be as much a source of rational division

[12] That is why the freedom of choice of an occupation is not a universal requirement of a rational agent. But we should not too readily identify being a beneficiary of others' productive efforts with being an exploiter or a parasite. There are difficult issues here about who exactly is productive as well as about entitlements. See Graham, 1989 and Van Parijs, 1995, ch. 5.

as of rational unity. And our materiality is so central that any political philosophy which does not explore whether it occurs is not worth the paper it is written on.

There is an obvious source for a comprehensive theory of our materiality, and especially conflictual aspects of it, in the writings of Karl Marx. I believe they contain insights about what it is to be a human agent which remain to be fully appreciated. But they are mixed up with more ambitious and less plausible theories about the dynamics of history,[13] and it is in any case an open question whether Marx's thought will recover from the appalling political misappropriation that it suffered in the twentieth century.

What I have tried to suggest in this paper is that there are sound reasons, arising from the nature of practical reasoning for creatures such as we are, for starting where he did. If we don't like Marx's theories about our materiality, then we need to find some others.[14]

[13] For some reasons why those theories are implausible, see Graham, 1994.

[14] I am indebted to Chris Bertram, Adam Morton and the participants in the Royal Institute of Philosophy conference on Pluralism and Philosophy, 1995, for helpful comments. I am also grateful to the University of Bristol Arts Faculty Research Fund for financial assistance.

Rawlsians, Pluralists, and Cosmopolitans*

ATTRACTA INGRAM

Some of us were introduced to political philosophy as an activity of identifying, criticising, and revising the moral basis of existing social institutions. We asked questions about the nature of the good or the just society, and some few of us thought that once we knew and advocated the truth, it would win out. We, or some appropriate revolutionary or reforming group or class, would with reason, truth, and history on our side, bring about the society of our ideals. When we first read John Rawls's *A Theory of Justice* we read it as continuing the traditional tasks of political philosophy. Justice as Fairness[1] was a moral theory which addressed a political subject matter. From the moral point of view it told us what any just society aiming to realise the values of liberty and equality would be like. This comported nicely with liberal cosmopolitanism, and also with more widely shared philosophical views that the task of political philosophy is to construct a vision of an ideal society, perhaps more sensitive to justice in implementation than would be required in pre-modern, pre-democratic societies, but nevertheless an ideal which in the long run we would hope to see all societies converge on. That kind of liberalism gave those of us who think that Rawlsian justice is the right or true justice a license to go on the offensive in promoting liberal ideals and practices in our own society, and, at the very least, a critical vantage point from which to judge other societies.

* The ideas for this paper were first tried out in Stephen Lukes's seminar on pluralism at the European University Institute, Florence, in April 1993. I thank Stephen Lukes for helpful comments and provocative questions. I am also grateful to the other participants in the seminar, especially Véronique Munoz-Dardé and Maurice Glasman. The present version has been improved by the responses of participants at the Royal Institute of Philosophy conference on Philosophy and Pluralism in Coleraine in 1995, and especially by Dave Archard and John Baker both of whom gave me written comments that showed me where the argument should be given more work. I thank Ian Cornelius for helping me to clarify some points and for socially necessary labour beyond the requirements of justice as fairness.

[1] The conception of justice presented in *Theory*. For the most recent restatement of the principles of justice as fairness, see (Rawls, 1993, p.5).

Rawls's self-interpretation in *Political Liberalism*, and in the writings that led up to it, sees the nature and tasks of political philosophy in a different way. Justice as Fairness is no longer a universal moral theory, but a political theory that is practical in being addressed to a distinctively modern problem: how to maintain over time 'a stable and just society of free and equal citizens profoundly divided by reasonable religious, philosophical and moral doctrines' (Rawls, 1993, p. xxv). The aim of political philosophy is no longer a theory of justice that is true and universal. Instead, it is to perform the practical social task of finding solutions to problems within a particular society or range of societies . For us, this is constitutional democracy. And our main problem is to establish the basis of social unity given the fact of pluralism, by which Rawls means the fact that modern society contains people who subscribe to a variety of different creeds and ideologies, which he calls different comprehensive conceptions of the good. Rawls sees this pluralism as more or less ineliminable from modern society. So the aim is a theory that 'may be shared by citizens as a basis of a reasoned, informed, and willing political agreement' (ibid. p. 9).

The new approach helps bridge the gap between theory and practice by making the political philosopher an agent of the constitutional politician. In this role we abandon any metaphysical hankering after truth and, instead, develop theory that serves certain practical aims. The theory must, of course, be a theory of justice, and in that respect it must be a principled moral theory and not merely a pragmatic solution to the problem of social unity in conditions of pluralism. But it need not be represented as true, that is, as expressing the conditions for realising deep moral truths and principles about how to live. If we, as philosophers, are to engage in the project of political liberalism, then we have to see the job, not as the traditional one of finding the true theory of justice but, rather, as confined to identifying, and extracting the meaning and consequences of, suitable premises for political justification in our society. In this search for the basis of agreement on justice, we abstain from insisting on the truth of our own contested, philosophically favoured premises for a theory of justice, for these are no less part of the pluralism of rival views than religious and moral views. Confronted with the fact of philosophical disagreement about fundamental values, we have to apply the principle of toleration to philosophy itself, abstaining from introducing our own unagreed premises for justice. Willingness to adopt this attitude of restraint is the condition under which we can engage in the project of political liberalism—of working out an acceptable justice for the institutions of our society. Given the aim of an agreed justice, and the existence of rival doctrines of the good, we have to be content with developing theory on the basis of whatever points of moral agreement in fact obtain among the rival views. We look for these shared ideas in the public political culture of democratic societies, and there we do find certain points of agreement—the idea that as citizens we are free and equal, that the principles of coercive social order should be justifiable to all who are forced to recognise them, that our institutions should reflect these core political values.

Now, these ideas are characteristically liberal ideas about social order. Hence the project of political liberalism is imaginable only because of the work of classical liberalism in creating liberal political culture. Given this fact, I want to examine two related questions: Why Rawls's project rather than continuing loyalty to classical liberalism? Can Rawls's project deliver on its promise to provide a principled basis for social unity in the conditions of pluralism that would obtain under full implementation of political liberalism? The considerations adduced in answer to the first question might loosen the hold of classical liberalism on us.[2] Should we then go with the project of political liberalism—the project of articulating a value-based conception of a political order (a political conception of justice) that is both 'independent of the opposing and conflicting philosophical and religious doctrines that citizens affirm' and capable of gaining the support of such doctrines (ibid.). But that would be impetuous, for unless we can see how social unity is even *imaginable* in a society regulated by political liberalism, given the likely presence of non-liberal[3] views about how to live, the project fails in its own terms, and liberals will have

[2] I assume with Rawls that the most appropriate conception of justice for a democratic society will be, in essentials, liberal. That is to say, it will protect individual rights and give them a special priority. See Rawls (1993, p. 156). This is not to prejudge the question of socialism versus liberalism, whatever that now means, for as G. A. Cohen has remarked 'a defensible socialist constitution must contain a bill of individual rights which specifies things which the community cannot do to, or demand of, any individual' (Cohen, 1986, p. 87).

[3] I use the term 'non-liberal' to refer to doctrines that give low priority to individualist (liberal) values like autonomy, choice, individuality, individual experimentation, critical and independent thought, and the like. Such views may be tolerant or intolerant of internal dissidents and of traditions other than their own. Illiberal views are intolerant in one or both these cases. The distinctions between liberal and non-liberal and between liberal and illiberal are matters of degree. For an exposure of oppressive elements in classical liberalism, past and present, see Parekh (1994). Illiberal doctrines drop out of contention for the political conception as I show below.

to fall back on the resources of classical liberalism when addressing the problem of social unity as it arises for us now and in the future. What we need to know, then, is how substantively non-liberal as well as liberal doctrines might be supposed to affirm political liberalism.

I

I shall deal with the first question by starting with the distinction between a comprehensive moral doctrine and a political conception of justice and then develop the argument for running with Rawls's project. A comprehensive view, Rawls tells us, 'includes conceptions of what is of value in human life, and ideals of personal character, as well as ideals of friendship and of familial and associational relationships' (ibid. p. 13). The major religions are examples. So too are substantive philosophical moral theories including the liberalisms of Kant and Mill. Comprehensive doctrines belong to the 'background culture' of civil society, the 'culture of the social, not of the political' (ibid. p. 14).

Rawls contrasts a comprehensive view with a political conception of justice. This has three characteristic features. First, it is a moral conception worked out for a specific subject, the basic structure of society—that is, the main social, economic and political institutions. It is not a conception for the whole of life. Second, while it has a justification by reference to one or more comprehensive doctrines, it is 'neither presented as, nor as derived from such a doctrine' (ibid. p. 12). Instead, it is presented as a freestanding view, 'a module, an essential constituent part, that fits into and can be supported by various reasonable comprehensive doctrines that endure in the society regulated by it' (ibid.). Third, the content of a political conception of justice is 'expressed in terms of certain fundamental ideas seen as implicit in the public culture of a democratic society' (ibid. p. 13). Rawls is here relying on the fact that, in the societies he is addressing, there are aspects of political culture and institutions that command widespread support despite the pluralism of doctrines of the good. These common ideas and values are worked up by the political conception into a theory of justice which can be the focus of an overlapping consensus among citizens despite their differences in comprehensive views. They can affirm the same political conception because its principles, being built on values they already accept, can be grounded in their own comprehensive views. The political conception may be reached by many paths of argument coming from many different philosophical, religious and moral directions. It does not matter what path is taken, only that some path is available to each citizen. But there is no privileged path, no single route they all must take.

In theory, there may be many versions of a political conception of justice. Rawls believes that his doctrine of justice as fairness, as laid out by his two principles of justice, is the most reasonable basis for social unity available to us. I am not concerned with the plausibility of this claim here, but with certain aspects of the very idea of a political conception. So, it is time to return to the question: why a political rather than a comprehensive conception of liberalism? Why the liberalism of Rawls rather than of Mill and his contemporary heirs?

It is not immediately obvious why the fact of pluralism should drive us to political liberalism rather than to a classical comprehensive liberalism. The accommodation of pluralism has been a steady mark of liberal doctrine since liberal advocacy of the principle of toleration provided the basis for a permanent end to the wars of religion in Europe. It is also evident that Rawls's project presupposes the cultural capital of shared political ideas that comprehensive liberal doctrines helped bring about. Since it abstains from truth, political liberalism itself cannot bring about its own conditions. So it offers no support to liberal agents in aspiring democracies which lack the public culture of shared implicit ideas on which it is built. This is not merely a problem of failing to provide justification for the establishment of liberal institutions in the first place; it may also undermine the defence of liberal institutions against illiberal forces in an existing liberal society (Barry, 1989, ch. 2; Scheffler, 1994).

Why then should we give up comprehensive liberalism? I think the answer has to do with the shift in liberalism's self-understanding which Rawls asks us to make. This is the shift from truth to reasonableness, and is made necessary by the need to widen the defence of liberal institutions in modern societies in order to appeal beyond the liberal faithful to citizens who have substantively non-liberal conceptions of the good. That is the practical reason. But it is a reason drawn from liberalism's own self-understanding as a family of doctrines which share an idea about political justification: that coercive social order be defensible to those who live under it (Waldron, 1993, ch. 2; Larmore, 1990). In conditions of contemporary pluralism, where we find, not merely a plurality of views within the same broad church (liberal pluralism), but also ones which are substantively illiberal and non-liberal, liberalism cannot meet its own demand for defensible coercive order by appealing to one or other of its own contested comprehensive doctrines. It could hold that some version of comprehensive liberalism is true or correct and so license acting against illiberal forces, containing their spread by active shaping of citizens' views and constitutive cultural matrices. I do not believe that any comprehensive liberalism has a license to sustain liberal institutions in this (Rousseauesque) way. For, that kind of social shaping involves either surreptitious or open tampering with cultural identities, in violation of liberalism's own commitment to transparent and non-coercive community. If citizens are to be free under liberal institutions this has to be because they endorse those institutions from within their own beliefs and values and not ones preformed by the state just so it can represent itself as non-coercive. Where substantial pluralism develops, no comprehensive liberal doctrine can serve as the basis of the state without forcing some people, perhaps many, to act contrary to their own comprehensive views.

Political liberalism offers to improve the defensibility of liberal institutions given the fact of pluralism, or reasonable pluralism, as Rawls now limits the domain. It tries to cut a deal that confines the play of liberal values to the political domain while leaving people free to pursue their comprehensive views, however substantively non-liberal, in their non-public lives. Its strategy is to raise politics above the fray of rival views, including rival philosophical views, while commanding their support by using only local building materials—the fund of shared ideas to be found in the public political culture. In that way it aims to satisfy, to a greater degree, the liberal demand of defensibility to all. The defensibility claim is expressed by Rawls in the idea that the political conception can become the focus of an overlapping consensus. That is, it can be accepted by people who affirm very different moral views, because they also accept, albeit for different reasons, the fundamental ideas out of which the political conception is constructed. In an overlapping consensus, Rawls writes, 'reasonable doctrines endorse the political conception, each from its own point of view. Social unity is based on a consensus on the political conception' (Rawls, 1993, p. 134.).

Underlying all of this is the liberal claim that what is really important for politics for us is consensus-based social unity. That is, 'informed willing agreement' and the absence of excessive coercion, is a moral ideal of such great value that we could not count a theory as a theory of *justice*, rather than say, of social stability if it did not rest on the ideal. (Raz, 1990, p. 14). On the face of it a theory built on this moral assumption should by that fact be true (ibid. p. 15). But we know that Rawls says that the political conception is not to be presented as true (Rawls, 1993, p. 129). And since it is a liberal conception this cannot mean that the truth-claim is suppressed in order to mislead people into support for the political conception. The explanation that Rawls offers is that 'holding a political conception as true, and for that reason alone the one suitable basis of public reason, is exclusive, even sectarian, and so likely to foster public division' (ibid.). Behind this is his analysis of classical and medieval thought as wedded to the idea of one good, one truth about how to live, and one justice—the effective promotion of the good—to be recognised by all fully reasonable and rational citizens. But since the Reformation, our situation is not at all like that. We are divided on the question of whether there is one conception of the good and of the right, or many (ibid. p. 37, pp. 134–135).

Those of us who accept that reason does not give us one good but a plurality of reasonable views may continue to think that our conception is true. But we can no longer think that our view *can* be recognised by all fully reasonable and rational citizens. So we no longer have the basis for enforcing one view of the good and the just as what all *should* recognise. For us, then, who want to share a political life in circumstances of profound disagreement about fundamental questions, there can only be justice without truth. Our justice has to be constructed on the basis of a few central shared ideas. But even these we cannot call true, that is, founded on true premises, for the premises from which we might derive them belong in our contested comprehensive doctrines.

Take, then, the ideal of a minimally coercive social order. What makes it a basis for the political conception is that it is widely shared. The apparatchiks of the political conception do well to avoid inquiring further into why that is. For that would open up a world of conflicting stories, and revive hostilities over which of them is true. All we need to know is that people accept it and that it is a *stable* acceptance because deeply part of their moral consciousness about the form of principles of political order (Larmore, 1994, p. 61). That can be so only if it is consonant with, or derivable from, their different comprehensive views. But from that, what follows is the reasonableness of the derived ideal, not its truth, (assuming, as I show below, the existence of reasonable disagreement). This, then, is the shift from truth to reasonableness that Rawls asks us to make. We can have justice without truth, because we have the idea of the reasonable.

Where does all this leave the question of comprehensive versus political liberalism? The issue, I think, is whether political liberalism can be the focus of a wider overlapping consensus than a comprehensive liberalism. If it can, it better realises the ideal of defensible social order in modern societies than a comprehensive doctrine. What matters for political liberalism is not the empirical question of how much non-liberalism survives in the well-ordered society—but whether such views can be treated as unreasonable if they fail to endorse the political conception. (Liberals do not expect to have to justify coercion to people who are irrational or unreasonable, for example, the proponents of views which are mad or fanatical.) So, in the end, the case for political versus comprehensive liberalism turns on whether it can be accepted by the adherents of reasonable non-liberal doctrines, in a sense of 'reasonable' yet to be defined.

II

If the case for political liberalism is that it widens the defensibility of liberal institutions in conditions of reasonable pluralism, it must provide an argumentative route to itself from premises of a general rather than a specifically liberal kind. Reasonable pluralism excludes doctrines that are mad, irrational, or simply blind to everyday needs and interests. But it is not confined to liberal pluralism, that is a pluralism of doctrines that give high priority to some subset of individualist values such as autonomy and choice, individuality, independence of thought and action, and the like.

So the first question is whether we can identify doctrines as reasonable without presupposing a liberal conception of reasonableness. Rawls uses the terms 'reasonable' and reasonableness' in several senses, three of which are particularly important. First he says what he means by a reasonable comprehensive doctrine. It has three main features:

> [i] a reasonable doctrine is an exercise of theoretical reason: it covers the major religious, philosophical, and moral aspects of human life in a more or less consistent and coherent manner. It organises and characterises recognised values so that they are compatible with one another and express an intelligible view of the world...
> [ii] In singling out which values to count as especially significant and how to balance them when they conflict, a reasonable comprehensive doctrine is also an exercise of practical reason...
> [iii] it normally belongs to, or draws upon, a tradition of thought and doctrine. (Rawls, 1993, p. 59).

In this first sense of 'reasonable', a reasonable doctrine displays the intelligibility that marks the exercise of reason. Call this 'the reasonable as *intelligible'* sense. In the second sense, 'reasonableness' means 'willingness to recognise the burdens of judgement and to accept their consequences for the use of public reason in directing the legitimate exercise of state power in a constitutional regime' (ibid. p. 54). Here reasonable means being willing to acknowledge the existence of 'conflicting reasonable judgements' (ibid. p. 58) in view of the circumstances that affect all reasoning about values, what Rawls calls the burdens of reason—lack of conclusive evidence, the difficulties of ranking values, and of estimating the weight of conflicting considerations, differences in individual experience leading to differences in assessing evidence and weighing values, and the impossibility of fitting all values into one moral space (ibid. pp. 54–57). In this, the *burdens* sense, a reasonable doctrine is one which acknowledges the fact of reasonable disagreement about values and its consequences. In the third sense 'reasonable' or 'reasonableness' means willingness 'to propose principles and standards as fair terms of co-operation and to abide by them willingly, given the assurance that others will likewise do so' (ibid. p. 49). Here the salient feature is willingness to moderate one's view, or the claims one makes on the basis of it, for the sake of co-operation with others. Call this the 'reasonable as *moderation'* sense. A view that is reasonable in this sense has the right shape to affirm the political conception.

On the face of it, it seems possible for there to be views which are reasonable in the sense of intelligible, without also being reasonable in the burdens sense, and also ones which are reasonable in the burdens sense that do not meet the standard of reason as moderation. What Rawls has to show is that views which are reasonable in the intelligible sense can find a path through the burdens sense to reasonableness in the reason as moderation sense. This he fails to do, explicitly anyway, hence the appearance of political liberalism as a doctrine that speaks only to the liberal faithful.

The needed argument is not like a non-stop train. The journey has several stops and fare stages, and adherents of different views may refuse to go on because they cannot find the fare, or because they think it represents bad value, given the way their view of life balances its various values. This is why all the argument seeks to establish is the main staging posts and considerations in favour of adopting reason as moderation for political life. People have to find their own way from stage to stage on the basis of ideas drawn from, or compatible with, their own comprehensive doctrines. Nevertheless I shall suggest that because there is something we might call the form of a reasonable view, though there is no single standard of reasonableness, there is an inbuilt tendency for views that set themselves up as reasonable to converge on the standard of reason as moderation.

The first step in the argument is to say that proponents of reasonable doctrines (intelligible sense) are reasonable (burdens sense) if they are prepared to acknowledge the existence of other similarly reasonable (intelligible) doctrines. Such acknowledgement is a consequence of accepting the burdens of reason. Rawls offers this doctrine as an explanation of the existence of a plurality of reasonable (intelligible) doctrines. We should note that its explanatory power derives from the idea that the exercise of reason, given the burdens, offers no guarantee of final agreement on fundamental questions about how to live. Indeed, it is very likely to produce diversity. '[O]ur most important judgments are made under conditions where it is not to be expected that conscientious persons with full powers of reason, even after free discussion, will all arrive at the same conclusion' (ibid, p. 58; see also Larmore, 1994, p. 74). So, we cannot expect thinking and arguing about values to lead to agreement rather than to disagreement. More significantly, we have no neutral way of privileging one over another of the diverse reasonable products of reasoning in these circumstances. That is why the proponents of reasonable views (intelligible sense) may be prepared to acknowledge the existence of other similarly reasonable views. Then they are reasonable in the burdens sense too.

The burdens criterion of reasonableness may be met by many of the comprehensive doctrines in society under free institutions. They can be expected to satisfy it because they are shaped by the paradigm of religious comprehensive views and we now take the differences between the major religions to be a matter of reasonable disagreement. But the criterion is unlikely to be met by all comprehensive doctrines, including certain versions of the major religious doctrines. For, the acknowledgement of reasonable disagreement entails that one's own doctrine is in certain respects deeply *problematic*. It may be true and the arguments for it sound, but one cannot hold it with the kind of fanatical intensity and intolerance of other views, that accompanies the pursuit of some comprehensive doctrines. So doctrines which are unable to accommodate the thought that 'truths' about how to live are deeply problematic, though reasonable in the sense of intelligible, will not even aim to satisfy the burdens sense. They will be classed as intolerant, and therefore illiberal. In the well-ordered society their adherents are not part of the overlapping consensus and they have to live by terms drawn up by those who acknowledge reasonable disagreement. In these cases political liberalism moves its defence from actual consent to hypothetical consent. It defends the jurisdiction of its terms of association by arguing for them as ones that could be endorsed by all as free and equal. So some or all fundamentalists, for example, are unfree in that the liberal political order does not have their actual consent. But their position with respect to unfreedom is not as bad as it would be for everyone else were *they* to set the terms of association. For that is a social order to which the consent of all as free and equal is not even imaginable (Waldron, 1993, p. 51).

The second step has to take us from willingness to acknowledge reasonable disagreement to political liberalism as a consequence. Here the crucial idea is that it is unreasonable to impose one's own (problematic) comprehensive view on others. The operative criterion of reasonableness here is the moderation sense. People who are reasonable in this sense are willing to moderate the claims they make on the basis of their comprehensive view in order to reach accommodation with others who do not share it.

The question is how many of the survivors of the burdens test respond to reasonable disagreement by adopting this new standard of reasonableness. The answer depends on how many are blown toward the liberal shore by winds they have raised themselves. There may, in the end, be many of those, as I hope the following considerations show.

The fact of reasonable disagreement, by itself, cannot contribute to the conclusion of political liberalism without the addition of a normative claim: people should not be forced to act contrary to their own reasonable views about how to live. In support of this proposition liberals appeal to a notion of moral integrity—the idea that we destroy people's stature as moral agents if we break the link between their deepest moral beliefs and their actions. People must be able to live their lives from the 'inside' as Kymlicka puts it, on the basis of beliefs and values they can call their own, not ones that have been imposed on them by others (Kymlicka, 1990, p. 204; Ingram, 1994, pp. 183–184). Sometimes the objection to external imposition is rooted by liberals in a Kantian claim that it forces on people a certain kind of heteronomy, in violation of their capacity for free moral thinking, the sole condition on which morality is possible. But some people do not accept the Kantian basis. After all, it is a clearly liberal basis. However, the objection to moral imposition is not specifically liberal. It can also be rooted in a much more broadly shared understanding of the significance of reason for morality.

To introduce the point consider Larmore's definition of reasonableness as 'thinking and acting in good faith and applying, as best one can, the general capacities of reason that belong to every domain of inquiry' (Larmore, 1994, p. 75). What I want to draw attention to here is the phrase 'in good faith'. We might substitute 'conscientiously' or 'in good conscience' (see Rawls 1993, p. 58). The idea that a conscientiously held view, one that is based on our best efforts to understand and think through its demands, deserves moral respect, and should not normally be overridden by others, is part of a long tradition of mostly non-liberal thought which holds that we learn about the good by reasoning about it, that the capacities of reason are human capacities, and that acting contrary to reason is bad for humans as thwarting a natural and distinctive excellence. If morality is 'acting in accordance with reason', that is, something that has the general form of reason, and people's views about the good are intelligible results of their exercise of reason, then people may be regarded as normatively free to live by those views, provided they grant a like freedom to all. To suggest otherwise might be thought to undermine the status of reason as something of fundamental moral significance which anything that counts as a moral view must finally honour, a position that few doctrines identifying themselves as reasonable want to adopt.[4] For, the whole point of the concern about being reasonable is to be able to claim the privileges that go with that status in western thought generally—respect, power, legitimacy, freedom, and so on.

Given the honorific role of capacities for reasoning and thinking in western thought, views that develop inside this tradition are likely to present themselves as, in some sense, reasonable. And in fact this is how many of the major comprehensive views do present themselves. The deep value of reason, as something it is good and right for humans to exercise, predisposes such comprehensive views to adopt whatever standard of reasonableness in conditions of pluralism best realises that abstract value. If Rawls is right, this is the standard of reasonableness as moderation on which political liberalism is based. The predisposition to reasonableness as moderation is likely to be most marked in doctrines that acknowledge the burdens of reason, and indeed the endorsement of something like the political conception, as shown by the willingness to separate church and state to be found in liberal democratic societies, suggests that a deep background commitment to honouring reason, leads to the effort to adopt the reason as moderation standard.

However, we need not suppose that all of the doctrines that are reasonable in the burdens sense are compelled to adopt reason as moderation. Having due regard for democracy, they may sustain a

[4] For an exception, see note 6 below.

claim to be expressed in the law of a state where they have overwhelming majority support. This is not an unfamiliar or even much frowned-upon situation. For all that we describe familiar states as liberal democracies, we also identify many of them by the main religious affiliation of their citizens, and that is frequently explanatory of why they have certain elements in their constitutions and laws.[5] In the context of the well-ordered society, such claims could take the form of a right to exit (secession) or to retreat (some level of political autonomy within the existing society), as Galston (1989, p. 717) has argued.

Other doctrines will not seek to accommodate to the reason as moderation standard for darker reasons. They may recognise reasonable disagreement in light of the burdens of reason, while insisting that opposing views embody an inferior exercise of reason as judged by the standard of self-assertion on the stage of history. In the grip of their world historical mission proponents of this sort of view will regard other views, other cultures, other nations, as without rights, as Hegel (1952, pp. 218–219) taught with respect to the right to dominate others of the nation that is the current vehicle of the development of world mind.[6] The potential for civil strife represented by such views hits the limits of toleration in Rawls's well-ordered society. Here, as in other cases where people claim that their pursuit of the good requires imposing it on others, by force, if necessary, 'we may eventually have to assert at least certain aspects of our comprehensive ... doctrine ... This will happen whenever someone insists, for example, that certain questions are so fundamental that to insure their being rightly settled justifies civil strife ... At this point we may have no alternative but to deny this, and hence to maintain the kind of thing we had hoped to avoid' (Rawls, 1993, p. 152). This is a revealing passage. It reminds us that the political conception draws its justification from the various comprehensive views that are willing to be regulated by it. It represents fair terms for peaceful coexistence. When

[5] An example is the Constitution of Ireland.

[6] 'The nation to which is ascribed a moment of the Idea ... is entrusted with giving complete effect to it . . . That nation is dominant in world history during this one epoch, and it is only once . . . that it can make its hour strike. In contrast with this its absolute right of being the vehicle of this present stage in the world historical mind's development, the minds of the other nations are without rights, and they, along with those whose hour has struck already, count no longer in world history' and 'The civilised nation is conscious that the rights of barbarians are unequal to its own and treats their autonomy as only a formality' (Hegel, 1952: sect. 347, p. 218 and sect. 351, p. 219).

another view puts itself into a state of war with our own comprehensive view the gloves come off and we defend our right to our own view and to a society that defends it, even though that may mean, for the moment, insisting on our standard of reasonableness (moderation).

The argument should not stop here. It should show that political liberalism leaves adequate space for the pursuit of comprehensive views in non-public life. Clearly there is going to be disagreement about this. And I cannot pursue the issue here. Suffice to say that political liberalism is likely to leave more space than classical liberalism, because it is not wedded to advancing a perfectionist ideal such as human autonomy, individuality, or the like. This is what makes political liberalism an attractive project for those concerned about the terms under which people can live together in the kind of multi-ethnic, multicultural, and multi-faith societies we live in. Justice as fairness may provide those terms. But even if it does not, it provides a model of what the terms should look like and, perhaps, also a standard, departures from which have to be justified.

I hope I have done enough to show the plausibility of the claim that Rawlsians need not be liberals, deep down. Non-liberal Rawlsians must however acknowledge the existence of reasonable disagreement. This allows me to say, finally, that while Rawlsians need not be liberals, they must be moral cosmopolitans. That is, they must regard every human being as a member of a global moral community in which each has a common moral status. In our tradition this global moral status is often based on common human reason. This is what explains the ability of adherents of many familiar comprehensive moral doctrines to accept that those who disagree about the good life are in reasonable rather than blind and irrational disagreement. This is also why they will tend to embrace the reason as moderation standard for political life. For, they are moved by the consideration of global human moral status, to seek to accommodate one another's peculiar efforts at reasoning about how to live.[7] But the idea of moral cosmopolitanism is not confined to doctrines wedded to something like common human reason. Other comprehensive doctrines may have different grounds. What matters for them, as for the 'rationalist' doctrines is whether they have or can develop a basis for recognising the integrity of other human beings in the cultural contexts in

[7] Moral cosmopolitanism does not entail a global political community. Empirical as well as normative considerations bear on questions about institutional structures and political boundaries (see Beitz, 1979, p. 183).

which their identities and their convictions about the good are formed. Political liberalism may be a doctrine for societies 'like ours'. But its feasibility rests on comprehensive doctrines which are able to accept the reasonableness of views and people who are not at all 'like us'.

Political Liberalism, Secular Republicanism: two answers to the challenges of pluralism

CATHERINE AUDARD

The main challenge facing democracies in the post-Communist era is probably not so much the threat of totalitarianism as the consequences of pluralism, of the existence within these societies of a plurality of incompatible cultural allegiances. How are they to survive their fragmentation into communities many of whom no longer share the basic moral requirements of a democratic regime: recognition of the liberty of conscience, of equality of rights, and the like?

Two main theories seem to provide a solution, republicanism on the one hand, liberalism on the other hand, but they may seem out of touch with the present situation. Would, nevertheless, a historical and conceptual survey of these two different options be of any help in shedding some light on the issues involved? What is their understanding of diversity and could each have something to learn from the other? The aim of this paper is to show that these two responses are both still very much alive; that they are much more similar than one might suspect; and that an examination of them shows very clearly that the root of the problem lies in the content of citizenship and in the dignity attached to it, rather than in diversity as such.

I shall, therefore, (1) try and explain the main features of the typical French view on diversity and its recognition, and the way in which republicanism has provided resources for successful cultural integration. I shall then (2) underline the similarities with aspects of the Rawlsian conception of political liberalism (Rawls, 1993) which may, at first, seem significantly far removed but which, in fact, are much less so when examined in detail. I shall conclude (3) by briefly suggesting a re-evaluation of citizenship that goes beyond the social meaning that it has in the French republican tradition and yet avoids the dangers of the 'politics of recognition' typical of contemporary liberalism.

The Main Features of the French Republican Model: integration as 'assimilation'

France, as a nation, has been the result of a political project, the formation of a community based not on 'blood', but on citizenship: the nation as a community of citizens. This project has been articulated most strongly by the French Revolution, but it has deeper roots, which I cannot explore here. The twin processes of modernisation and universalisation during and since the French Revolution have meant that to be or to become French was not simply to enter a particular ethnic group or nation, but to become an actor in a wider drama, that of an emancipatory process which was to lead eventually to a federation of democratic and peaceful nations, to universal reconciliation, to the dissolution of particularities and differentiations as sources of conflicts, to the recognition of a kind of universal brotherhood or world citizenship. This idea was, for instance, the inspiration of Kant's 'Perpetual Peace' (Kant, 1991, pp. 99–100):

> A *republican constitution* is founded upon three principles: firstly, the principle of freedom for all members of a society (as men); secondly, the principle of the *dependence* of everyone upon a single common legislation (as subjects); and thirdly, the principle of legal *equality* for everyone (as citizens) ...The republican constitution offers a prospect for a perpetual peace ... as it is inevitably the case that under this constitution, the consent of the citizens is required to decide whether or not war is to be declared, and they will have great hesitation in embarking in so dangerous an enterprise.

The ideal Republic as a civic nation appears, therefore, to be the best protection against nationalism and war. The French Revolution had had the privilege of being the prime mover in this process by freeing the people from their particular roots and bonds and by 'recreating' them as the abstract bearers of rights: no more a Breton or an Auvergnat or a Jew or a Pole, but a French citizen with equal rights and dignity. To be French, therefore, implied special responsibilities, very similar to those carried by the American notion of citizenship, those of enlightening the rest of the world as to the benefits of free and equal citizenship, beyond the differences of class, ethnic origins, language and religion. France had invented the notion of the 'civic nation' and, as such, exemplified one particular instance of the 'universal Republic'.

Let us consider first, the exact meaning of the civic nation, of the Republic as a community of citizens, united and integrated in spite of their different cultural origins. By contrast with the 'ethnic nation', embodied in contemporary united Germany, for instance, the political project of the civic nation does not take political homogeneity to be 'given' as a kind of natural phenomenon, a second nature, as it were, but sees it as the result of a voluntary and conscious allegiance. The nation is not given as such by the past, by culture or by tradition, but this does not mean that the political superstructure is superimposed or, so to speak, forced upon a divided, fragmented civil society. It is created at any given time by the tacit adhesion of the citizen to its political institutions: the nation, as Ernest Renan famously said, is *a daily plebiscite*. This is the best definition of the Republic as a voluntary political creation, the result of an endlessly renewed social compact or 'pacte républicain'. Consequently, cultural pluralism and the fragmentation of society into distinct communities are threatening for such a project. The many different components would remain untouched by the social contract. They would remain what they were at the beginning: particular communities and individuals without a common political project. This is why if France is effectively as multicultural a society as Britain or the United States, it does not see itself as such, but rather as having the mission to assimilate this diversity into the one and indivisible Republic, to transform these individuals into equal and similar citizens, to dissolve the remaining small local communities into the undifferentiated body politic.

We have, then, two possible readings of the myth of a universal Republic. Either we can see the French model of integration as nationalist and illiberal in that its real intent, beyond the rhetoric of equality, is to 'Frenchify' its population, to impose on it one single culture, one language, one way of thinking, irrespective of its various distinct identities, and all this in the name of emancipation. More importantly, we can see it as wanting to create the conditions necessary for the exercise of a strong central political domination. From this point of view, it is clearly an instrument of internal and external colonisation and imperialism. Or we can see it as an effective way of avoiding nationalism, because of the *political* nature of the nation. The strength of the nation as a united community comes from its political institutions, not from its language or racial purity. This is a very important feature that one should keep in mind before criticising too strongly the republican ideal, especially when one thinks of the attempt at articulating a similar conception in contemporary Germany, that of Habermas's 'constitutional patriotism' and its recent failure to win widespread acceptance, since the reunification of Germany and the rise of German nationalism in the Nineties. Maintaining a balance between universality and particularity is or could be one of the merits of this model; ethnocentricity may be avoided if universality is attributed only to the political institutions of the state and not to the cultural traditions within which they have emerged.

Assimilation which, since the advent of the 'politics of recognition', we tend to see now as involving the loss of precious and irreplaceable identities, of valuable attachments and traditions, has not always been seen in such an unattractive light. On the contrary, depending on the features of the immigrant population, on the balance of powers and mostly, on the extent of the rights and benefits attached to citizenship, it has long been synonymous with a kind of emancipation and modernisation that does not so much mean the painful loss of identity as the creation of a new breathing space in which to develop it in a new idiom.

Of this we could find many eloquent examples. One such is that of the Jews and of the French Revolution which granted them, in 1789, the status of equal citizenship for the first time during the history of the Diaspora. This meant a huge gain in security, dignity and basic life-prospects. For instance, the right to full ownership of property which, for centuries, had been denied to non-Christians in Christian countries (and is still denied to Jews and non-Muslims in many Muslim countries) was for the first time granted to the Jewish population. This has been a historical landmark for the Jewish people all over Europe and is still fondly remembered as a significant event, as witnessed by the famous saying: 'Happy as God in France!'. Here, we have a case of assimilation without, on the whole, a loss of identity (though this claim obviously needs a careful analysis of the very notion of a Jewish identity), partly because of the special features of the Jewish religion, partly because of the content of the citizens' rights. As citizenship included the right to worship, it allowed for the possibility of carrying on being both a Jew and a French citizen. The only restriction the secular Republic imposed on the citizens and their right to worship was that the exercise of religion should be kept private, so that it would not invade the public domain. Because of the non-proselytising nature of the Jewish religion, this restriction has never really been a source of conflict. Secularism has benefited the Jewish religion because the latter had no ambition to transform the public life of the country, to intervene as such outside the limits of the Jewish community. (Of course, this optimism is challenged by that ever louder minority of very Orthodox Jews who, at least in Israel, would not wish to live in a secular State and who want rather to impose their conception of a truly Jewish life on the whole of society.)

All that was required was the possibility of leading a Jewish life within the community without any hindrance. The same should have been true of Islam in France, but this, for reasons that we shall see later, has unfortunately recently proved very difficult. By contrast, secularism during the nineteenth century has caused a burning and still on-going conflict with the Catholic Church mainly because of one of the latter's most prominent features, its one time and to some extent still avowed aim to transform French society into a Catholic one, to impose its specific values on the whole of the public sphere, irrespective of the basic rights and freedom of conscience of the rest of the population.

One should, thus, never underestimate the attractions of assimilation when it means a wider range of basic rights and freedoms, including the freedom to cultivate one's own identity and to gain recognition and respect for it within the framework and the constraints of citizenship. The politics of assimilation have been resented mostly when the content of citizenship has become thinner, when the value of fundamental rights has been eroded as in the contemporary case of North African immigrants in France. Assimilation can be seen from the outside as a very illiberal process, but for the population the benefits can be enormous as long as the political and social value of citizenship is sustained. My thesis is that its moral value should be taken into account as well.

It is when the process of assimilation is forced upon the people without the compensation of full citizenship that things go wrong. The French colonial enterprise in Algeria was characterised by an extraordinary ambiguity: the values of the Republic, equal citizenship, etc. were granted only to the colonists, not to the colonised Algerians. Algeria was part of France, but not all French nationals were full citizens: in 1862, the Court in Algiers stated that 'while not being a citizen, the native was nevertheless French'. All through the period of the French colonisation, the discrepancies between the phraseology of rights and equality and the actual inequalities of status went uncriticised, all in the name of the benefits of 'assimilation' (Schnapper, 1994, p. 152). This treachery is one among many betrayals that explain the intensity of the rift between France and Algeria and the subsequent difficulties of the Algerian immigrants in France.

The primary and most visible instrument of these politics of assimilation has been the powerful and centralised French state. The State should not be confused with the nation nor with the people itself. The State is *par excellence* the instrument of the nation. It has been, first, the instrument of its creation, then of its consolidation. It secures the permanence of the nation as the latter is faced by internal and external dangers. The legitimacy of the State power is grounded on the fragility of the civic nation as an abstract ideal. The State has to be powerful because, as the nation is *not* grounded on a 'natural' or ethnic community, by contrast with the civic or 'cultural' nation (Anderson, 1983), the factors of dissolution are numerous. One could easily explain the 'statocracy' in France by giving historical reasons, but also by reference to the importance of destabilising factors and to the number of the various regional communities which had to be absorbed and 'Frenchified' through a kind of internal colonisation since the Middle Ages. In modern Britain, by contrast, the process of absorption has, on the whole, been smoother and less authoritarian with the major exception of Ireland.

One sees clearly, then, why the creation by the State of a public, compulsory, secular and completely free educational system between 1880 and 1905 was an absolute necessity for the Republic: it was the best way in which to assimilate the diverse populations and to create a solid basis for the civic nation. But, again, these politics can also be interpreted as aiming at political domination, not at the creation of a civic nation. It would be wrong to underestimate the ambiguities of the Republic. The role of the school system, in accordance with the function of the State, has undoubtedly been to shape the mentality and the instincts of the ordinary people in order to produce 'good citizens'.

One should pause here and reflect on a striking feature of the Republican ideal, namely the permanent conflict between the individual and the citizen or, in Rousseauist terms, between the particular will and the general will. The meaning of this conflict is more historical than is conveyed by the Rousseauist vocabulary; it is actually a conflict between the regional and social particularities which were the hallmark of the Ancient Regime and of its deep inequalities, on the one hand, and the abstract unity of the civic nation, on the other. The confusion between diversity and inequality, where the former becomes synonymous with servitude, is conceptually absurd, but has nevertheless very deep historical roots. Here is what Jacques Muglioni, chief Inspector of Secondary Schools, writes in 1994 in an article entitled 'The Republic and the School': 'A human being, characterised by his allegiances, identifying himself with particular groups, with collective or individual interests, cannot be a good citizen since *a good citizen, first and for all, does not belong to anyone*' (my emphasis). And he goes on,

> But is it the citizen that makes the Republic or the Republic that makes the citizen? The reciprocal link is only made possible by the school, beyond any respect for family, work or community links, even for traditions, however great they may be. The school is at the service neither of the family nor of the employers. Its only function is to shape the mind, without any consid-

> eration for interests or beliefs and to bring it to its highest level of freedom. The Republic admits of individual beliefs, but only as what is due to any human being, not in the name of pluralism; this would go against integration and lead to discrimination when the particular religious or racial origins are being signalled by the institution, even by the identity card! (Muglioni, 1994, p. 75)

There is a lot to comment on here. Beyond the totalitarian tone: 'The school has thus an essential link to truth' (ibid. p. 77), one should recognise the will to create a new type of human being, the citizen, that is someone who is no longer a particular individual, Alsatian, Breton or Provençal, but first of all French. This is, of course, the most striking and fascinating difference with the British liberal tradition where the emphasis is on the individual and on 'the culture of the self', as Mill so eloquently shows in *On Liberty*. One learns how to become French through the study of the great masters, great writers, figures of the past, not through Socratic self-discovery. This explains why, in the very syllabus of the schools and in the methods of teaching, the emphasis is on theoretical, abstract knowledge and on competence, rather than on personal experience, because that would mean diversity, heterogeneity, anarchy, perhaps, anyway a challenge to the forces of unification. It says a lot about the ideology of emancipation according to the Republic that the Founding Fathers of the schooling system, the most famous of whom was Jules Ferry, should be disciples of Auguste Comte, not of John Stuart Mill (Kriegel, 1985, p. 84)

But once again, one should not see the Republic only as the enemy of personal, 'negative' freedom, but also as a political instrument of integration within a civic, not an ethnic nation, where citizenship is the substitute for cultural homogeneity. One is not born French, one becomes French, to paraphrase Simone de Beauvoir. The birth of a democratic community is made possible by a seemingly totalitarian ideology. The question is to what extent it actually is illiberal.

The most sensitive issue, even now, is, of course, that of religious peace in France. This is a very difficult question as the kind of secularism developed in France has had contradictory aspects. There is a pragmatic secularism, which is based on an on-going compromise between the Church and the State that attempts to satisfy contradictory basic claims; there is also an aggressive secularism, which wants to 'liberate' the people from their attachment to Catholicism and to the forces of obscurantism. This secularism becomes all too easily the caricature of the civil religion dreamed of, for instance, by Rousseau (Rousseau, 1991, IV, ch. 8). Between passions and compromises, the true story of the relations between the State and the Catholic Church is that of the emergence of neutrality with respect to the various beliefs now recognised as 'personal, free and changing'. It is worth noting here that secularism or 'laïcity' in French has two spellings: (1) 'Laïc' (lay) refers to the status of someone religiously active, but within a secular order, by contrast with the regular orders. (2) 'Laïque' (secular) means the status of institutions like schools or of ideas that are independent of or opposed to the hegemony of the Catholic Church in the civil society. One could conclude from this that secularism has close if not ambivalent links with the Church or that it is, at least, an ambiguous concept.

Of that long and complex story, I shall only take two very recent examples, those of the toleration of the Islamic scarf and of the Jewish Sabbath in French State schools. Since 1986 there has been a growing and often bitter polemic, first between parents, teachers and headmasters, then throughout the whole of the country, as to whether the correct interpretation of the principle of neutrality should allow or forbid the wearing of the Islamic scarf in school. In the end, in November 1989, the State Council (the court of arbitration for conflicts between the state and the citizens) laid it down that symbols of religious affiliation as such are not incompatible with the neutrality (*laïcité*) of the school on condition that they do not constitute a flagrant act of 'proselytism' and that they do not threaten the public order. But, in 1994 (when the full extent of the Islamic guerilla conflict in Algeria and its possible extension to France among the immigrant population began to be known), the Minister for Education issued a circular forbidding the wearing of 'ostentatious religious symbols' in school. By contrast, a strong minority of public opinion claimed that the right to education was more important than a strict application of the neutrality requirement and that young Muslim girls should not be excluded from school because of their religious identity. A comparison with the possibility for Jewish students to respect the Sabbath when there is school on Saturdays shows the same ambiguity. On the one hand, Jewish students may be allowed to miss school on some Jewish festivals, but, on the other hand, this is not a right as it conflicts with the requirements of school attendance. Thus, the Republican ideal can be the source of two conflicting interpretations. This is another argument to show that the republican model is not, as such, necessarily illiberal and intolerant, but that it provides a contradictory programme, as, indeed, it has done from the start.

Republicanism and Political Liberalism

Beyond the contrasts, however, the similarities between republicanism in the French sense and political liberalism are real and should lead us to see both as similar answers to the same challenge. Historically, the two conceptions share the same project of creating a civic nation embodying moral ideals and leading to peaceful coexistence, even though the embodiment of the project has taken different forms. Conceptually, they originate in similar sets of ideas dating from the Enlightenment: the idea of a social contract; the concept of procedural justice; the priority of the right over the good; the priority of basic liberties over utility; the definition of autonomy as a source of self-validating claims; the necessary tension between equality and liberty within the liberal tradition of natural rights (which does not mean, as Rawls tends to think, a conflict); the separation between the public and the private spheres. All these ideas are familiar enough. It is more interesting to stress that the problems encountered recently by liberalism are also those of republicanism.

I take political liberalism to mean what John Rawls has emphasised in his latest book (Rawls, 1993, chs. IV and VI), that is, a political conception of justice that can serve as the basis for an overlapping consensus between deeply divided and conflicting views of the good held by reasonable and cooperating citizens. His aim is to contrast it with comprehensive liberalism. Comprehensive liberalism, such as that of Kant or Mill, is a view not only of the basis of political association, but of the whole of human life. Its affirmation of the priority of freedom has metaphysical foundations in an individualistic conception of rationality and of the will. To ground philosophically the institutions of a democratic pluralist society on such a view would be both unjust and inefficient as people not sharing an individualistic secular doctrine would deeply resent its influence on the major institutions that shape their lives and those of their families. What about a liberal education, if you are a deeply traditional religious person? To this question Rawls presents political liberalism's answer: 'Political liberalism has a different aim and requires far less. It will ask that children's education include such things as knowledge of their constitutional and civic rights so that, for example, they know that liberty of conscience exists in their society and that apostasy is not a legal crime' (Rawls, 1993, pp. 199–200). This means that political liberalism concerns itself only with the citizen, with the political domain, not with what happens in the non-public sphere as long as the first principles of justice are complied with. In that sense, political liberalism is closer to republicanism than to what is known as comprehensive liberalism.

Now, both liberalism and republicanism claim that citizenship has a moral content, a dignity attached to it, but a 'thin' content, not one involving any religious or philosophical view. This 'thin' moral content lies in the recognition of the individual's reasonableness which is what allows for the possibility of a political consensus. The interpretation of this reasonableness leads, however, to different answers. For republicanism, in politics as in educational matters, republicans divide themselves into the religious who want to teach a republican catechism, and the moderates who wish to respect the liberty of conscience. On the one hand, we have the Jacobin tradition and the pervasive influence of Rousseau's suspicion of the individual; it is only the citizen, educated by the State and exhibiting the civic virtues necessary for the general will, by contrast with particular desires, who can be trusted to 'obey reason and not instinct'. On the other hand, we have Condorcet (Condorcet, 1889) and his followers during the Third Republic. For both Gambetta and Jules Ferry, the protagonists of an 'open' republic, the individual is a progressive and social being, following Auguste Comte's views on the social determination of human nature; reasonableness is not an expression of virtue, but the result of instruction and sociability. This second version is not, in its essence, as illiberal as the Jacobin one, even if we find in it tendencies to authoritarianism, as the exchanges between Auguste Comte and J. S.Mill show in an extremely illuminating manner (Mill and Comte, 1899) and it is not at all opposed to the main features of political liberalism.

What has been called reasonable pluralism (Cohen, 1993, pp. 281–282, Rawls, 1993, p. 36) should, then, make it possible both for the State and its citizens, to respect the plurality of conflicting views that make up the culture of contemporary democracies. If the people are able to recognise that others may have different beliefs from their own while remaining reasonable, they can all constitute a 'community of justification' in spite of their differences because they all recognise the limits of what can be justified, what Rawls calls the 'burdens of judgment' (Rawls, 1993, pp. 54–58). In other words, they recognise that 'reason does not mandate a single moral view' (Cohen, 1993, p. 284). This attitude is part of what Rawls calls the 'duty of civility'. 'This duty involves a willingness to listen to others and a fairmindedness in deciding when accommodations to their views should reasonably be made' (Rawls, 1993, p. 217).

Scanlon has described it as the principle for moral motivation in its relation to rationality: we have a basic 'desire to be able to justify one's actions to others on grounds that they could not reasonably reject' (Scanlon, 1982, p. 117 and Rawls, 1993, pp. 49n and 81–86). This ability to recognise reasons other than our own as acceptable reasons, even if we cannot share them, is the basis for a moral participation in the political association. This conception of toleration is at the heart of political liberalism. It means that without the existence of a community of justification, there cannot be a political association. But this community does not have to be united by a common vision of the good, as this would impinge on the freedom to choose his or her own ends that each member can rightly claim as their due. In the name of justice, the consensus has to be limited to a view of the principles regulating the political association as such and it must not go beyond.

This view of respect as the reasonable basis for a moral consensus is common to the political project of both liberalism and republicanism. The common enemy of both is a conception that takes political membership to be based on cultural allegiance. In such a perspective, self-respect can all too easily be sacrificed to the higher goals of the community and may never appear as a political value. One should then keep in mind that for the most part it is the historical embodiments of the project of a civic nation that have been so extremely different that they have tended to hide their common ideological ground. The real divide is between the civic and the ethnic nation, not that between republicanism and liberalism who, in fact, share a common conception of citizenship and of the dignity attached to it.

The Democratisation of the Republic and the Re-evaluation of Citizenship

The main idea that I should like briefly to stress here is that there is a need for a re-evaluation of the concept of citizenship within both the republican and the liberal traditions not so much as a development of the 'politics of recognition' as in order to provide a proper answer to the challenges of pluralism (Taylor, 1994, p. 37). Such a transformation of the content of citizenship would lead to greater democracy, that is, as Rawls rightly shows, to more respect for the needs, interests and development of the citizen as a moral person.

We saw earlier that one of the main benefits of integration, according to the French conception of the nation, has been education and the social value attached to citizenship. This should make up for the loss of local identities and attachments in the name of access to a new dignity. What is not present in the idea of the Republic is the moral value of this dignity. The French story has been more one of social mobility, social status acquired through citizenship than one of personal moral development. The Republican model, inspired by Greek and Latin antiquity, talks about the civic virtues and the value of political participation as the source for dignity. But this rests on a confusion between self-esteem, which is generated essentially by public recognition, and self-respect, which adds to this dimension that of internal appreciation (Sachs, 1981). The liberal model of citizenship and of the dignity attached to it, especially that of John Stuart Mill, is, by contrast, not so much based on political participation as on self-development and on its public acknowledgement. Self-respect and the recognition of the valuable character of our life and of our activities do not necessarily stem from acting together with others, but from the recognised value of autonomous behaviour in a free society. Thus, political institutions, in particular those concerned with the protection of the liberty of conscience, are sustained by free and equal citizens not only as instruments of their own well-being, but also because they protect their own personal moral development.

When Judith Shklar (1991, p. 96) talked about the necessity of dissociating productivity, work or utility, on the one hand, and citizenship, on the other, in the special case of the unemployed, following Rawls's concept of citizenship, she meant exactly that; citizenship should be valued as a means to personal and moral fulfillment and standing; you enjoy it not because you are useful to the community, but because you are an equal part of it and have been granted the same rights to develop and become an autonomous person and the same duties as any other member, employed or unemployed, useful or less useful. This is the central moral political value of self-respect which is destroyed if measured against the goods you produce, own, etc., just as it is destroyed if seen only in terms of social status.

In concentrating on the value of citizenship, both political liberalism and republicanism are answering the challenges of pluralism. One way to teach tolerance and respect for others is to stress the equal dignity of citizens as autonomous and reasonable persons: this is the liberal solution. Another way is to stress the equal dignity created by political participation: this has been the republican answer. Both have in common the long-term objective of a civic nation as a community of citizens, irrespective of their cultural origins and affiliations. This objective should be attainable if the necessary emphasis is placed on the major problem, that of bringing into focus the real value of citizenship and of equal rights. The desire for cultural differentiation and separation is created by a deficit in citizenship and in the dignity attached to it, not by a sudden and inexplicable longing for recognition.[1]

[1] This is a shortened and partially revised version of a paper given under the title 'French republicanism and thick multiculturalism' at a conference on 'Human Security in Multicultural Societies' held in Kasauli, India in March 1995.

'Race' in Britain and the Politics of Difference

TARIQ MODOOD

I Introduction

It was only a few years ago that the central topic of academic political philosophy, at least in the English-speaking world, was distributive justice. The focus was very much on economic or material goods; the question being whether people were entitled to have what they had, or did justice require that someone else should have some of it. That the arguments about justice led to investigating the conceptions of self, rationality and community that underpinned them meant that the debate was far from governed by economics and welfare, and was capable of moving in many directions and far from its starting-point. Yet that many of the leading participants in the 'liberalism *v.* communitarianism' debate should now have come to place diversity, pluralism and multiculturalism at the centre of their theorising, with the emphasis being on the justness of cultural rather than economic transactions, is surely not just a product of 'following the argument to where it leads'. The change in philosophical focus is also determined by changes in the political world; by the challenges of feminism, the growing recognition that most Western societies are, partly because of movements of populations, increasingly multi-ethnic and multi-racial, and the growing questioning of whether the pursuit of a universal theory of justice may not itself be an example of a Western cultural imperialism. The politics I am pointing to is various and by no means harmonious, but a common feature perhaps is the insistence that there are forms of inequality and domination beyond those of economics and material distributions. An insistence which can highlight the multi-dimensional nature of some forms of oppression, for instance when social relations are simultaneously structured by economic, gender and racial inequalities; but which can also point to forms of inequality even when economic parity is achieved, as in the relations between some men and women.

It is because I believe that the new debates about pluralism, about 'equality and difference'—no less in post-structuralist cultural theory than in Anglo-American political philosophy—are informed, and rightly so, by personal and local interests, that we should be extremely cautious in applying such theorising to a society or situation other than ones that inform it. The difficulty here is not just the one of interpreting the general so as to apply it in a particular case, as for instance a law must be interpreted in court in relation to a specific case. It is that what looks general and sufficiently abstract for transportation from one society to another may in fact be constructed in response to specific contexts. Perhaps this is just stating the obvious. Theorists of 'difference', in spite of the generality of the language of their theories, usually make very clear the specific forms of difference and inequality they are responding to. Titles as general as *Liberalism, Community and Culture* (Kymlicka, 1989), *The Politics of Recognition* (Taylor, 1994) and *Democracy and Difference* (Phillips, 1993) name texts which, notwithstanding their intellectual creativity and rigour, are openly driven by a reading of the circumstances and the political struggles of an exemplar: aboriginal peoples, in particular Native Canadians; the Québecois; and women in North West Europe and North America respectively. My own 'equality and difference' interest is in the circumstances of people of recent extra-European origins in Britain. The theoretical work that I have so far named or alluded to is of course relevant to their circumstances; what is important, however, is that British ethnic minorities not just be interpreted in the light of theories constructed with other groups and other jurisdictions in mind. Ideally, what I hope someone will do is to develop a political theory of multiculturalism which utilises the British experience in the way that Will Kymlicka and Charles Taylor do the Canadian, for I strongly believe that philosophy should be built from the ground upwards. What I offer here however is much more modest. I would like to point to what I think are some of the principal contemporary developments in British race relations which call for a rethinking of 'race' and of 'equality' as they apply to Britain today.

The task here is perhaps a preliminary to a philosophical engagement rather than the engagement itself. Preliminaries should not however be under-appreciated. Those who are cavalier about empirical detail are likely to not just risk irrelevance but allying philosophy with prejudice. Their philosophies will either fail to engage with some important British concerns, or will engage on the basis of ill-informed pronouncements. Let me give some examples. Over the last few years, especially since the publication of Salman Rushdie's *The Satanic Verses* in 1988, discussions in Britain about majority–minority relations—at all levels, from the least to the most intellectual, from the most courteous to the most violent—have been dominated by issues to do with the behaviour and political demands of Muslims. I suppose that this has not been the case in North America. Hence North American political philosophers, amongst whom some of the best work in the field is being done, either ignore what is happening in Britain or reveal an ignorance-cum-prejudice about it. An example of the first is Iris Marion Young. In a book which makes considerable progress in systematising the varied ways in which different kinds of minorities are harmed and which continuously refers to contemporary cases and offers long lists of relevant groups, there is not a single reference to Muslims (Young, 1990). Examples of leading theorists making false accusations against Britons include Will Kymlicka's remarks about arranged marriages and sex-segregated education (made in Kymlicka, 1992, p. 38; discussed in Modood, 1993a and Kymlicka, 1993), and his suggestion that 'some British Muslim groups have demanded the same sort of exemption from a liberal education granted to the Amish', which he describes as the withdrawal of children from school before the age of 16 (Kymlicka, 1995, pp. 177 and 162). Or consider Stephen Macedo's assertion that '[i]n Great Britain, violent Moslem [sic] demonstrations against Salman Rushdie's depiction of Mohammed in *The Satanic Verses* helped provoke the Ayatollah Khomeni into pronouncing a death sentence on the author' (Macedo, 1993, p. 622). In fact the first Muslim demonstration in Britain at which there was any violence was in London at the end of May 1989, three and a half months after the death sentence; what provoked Khomeni were the deaths of Muslims in demonstrations in Pakistan and India (Horton, 1993, pp. 109–110).

I call these factual errors an 'ignorance-cum-prejudice' for they betray an intellectual carelessness and an appeal to taken-for-granted stereotypes that would not be tolerated if instead of Muslims, it was, say, women, Jews or African-Americans that were the topic of discussion. The problem is not simply about the uses of factual error, it can also take the form of obfuscation. An example can be found in the otherwise stimulating essay by Charles Taylor referred to above. He argues, rightly I believe, that liberalism is not a 'neutral ground on which people of all cultures can meet and coexist' (Taylor, 1994, p.62). The only example he gives of where 'one has to draw the line' is 'incitement to assassination'. So far there is likely to be no conflict. He reaches this conclusion however by arguing that the controversy over *The Satanic Verses* shows that '[f]or mainstream Islam, there is no question of separating politics and religion the way we have come to expect in Western liberal society' (ibid.). My objection is that it is far from obvious that this is what the controversy showed or needs to show in order for anyone to reach the conclusion that liberalism ought not to tolerate incitement to murder. Taylor offers no evidence that 'mainstream Islam' involves an acceptance of incitement to assassination; nor that if you hold that politics and religion do not have to be separated (in the way that Taylor himself argues that politics and culture do not have to be separated), then you have no argument against incitement to assassination. The reference to mainstream Islam is in fact a *non sequitur*, but the impression is created that liberalism cannot accommodate mainstream Islam, that mainstream Muslims are not to be included in 'the politics of recognition'.

II Racial Equality

It is generally recognised that 'race' interpreted as 'white' and 'black', paradigmatically those of European and African descent respectively, is perhaps the most important historical and contemporary divide in the United States—suggesting not a pluralism but a dualism. It is a racial division that certainly has some parallel in the British colonial experience, not least because the two histories were once one and the English gave birth to what happened in America. From the 1970s onwards, in the wake of immigration into England from some parts of the former Empire, a growing body of opinion, especially expert opinion, came to the view that a racial dualism had emerged in Britain too. It is most succinctly expressed in a sentence from Salman Rushdie:

> Britain is now two entirely different worlds and the one you inherit is determined by the colour of your skin (Rushdie, 1982).

The truth in this view was somewhat exaggerated and is now increasingly inappropriate. For example, while in the early 1980s it just about made sense to say that non-white people shared similarly disadvantaged economic circumstances, this was not the case by the end of that decade (Modood 1992; Jones,1993; Ballard and Kalra, 1994). Using the three key indicators of unemployment, job hierarchies and educational qualifications shows that there is a dualism, but that it is not a colour dualism. Bangladeshis, Pakistanis and Caribbeans have made some progress but continue to have the disadvantaged profile of a decade earlier. The Chinese, African Asians and Indians, on the other hand, have or are developing a socio-economic profile which is similar to or better than that of the White population.

A stronger case can be made for a racial dualism on the basis of discrimination rather than disadvantage; that the non-white groups are not doing as well in employment terms as might be expected in terms of the qualifications they hold. It may be suggested that regardless of their *position* in the occupational hierarchy all or most non-white groups are in a lesser position than they should be and that the cause of this is racial discrimination. There is indeed some truth in this and it has some important implications for how we measure equal opportunities and hypothesise discrimination. In practice we often take the statistics of disadvantage as a proxy for discrimination, or at least as an indicator of discrimination. However, once we unbuckle discrimination from disadvantage, we are open to the possibility that successful groups may not only continue to suffer discrimination (if we had borne the example of the Jews in mind there would hardly be a sense of discovery), but that in principle advantaged groups might sometimes even suffer more discrimination than disadvantaged ones. Secondly, even this sort of analysis does not yield a racial dualism. One study found that the comparative gap between qualifications and subsequent careers varied for different groups and did not affect the Chinese (Cheng, 1994); another that the comparative gap between identically qualified candidates and entry into higher education affected only the Caribbeans and Pakistanis and not others that were 'racially' or in appearance similar to them (Modood and Shiner, 1994); and yet another that the gap as it related to the most difficult to enter section of higher education, medical schools, was statistically identical to a penalty for having a non-European name, which is odd, because this line of enquiry began with the assumption that skin-colour is fate in Britain, whereas in Britain, as in the US, most black people have European names (McManus *et al*. 1995).

The most important fact the new data on socio-economic diversity should help us to see is that racial discrimination is not a unitary form of disadvantaging because not all non-white groups are discriminated against in the same way or to the same extent. Colour-racism may be a constant but there are other kinds of racism at work in Britain. Colour-racism is the antipathy, exclusion and unequal treatment of people on the basis of their physical appearance, above all on their not being 'white' or of European-origin appearance. Cultural-racism builds on colour-racism by using cultural difference from an alleged British or civilised norm to vilify or marginalise or demand cultural assimilation from groups who also suffer colour-racism. Post-war racism in Britain has been simultaneously culturalist and biological and, while the latter is perhaps essential to it being racism, it is in fact the more superficial aspect. As white people's interactions with non-white individuals increased, they were not necessarily less conscious of group differences but they were far more likely to ascribe group differences to upbringing, customs, forms of socialisation and self-identity than to biological heredity. So, for example, white people who continue to be racists towards some ethnic groups, can come to admire other ethnic groups. Several ethnographic studies have found for example that white working class boys who are anti-Asian admire Afro-Caribbean sub-cultures because of their positive masculine and class associations (Cohen, 1988; Back, 1993). Opinion surveys, such as the annual Social Attitudes Survey, point in the same direction. They began in 1982 and have consistently recorded that white people think there is more extreme prejudice against Asians than against Afro-Caribbeans. The gap is most amongst younger people and is widening (Airey and Brook, 1986, p. 163). A survey we are currently analysing at the Policy Studies Institute found that all ethnic groups believe that prejudice against Asians in general, and Muslims in particular, is much the highest of any ethnic, racial or religious group (Modood *et al.* forthcoming 1996).

Perhaps unlike in the United States, there has been a significant growth in black-white sociability and cultural synthesis, especially amongst young people. This is evident in the high prestige that black cultural styles are held in, and in the hero-worship of successful black 'stars' in football and sport, music and entertainment (Boulton and Smith, 1992). As also in the high rates of black–white marriages and cohabitation: nearly half of Caribbean men under the age of 44, and nearly a third of women have a white partner, compared to less than 10% and less than 5% of Asian men and women respectively (Labour Force Survey 1988–1990; for details see Modood *et al.* 1994, pp. 77–78). It is particularly important to note that this sociability is not necessarily in a colour-blind assimilationist, 'passing for white' context in which racism is ignored. For some young people it can take place in ways in which black ethnicity and anti-racism is emphasised, indeed is the point. Black persons can be admired, not in spite of, but because of their blackness, for their aesthetics, style and creativity as well as for their anti-racist resistance: for example, at a typical performance of the controversial black nationalist rap band *Public Enemy*, more than half of the audience will be white. Of course, there is also much negative stereotyping and racism against black people (and some positive stereotyping of Asians). My point is that different groups suffer different, as well as similar kinds of racism, and one kind depends upon cultural acceptability.

I am aware that the concept of cultural-racism will seem perverse to some. It will seem yet another example of what Robert Miles calls an 'inflation of the meaning of racism' (Miles, 1989) by bringing together two things, racism proper and cultural prejudice or ethnocentricism, that are apparently quite distinct, thereby obscuring the real nature of racist thinking and practices. It is true there is no necessary connection between cultural prejudice and colour-racism; but there is no more a connection between racial discrimination and class inequalities, and yet when the two do come together the concept of racial disadvantage is a good one to describe the situation. Or again, there is no necessary connection between racism and sexism (for the opposite view, see Balibar, 1991, p. 49) but we know they can be connected, and when they are, a distinctive phenomenon is created in the form of stereotypes about submissive Asian women and the strong black woman who cannot keep her man (Anthias and Yuval-Davis, 1992, p. 125). So similarly, there may be only a contingent, as-a-matter-of-fact connection between colour prejudice and cultural prejudice, true for only certain times and places; nevertheless when the two kinds of exclusionism and oppression come together, we have a distinctive phenomenon worthy of its own name and conceptualisation. In this conceptualising, far from obscuring racism we learn something about it. Namely, that contemporary British racism is not dependent upon any (even unstated) form of biological determinism. There must be some reference to differences in physical appearances and/or a legacy of the racism of earlier centuries, otherwise we would not be speaking of a racism but of an ethnicism. The reference however is not necessarily to a deep biology; a superficial biology is all that is required to pick out racial groups, to stereotype them and to treat them accordingly. Being able to pick individuals out on the basis of their physical appearance and assign them to a racial group may be essential to racism but physical appearance may stand only as a marker of a race not as the explanation of a group's behaviour. The racist will want to impute inferiority, undesirability, distinctive behavioural traits and so on to a group distinguished by the use of phenotypes; but the racist does not have to believe, and by and large in contemporary Britain it is not believed, that the behavioural qualities are produced by biology rather than by history, culture, upbringing, by certain norms or their absence. I suggest therefore that a notion of cultural-racism is essential to understanding and opposing racism in Britain (Modood,1994a).

III Multiculturalism

Minority ethnicity, albeit white ethnicity, has traditionally been regarded in Britain as acceptable if it was confined to the privacy of family and community, and did not make any political demands. Earlier groups of migrants and refugees, such as the Irish or the Jews in the nineteenth and the first half of the twentieth century, found that peace and prosperity came more easily the less public one made one's minority practices or identity. Perhaps for non-European origin groups, whose physical appearance gave them a visibility that made them permanently vulnerable to racial discrimination, the model of a privatised group identity was never viable. Yet, additionally, one has to acknowledge the existence of a climate of opinion quite different from that experienced by the earlier Irish or Jewish incomers.

In association with other socio-political movements such as feminism and gay rights which challenge the public-private distinction or demand a share of public space, ethnic difference is increasingly seen as something that needs not just toleration but also public acknowledgement, resources and representation (Commission for Racial Equality, 1990). Iris Young expresses well the new political climate when she describes the emergence of an ideal of equality based not just on allowing excluded groups to assimilate and live by the norms of dominant groups, but based on the view that 'a positive self-definition of group difference is in fact more liberatory' (Young, 1990, p. 157). An example she gives is of the black power movement which 'encouraged Blacks to break their alliance with whites and assert the specificity of their own culture, political organisation and goals' (ibid. p. 159). Another is of the 'gay pride assertion that sexual identity is a matter of culture and politics, and not merely "behaviour" to be tolerated or forbidden' (ibid. p. 161); and certainly one of the most important movements to contribute to this contemporary climate of opinion is 'gynocentric feminism' which, with its emphasis on the positivity and specificity of female experience and values has successfully contested the gender blindness of an earlier wave of feminism so that '[m]ost elements of the contemporary women's movement have been separatist to a degree' (ibid. p. 161).

These movements have not had the same impact in Britain as in parts of North America, but are certainly present here. In particular I think there is an ethnic assertiveness in Britain which has parallels with North America, and which has been less evident amongst recent migrants and their descendants in other European Union countries, where cultural assimilation is still regarded as integral to citizenship and political equality (Baldwin-Edwards and Schwain, 1994). This assertiveness, based on feelings of not being respected or of lacking access to public space, often consists of counterposing positive images against traditional or dominant stereotypes, of projecting identities in order to challenge existing power relations or to negotiate the sharing of physical, institutional and discursive space. At the very least one would have to say that a significant anti-racist challenge is taking place to the presumed stigma associated with not being white or conventionally British (Modood *et al.* 1994).

The movement is from an understanding of equality in terms of individualism and cultural assimilation to a politics of recognition, to equality as encompassing public ethnicity. Equality as not having to hide or apologise for one's origins, family or community but requiring others to show respect for them and adapt public attitudes and arrangements so that the heritage they represent is encouraged rather than contemptuously expected to wither away. This movement, including the tension between the older and newer versions of equality and attempts to achieve compromise or synthesis, has influenced British race relations and anti-racist debates. It has also influenced one of the newcomers to this debate, Muslim assertiveness. A study of some of Muslim activism shows close parallels with the main contemporary American and British racial equality perspectives (Modood, 1993b). Three broad approaches stand out: a colour-blind human rights and human dignity approach; an approach based on an extension of the concepts of racial discrimination and racial equality to include anti-Muslim racism; and, finally a Muslim syndicalism or Muslim-power approach. What is revealed is less obscurantist Islamic interventions into a modern secular discourse, but typical minority options in contemporary Anglo-American equality politics. Certainly, British Muslim community activism mirrors much more closely other related contemporary equality debates than it does any Muslim polity (past or present) or any particular sectarian differences (such as Shia or Sunni).

The multiculturalism that I see emerging in Britain or at least pushing its way into debates, is then, in some important ways similar to that being elaborated by some North American political theorists. It is developing a notion of public ethnicity, of redrawing our understanding of the private and the public. This is hardly a simple matter. Indeed, there is a body of theoretical opinion which argues that the public-private distinction is essential to multiculturalism. John Rex, for example, argues that the fundamental distinction between a pluralist society without equality and the multicultural ideal is that the latter restricts cultural diversity to a private sphere so that all enjoy equality of opportunity and uniform treatment in the public domain (Rex, 1985, 1986). He readily recognises that this is a far from watertight distinction; education, for example, is an area in which both the claims of the public (the teaching of a civic culture) and the private (the teaching of minority religious and linguistic heritages) have to co-exist, and Rex is open to the idea of state funding of schools which besides teaching a core curriculum are designed to meet the religious and cultural needs of minorities. He sees such state support for minorities as analogous to the many welfare and economic responsibilities assumed by the modern social democratic state. For him, therefore, the public-private distinction is not about a policy of laissez-faire in relation to culture, a state neutrality about conceptions of the good, but an insistence that while there may legitimately be a sphere of differential rights, it does not extend to law, politics, economics and welfare policy. Yet Rex believes that as a matter of historical fact, European societies have managed to extract a 'rational', 'abstract' morality and legal system out of the various 'folk' cultures, and that all citizens can share this without betraying their folk culture, for all folk cultures have been subordinated to this civic culture, which is the basis of the modern state and capitalist economy. 'Thus multi-culturalism in the modern world involves on the one hand the acceptance of a single culture and a single set of individual rights governing the public domain and a variety of folk cultures in the private domestic and communal domains' (Rex, 1985, p. 6). On this view the multicultural state might be supportive of some or all folk cultures, but it effectively limits their scope and makes itself immune to folk criticism.

An important implication of this way of seeing the public-private distinction is found in a discussion by Habermas. To the question of to what extent a recipient society can require assimilation from immigrants, he answers that immigrants cannot be required to conform to the dominant way of life, but a democratic constitutional state must

> preserve the identity of the political community, which nothing, including immigration, can be permitted to encroach upon, since that identity is founded on the constitutional principles anchored in the political culture and not on the basic ethical orientations of the cultural form of life predominant in that country. (Habermas, 1994, p. 139)

But surely there is not a valid distinction here : politics and law depend to some degree on shared ethical assumptions and inevitably reflect the norms and values of the society that they are part of. In this sense, no state stands outside culture, ethnicity or nationality, and changes in these will need to be reflected in the arrangements of the state. Indeed, Habermas goes on to recognise that, following immigration, 'as other forms of life become established the horizon within which citizens henceforth interpret their common constitutional principles may also expand' (ibid. pp. 139–140). But then, what is the point of his initial distinction? It cannot simply be to state that the status of law is different from customs and lifestyles, that immigrants must obey the law and (like everybody else) use constitutional means to change it and the political system, because that neither requires nor implies that the preservation of a recipient society's political identity is more essential than other collective identities, say, the recipient society's linguistic or religious identity.

David Miller shows a much better appreciation that a political system is likely to be inseparable from a wider national culture (Miller, 1995). In arguing for the existence and political importance of a British national identity he too believes that a public-private distinction is essential in order to avoid a narrow, exclusivist, authoritarian nationalism. A form of the latter involves elevating 'cultural Englishness'—such things as drinking tea and patronising fish and chip shops—into public principles and institutions. He rightly wants to locate a national identity elsewhere, but there is an ambiguity in where it is. On the one hand, '[t]o have a national identity is to take part in a continuing process of collective self-definition which is expressed in essentially public ways—in political institutions, in the policies of a government, and so forth' (ibid. pp. 161–162); on the other hand, it involves 'an essentially historical understanding' which recognises, for instance, the importance of a residual Protestantism in British political culture (ibid. p. 163). The two descriptions are not incompatible with each other but point respectively to a narrow and broad view of political culture.

It seems to me that to participate in political institutions presupposes a great deal of commonality; language or languages, for instance, including an understanding of the rhetorical and symbolic force of words, gestures and silences, the evocation of names and so on. Just as tea-drinking and cricket must not be allowed to define membership of the national community, so too perhaps we ought to be wary of over-politicising national identity, of as it were putting all the burden of our commonality on the commonalty. The open and complex character of a rich and varied nationality must not be essentialised into a few quaint customs; but nor can it be reduced to a political system. People have a sense of constituting a society or a nationality or, as it were, a federation of communities by living and working and knowing each other in numerous and complex ways, from using the same local shops to reading the same newspapers; admittedly, none of these has the same formal status of membership as the rights of citizenship, and the points of trust and shared interests usually exist within a political and legal framework. My point is that even if some conditions are necessary to a participation in a shared public culture, such as the rights of citizenship, a public culture or a national identity cannot be equated with the formally legal or institutional. A sense of society, of effective as opposed to nominal membership in a shared public culture, over and above private and communal affiliations, may be dependent on many different points of contact and of sharing different things with different people. It may be like the philosophically proverbial cord, the strength of which does not depend upon a single thread.

Public and private, national and ethnic, then may mark different spheres of activity, and different ways in which we relate to people, but they are not strict divisions. There are bound to be dialectical tensions, and, as Rex recognises, points of dependency; communities may look to the state to support their culture, for example through schools and other educational institutions, and the state may, for example, look to communities to inculcate virtues such as truth-telling, respect for property, service to others and so on without which a civic morality would have nothing to build on. If the public and private mutually shape each other in these ways, then however 'abstract' and 'rational' the principles of a public order may be, they will reflect the 'folk cultures' out of which the particular public order has grown, which provides its personnel and sustains it in all kinds of ways. There can then be no question of the public sphere being morally neutral; rather, it will appeal to points of privately shared values and a sense of belonging, as well as to the superstructure of conventions, laws and principles. Those whose ethnic or community identities, for reasons of conquest or genius, are most reflected in the national, those who are most comfortable in these complementary identities, will feel least the force of a public–private distinction; they may feel it more when they have to share the public domain with persons from other communities, persons who also wish the national to reflect something of their own community. The elaboration of a strict public–private spheres distinction at this point may act to buttress the privileged position of the historically 'integrated' folk cultures at the expense of the historically subordinated or the newly migrated folk. In this context the public–private division, far from underpinning multiculturalism will work to prevent its emergence.

If we recognise that the public order is not morally neutral, is not culture- or ethnic-blind, we can understand why oppressed, marginalised or immigrant groups (in Britain if not in North America, immigrants and former subjects of the Empire will be synonymous terms) may want to see the public order, in which they may for the first time be coming to have rights of participation, to 'recognise' them, to be user-friendly to the new folks. The logic of demanding that public institutions acknowledge the gender-bias of their ways of doing things, and allow for female insights and perspectives, becomes readily intelligible, as does the whole phenomenon of minorities seeking increased visibility, of contesting the boundaries of the public, of not simply asking to be left alone and civilly tolerated. To recognise what lies behind challenges to the public–private distinction is not however necessarily to know how to meet the various challenges in a principled way, what kind of institutional recognition or political representation is merited by the various claims. One normative ideal of a plural public is where 'each of the constituent groups affirms the presence of others' (Young, 1990, p.188). Committed people sometimes speak of 'celebrating' diversity. For Taylor the critical 'recognition' is for a polity to commit itself to ensuring the survival of cultures or nations within its boundaries, as he would like Canada to guarantee the cultural survival of the Québecois (Taylor, 1994, pp. 58–61).

While I too strongly feel that multiculturalism means something more than negative tolerance or 'benign neglect', a cultural laissez-faire, it seems certain that while we all have to learn to live with groups of people and their norms that we may in various ways disapprove of, many people will not want to affirm or celebrate or publicly fund other people's religions or their hedonism, and I do not know what argument there is which says that one ought to celebrate ways of life that one regards as wrong or irresponsible. Perhaps, as the challenge of the politics of recognition is at many different points of the public–private boundary, such as gender, race, religion, sexuality, the normative character of the challenge may vary, and so then ought the institutional response. But if so, we must seek principles to guide us here. For otherwise what we may have in practice is a kind of 'differential incorporation', a pragmatic-cum-prejudiced response based on how much power a minority is able to exert, how much hostility there is to it, the structure of existing institutions, and so on. Thus a political party might find the will to address the under-representation of women in public office but not of ethnic minorities. Or, as Amy Gutmann suggests, public institutions should actively recognise the particular cultural identities of those they represent, but should be neutral as regards religious identities (Gutmann, 1994, p. 12). Perhaps this is just realism, but Gutmann believes that there is a principled basis for treating cultural and religious identities differently. I can see that there is a principled argument in favour of state neutrality, and there is another principled argument in favour of public recognition. Gutmann applies the former to religious identity, the latter to other identities, but no criteria are offered which justify this differential application. The pragmatic approach may be the best that we have, but given the specific focus of my concerns, I worry about a politics of recognition that begins with a structural bias against disadvantaged religious minorities (Modood, 1994b).

Tragedy, Moral Conflict, and Liberalism

SUSAN MENDUS

The central question of this paper is how modern liberal political theory can understand and make sense of value pluralism and the conflicts upon which it is premissed. It is a commonplace that liberalism was born out of conflict, and has been partly characterised ever since as a series of attempts to accommodate it within the framework of the nation state (Lukes, 1989, p. 139). However, it is also true that liberals have proposed many different routes to the resolution, or containment, of conflict, and these different routes are manifestations of different understandings of conflict itself both within an individual life and between lives. Thus, some assert the irreducible heterogeneity of value: John Stuart Mill famously inveighs against the attempt to model all human life on a single pattern and tells us that 'human beings are not sheep, and even sheep are not indistinguishably alike. A man cannot get a coat or a pair of boots to fit him unless they are either made to his measure or he has a whole warehouseful to choose from; and is it easier to fit him with a life than with a coat?' (Mill, 1978, p. 133). On Mill's account, plurality is the natural (and indeed desirable) condition of humanity. We should neither hope for nor expect the elimination of conflict, and a world in which there is diversity is richer and better for it.

Others take pluralism to be allied to scepticism: there just are conflicting values, but since we have no justification for deeming any particular way of life 'the best', we must acknowledge conflict as an ineradicable part of the human condition. This latter view does not assert the superiority of a world containing plural values: it merely accepts that where there is a plurality of conflicting values, we will have no basis on which to deem one value preferable or superior to another.

These distinct understandings of the nature of conflict generate distinct responses to its resolution: for the sceptic, conflict is simply a fact, and (often) an unfortunate fact insofar as it generates social and political discord, whereas for the committed pluralist, conflict is, if not itself valuable, at least a necessary concomitant of the heterogeneity of value. The pluralist therefore sees conflict as something inevitable and not wholly regrettable. Probably the most famous modern exponent of this position is Sir Isaiah Berlin, In his seminal essay, 'Two Concepts of Liberty,' Berlin writes; 'If, as I believe, the ends of men are many, and not all of them in principle compatible with one another, then the possibility of conflict—and of tragedy—can never wholly be eliminated from human life, either personal or social' (Berlin, 1969, p. 169). Additionally, Berlin argues that the attempt to eliminate conflict is itself one of the most pernicious forces in politics. He inveighs against those who pretend that conflict resolution can be costless and insists that we cannot conceive of a situation in which all value conflict has been eliminated and there has been no loss of value on the way. Moreover, he implies that the elimination of conflict is problematic not only inter-personally but also intra-personally. This, I take it, is the force of his emphasis on the permanent possibility of tragedy at both the personal and the social level.

However, Berlin's emphasis on the dangers of loss inherent in conflict resolution appears to be denied by a rather different characterisation of pluralism—one provided by Steven Lukes. In the course of a discussion of the incommensurability of values Lukes writes: 'the very assumption of commensurability would subvert certain values which are what they are in part just because they deny it'. And he goes on to explain this by citing the examples of friendship and family relations, arguing that 'if I were prepared even to consider ... whether my parental duties can be traded for some greater overall benefit, or against, say, some promise I have made, that might only go to show that I am not a true friend or parent' (Lukes, 1989, pp. 138–139). On Lukes's account, therefore, pluralism need not generate conflict, for incommensurability implies a refusal to trade-off or weigh one value against another: faced with a choice between familial duty and keeping a promise, the agent ought not even to consider the weight carried by the promise, but should simply act as a good parent.

In order, therefore, for pluralism and incommensurability to generate conflict, something more is required, and this is to be found, I think, in Alasdair MacIntyre's analysis of the tragic. MacIntyre writes:

> The interest of Sophocles lies in his presentation of a view equally difficult for a Platonist or a Weberian to accept. There are indeed crucial conflicts, in which different virtues appear as making rival and incompatible claims upon us. But our own situation is tragic in that we have to recognise the authority of both claims. There is an objective moral order, but our perceptions of it are such that we cannot bring rival moral truths into complete

> harmony with each other, and yet the acknowledgement of the moral order, and of moral truth, makes the kind of question which a Weber or a Berlin urges upon us out of the question. For to choose does not exempt me from the authority of the claim I choose to go against. (MacIntyre, 1981, p. 134)

The Platonist cannot admit of tragedy because, for him, all value must ultimately be harmoniously reconcilable. Equally, however, emphasis on incommensurability is not sufficient for tragedy because incommensurability, at least in the form in which Lukes discusses it, denies the conflict which is essential to tragedy. Nor, on MacIntyre's account, can pluralism of the form advocated by Berlin fully acknowledge the authority of the value the agent decides against, and therefore it too denies tragic conflict. For tragic conflict, therefore, we require both pluralism and a denial of the possibility of harmonious reconciliation and an acknowledgement that the value which is decided against has authority: we require pluralism, plus conflict, plus loss.

In modern liberal political theory, the facts of pluralism, conflict and loss appear to be acknowledged to high degree. Indeed, and as has been noted already, modern liberalism begins from these facts and asks how such conflict may nevertheless be accommodated. My concern in this paper will be to suggest that, in answering this question, liberals have a tendency to deny the premise from which they began. They respond to pluralism, conflict and loss by constructing a political theory which denies their significance, and hence renders tragic conflict irrational or incomprehensible. More specifically, they aspire to 'tame' conflict, firstly by insisting that the private should be subordinated to the public in any conflict between the two, and secondly by attempting to substitute principles of justice for the operation of fate.

However, in so doing, modern liberalism creates the seeds of a new, and essentially modern, tragic situation.

Modern Liberalism and the Nature of the Tragic

I have noted that liberalism was born of the recognition of conflict and that its central aim is to demonstrate ways in which such conflict may be accommodated within the framework of the state. This 'fact' of plurality, and of the conflict attendant upon it, is the starting point of John Rawls's *Political Liberalism*, and in the introduction to that book Rawls declares that; 'a modern democratic society is characterised not simply by a pluralism of comprehensive religious, philosophical and moral doctrines, but by a pluralism of incompatible yet reasonable comprehensive doctrines. No one of these doctrines is affirmed by citizens generally. Nor should one expect that, in the forseeable future one of them, or some other reasonable doctrine, will ever be affirmed by all, or nearly all, citizens' (Rawls, 1993, p. xvi). Pluralism, then, is a fact—and not one which can be expected to go away. Since that is so, the task of liberal political theory is to show how the conflict attendant upon it may be channelled and accommodated.

The Separation of the Political

One very familiar way in which liberalism has attempted to cope with conflict is by insisting upon a separation between the public and the private spheres: within the private realm, individuals may pursue their own conceptions of the good, but in public life those conceptions must be subservient to an over-arching conception of the right, or of justice. This distinction between public and private has been extensively criticised, particularly by feminist commentators, who draw attention to the way in which it characteristically construes the private realm as the realm of the family and thus removes women, and women's concerns, from the sphere of justice. These problems are familiar and I shall not dwell on them here, though I shall refer back to them later in the paper. What I now wish to concentrate on is a slightly different aspect of the public–private distinction, which is the tendency, prevalent in more recent liberal political philosophy, not merely to distinguish between public and private, but also to privilege the former over the latter. In *Political Liberalism* Rawls asserts that under reasonably favourable conditions that make democracy possible, 'political values normally outweigh whatever non-political values conflict with them' (Rawls, 1993, p. 139). The claim is made yet more starkly by Brian Barry in his recent book, *Justice as Impartiality*. Commenting on the Irangate controversy, and the question of whether Oliver North's secretary should have shredded the secret documents, Barry says; 'the answer is obvious: principles of justice win … to regard loyalty to one's boss as a genuine moral counterweight is simply to show a frightening lack of common sense' (Barry, 1995, p. 251). And he seems prepared to generalise this conclusion, arguing that considerations of loyalty, love, and commitment to others enter into the picture only when considerations of justice do not yield a determinate answer. When, however, they do yield a determinate answer 'Justice wins'.

It is interesting to note that although the claims made by Rawls and Barry for the priority of justice over loyalty contradict Lukes's claim, mentioned earlier, they nevertheless result in a similar problem for those who aspire to accommodate both pluralism and conflict. Like Lukes, they do not explain the conflict which is consequent upon pluralism, rather they remove it by establishing a hierarchy of values. Thus, where Lukes insists that a willingness to consider the relative weight of familial loyalty may bespeak a misunderstanding of it as a value, Barry insists that a willingness to consider the importance of loyalty bespeaks a 'frightening lack of common sense'. For Lukes, loyalty must win, else we do not understand what loyalty is; for Barry, justice must win else we show a lack of common sense. But the result is the same in both cases: what begins as an acknowledgment of plurality ends, quite rapidly, in a denial that plurality generates real conflict.

It is, then, the insistence on a distinction between public and private values, coupled with a priority ordering, which enables modern liberalism to cope with pluralism and the conflict of value attendant upon it. But this strategy threatens the very premise on which liberalism itself is initially based: namely that there are values which are irreducibly conflictual and that the conflicts cannot be resolved without loss. To return to the point made by MacIntyre, and quoted earlier, modern liberalism begins by asserting the 'fact' of plurality, and attempting to show how the conflict consequent upon it may be accommodated, but it soon ends by denying conflict altogether, since its insistence on a priority ordering is a covert way of refusing to acknowledge the authority of the claim we choose to go against. Thus, Lukes's argument results in a denial of justice when it is pitted against personal or familial loyalty; and Barry's argument results in a denial of loyalty when it is pitted against justice. Either way, though, the resolution of conflict is purchased at a price—and the price is a genuine recognition of the facts of conflict which motivated liberalism in the first place.

Perhaps none of this would matter were the realm of justice and the realm of personal morality uncontroversially distinct. But notoriously they are not. In a footnote in *Political Liberalism* Rawls discusses the appropriate political response to the problem of abortion. He writes:

> suppose we consider the question in terms of these three political values: the due respect for human life, the ordered reproduction of political society over time, including the family in some form, and finally the equality of women as equal citizens ... I

> believe that any reasonable balance of these three views will give a woman a duly qualified right to end her pregnancy during the first trimester ... any comprehensive doctrine that leads to a balance of political values excluding that duly qualified right [the right to termination] in the first trimester ... is unreasonable. (Rawls, 1993, p. 243, fn.32).

This passage is notable both for its (much discussed) insistence that a denial of the right to abortion would be 'unreasonable', and for its (less discussed) assumption that the question falls uncontroversially within the scope of a theory of justice and therefore (presumably) constitutes an example of a case in which private views must be subsumed beneath the requirements of Rawlsian justice. But as Simon Caney has pointed out, it is not clear why Rawls believes that there will be no 'fact of reasonable pluralism' about justice and the right (Caney, 1995, p. 256). Roman Catholics, who see abortion as simply murder, will be disinclined to interpret their belief either as one which must be dismissed as unreasonable, or as one which should be 'privatised' within a Rawlsian conception of political value. What is much more plausible is that the Roman Catholic insistence that abortion should be made illegal is evidence of a different conception of justice. In short, it is evidence of the fact of pluralism about the right.

Caney's point occurs in the context of a discussion of Rawls's requirement of reasonableness, and he suggests that, in at least some places, Rawls adopts the following understanding of reasonableness: 'reasonable persons think that political decisions may not be based upon claims about which intelligent persons disagree'. However, if this is a correct interpretation, Caney notes, the requirement of reasonableness is far too strong: if consistently applied, it would preclude the state taking any position on abortion, since this is precisely a subject about which intelligent people disagree vigorously. Yet Rawls insists that the state may legitimately take a position on abortion. Additionally, his commitment to the difference principle rests upon a controversial assumption—namely that the distribution of talents is 'arbitrary from a moral point of view'. However, this assumption, too, is one on which intelligent people can (and do) disagree. Therefore, Caney concludes, if Rawls really means to adopt the strong interpretation of reasonableness, he will find himself precluded from implementing some of the central tenets of his own theory of justice.

Caney is concerned to draw attention to the difficulties inherent in interpreting Rawls's requirement of reasonableness, but his reference to the difference principle may alert us to further problems consequent on Rawls's account. The difference principle flows from the contention that the distribution of talents is arbitrary from a moral point of view. But this claim can be sustained only by insisting upon a particular understanding of the distinction between justice and fate: one which is not wholly implausible, but which is controversial and which, again, has consequences for the understanding of pluralism, conflict and loss inherent in modern liberalism. It is to this I now turn.

Justice and Fate

I begin my discussion here, not with a piece of philosophy, but with a quotation from the playwright Arthur Miller:

> There are a thousand things to say about that time [the Depression] but maybe one will be evocative enough. Until 1929 I thought things were pretty solid. Specifically, I thought—like most Americans—that somebody was in charge. I didn't know who it was, but it was probably a businessman, and he was a realist, a no-nonsense fellow, practical, honest, responsible. In 1929 he jumped out of the window. It was bewildering. His banks closed and refused to open again, and I had twelve dollars in one of them. More precisely, I happened to have withdrawn my twelve dollars to buy a racing bike from a friend of mine who was bored with it, and the next day the Bank of the United States closed. I rode by and saw the crowds of people standing at the brass gates. Their money was inside! And they couldn't get it. And they would never get it. As for me, I felt I had the thing licked.
>
> But about a week later I went into the house to get a glass of milk and when I came out my bike was gone. Stolen. It must have taught me a lesson. Nobody could escape that disaster. (Miller, 1994, pp. 176–177.

The final line, 'nobody could escape that disaster', introduces a pervasive theme in Miller's writing, which is that what, from one perspective, is most naturally represented as a disaster can, from another perspective, be seen only as the deliverance of justice. For Miller, the distinction between justice and fate is, in part at least, agent–relative, and many of his plays take this fact as central. Thus, discussing *Death of a Salesman* he writes:

> To me, the tragedy of Willie Loman is that he gave his life, or sold it, in order to justify the waste of it. It is the tragedy of a

> man who did believe that he alone was not meeting the qualifications laid down for mankind by those clean-shaven frontiersmen who inhabit the peaks of broadcasting and advertising offices. From those forests of canned goods high up in the sky, he heard the thundering command to succeed as it ricocheted down the newspaper-lined canyons of the city, heard not a human voice, but a wind of a voice to which no human being can reply in kind except to stare into the mirror at a failure. (Miller, 1994, p. 15)

We may see Willie Loman as a victim, seduced by the illusions of a corrupt society, but he himself cannot see things that way: he is consumed by the American Dream which dictates that merit is always rewarded by success and that therefore his own failure is a just consequence of his own inadequacies.

The point can and has been generalised: it is an implicit premise of much modern liberalism that a clear line can be drawn between what counts as an injustice and what counts as a misfortune. Rawls explicitly expresses the expectation that in a just society 'our loves will expose us mainly to the accidents of nature and the contingency of circumstances' (Rawls, 1972, p. 574). But what we are disposed to attribute to the accidents of nature or contingency of circumstances depends partly on the role we ourselves occupy and partly on the scheme of justice within which we situate ourselves. Thus, many are inclined to construe famine, poverty and unemployment as accidents of nature but, as Judith Shklar has pointed out, the people most likely to do so are those who fear that they may be potentially or actually blameworthy: 'for them, it is a self-protecting move, with a view to similar future events' (Shklar, 1990, p. 57). Here, the tendency to declare in favour of fortune rather than injustice is a product of one's own place in the wider scheme of things. But it may also be a product of a particular political ideology.

To take a central case in modern political theory, Hayek's 'invisible hand' interpretation of the market results in a clear distinction between fate and justice, but the line between the two is drawn in the place dictated by his understanding of the market as something akin to a force of nature: 'his market is neither fair nor unfair; it knows only winners and losers. It has no will, no purposes, no personality. We cannot hold it responsible for anything at all. Because the market is an impersonal force of nature, those who are injured by it cannot claim that they have suffered an injustice, although many of their normal expectations may have been shattered' (Shklar, 1990, p. 80).

Both sorts of difficulty are exhibited by Miller's Willie Loman: Willie's moral assessment of his situation is partly a function of his own position in the larger scheme of things and partly a function of his acceptance of a particular political ideology. Thus, the tragic power of the play depends on our ability, as audience, to see what Willie himself cannot see—namely that he has been harshly dealt with. Additionally (and this, I take it, is a central point for Miller) the very fact that we see him as one who has been harshly dealt with, casts doubt upon our willingness to concede that the distinction between justice and fate is clear and uncontroversial: on the contrary, the playwright suggests that the line between the two is value-laden. It is a consequence of specific political commitments, not something which hangs free of them.

All this, of course, arises in the context of a specific tragic play. However, the same point is emphasised in a philosophical context by Bernard Williams, who argues that the ancient Greek understanding of slavery was not, or not most significantly, that it constituted a necessary identity, but that it was a piece of individual bad luck. For the Greeks, he says, being a woman was a necessary identity, but being a slave was a misfortune, even a disaster. Indeed, it was the paradigm case of misfortune, the kind of thing which could befall anyone and which was characterised precisely by its violence and arbitrariness. Williams takes the difference between our understanding of slavery (as a fundamentally unjust institution) and the Greek understanding of slavery (as both socially necessary and personally disastrous) to be indicative of a more general difference in attitude towards the world and our place in it. The Greeks, he claims, did not suppose that because something was necessary it was therefore just, and in this respect their approach to the moral world was more wholesome—less corrupt—than that of much modern liberal political philosophy, which does assume that what is necessary is just, or at least not unjust:

> We, now, have no difficulty in seeing slavery as unjust: we have economic arrangements and a conception of a society of citizens with which slavery is straightforwardly incompatible. This may stir a reflex of self-congratulation, or at least of satisfaction that in some dimensions there is progress. But the main feature of the Greek attitude to slavery was not a morally primitive belief in its justice, but the fact that considerations of justice and injustice were immobilised by the demands of what was seen as social and economic necessity. That phenomenon has not so much been eliminated from modern life as shifted to different places. (Williams, 1993, p. 125)

The point is reinforced by Shklar, who singles Hayek out as someone who, unusually, does not blame the poor for their poverty, 'nor does he claim that their situation is not only necessary but also just. It is', she says, 'much to his credit that he does not yield to the urge to blame the victim' (Shklar, 1990, pp. 79–80). On the contrary, and for Hayek, the operation of the free market is like a force of nature: its results are unintended and need carry no implication of praise or blame. But the desire to rid the world of such random forces and to deny that we are, any longer, under the thrall of circumstances which are outside our control, is pervasive in much modern liberal political theory. It is also, in large part, commendable, for it militates against a tendency to attribute to fate what is in fact the remediable consequence of political policy.

Nevertheless, there are dangers inherent in supposing that the effects of fate can be completely eliminated or, more particularly, that moving the line between justice and necessity is tantamount to removing it. Just as the ancient Greeks had no idea how to continue their own way of life without perpetuating the institution of slavery, so we now may have no idea how to continue our way of life without permitting continued poverty in the Third World. But it does not follow, and it is not true, that our inability to reconcile these two renders Third World poverty just, any more than the ancient Greeks' inability rendered slavery a just institution. This is the deep point behind Williams's discussion: like the ancients, we find our sense of justice and injustice 'immobilised' by some problems, but unlike them we are inclined not simply to concede our impotence, but to conclude that what has no political remedy cannot be unjust. And this, in the end, is the source of Willie Loman's tragedy—he cannot admit that his own situation is anything other than the deliverance of justice. In this respect, therefore, modern liberalism not only attempts to substitute justice for fate but, in so doing, gives rise to a new, and distinctively liberal, form of tragedy. For now tragedy arises not from the operation of a cruel and arbitrary fate; it arises from the belief that we can escape fate by extending the power and scope of justice.

In *The Death of Tragedy* George Steiner remarks that 'tragedy is that form of art which requires the intolerable burden of God's presence. It is now dead because His shadow no longer falls on us as it fell on Agamemnon or Macbeth or Athalie' (Steiner, 1961, p. 353). More generally, we might say that tragedy is impossible in the modern world because we no longer recognise something beyond ourselves: something authoritative and compelling which nevertheless cannot be brought into harmony with our own understanding of the moral order. As we have seen, modern liberalism aspires to 'tame' plurality by the twin strategies of prioritising the political and rendering us immune to all but the accidents of nature and the contingency of circumstance. What I have suggested, however, is that these strategies are simultaneously untrue and distorting. The distinction between the political and the private is fundamentally unstable, and even if it were not there is no compelling argument for giving the political priority over the private. On the contrary, the cost of giving priority to the political is that we are forced to neglect rather than accommodate the facts of plurality, conflict and loss.

The second strategy for accommodating conflict also depends upon an unstable distinction: this time, the distinction between justice and fate. I have suggested that what we see as the deliverance of fate is not value-free, but must depend in some part on the wider system of value within which we operate and to which we subscribe. Much liberalism, however, depends upon there being a clear and stable distinction between what is attributable to fate and what is within the domain of justice. It aspires, moreover, to reduce the domain of fate and substitute justice for it. But in this lie the seeds of a new form of tragedy. Arthur Miller tells us that modern tragedy 'is the consequence of a man's total compulsion to be evaluated justly'. In the context of my argument, I take this to mean two things: tragedy is a consequence of our belief that the world can be rendered fundamentally just, and it is a consequence of our further belief that justice has priority over all other values—that in any conflict between values 'justice wins'. But the tragedy of Willie Loman is precisely that he has learned these lessons too well: believing that the race genuinely is to the swift and the battle to the strong, he cannot explain his own failure to himself and therefore he must 'sell his life in order to justify the waste of it'. He is, for these reasons, the tragic (and the ironic) hero of modern liberal political philosophy.

References

Airey, C. and Brook, L. 1986. 'Interim Report: Social and Moral Issues', in Roger Jowell, *et al.* (eds.), *British Social Attitudes*, SCPR. Aldershot: Gower.

Anderson, B. 1983. *Imagined Communities: Reflections on the Origin and Spread of Nationalism.* London: Verso.

Anscome, G. E. M. 1958. *Intention.* Oxford: Blackwell.

Anscome, G. E. M. 1968. 'The Intentionality of Sensation: A Grammatical Feature', in R. J. Butler (ed.). *Analytic Philosophy.* Oxford: Blackwell.

Anscombe, G. E. Balibar and Wallerstein I. *Race, Nation, Class: ambiguous identities* London: Verso.

Anthias, F. and Yuval-Davis, N. 1992. *Racialised Boundaries: race, nation, gender, colour and class and the anti-racist struggle.* London: Routledge.

Aquila, Richard. 1977. *Intentionality. A Study of Mental Acts.* University Park & London: The Pennsylvania State University Press.

Aquinas, Thomas. 1952. *The Summa Theologica of Saint Thomas Aquinas.* 2 volumes, trans. Fathers of the English Dominican Province. Chicago: Encylcopaedia Britannica.

Aquinas, Thomas. 1955. *On the Truth of the Catholic Faith: summa Contra Gentiles,* 4 volumes, trans. Anton C. Pegis. New York: Image Books.

Arberry, A. J. 1957. *Revelation and Reason in Islam.* London: Allen & Unwin.

Aristotle 1984. *The Complete Works of Aristotle,* the revised Oxford translation, (ed.) Jonathan Barnes, 2 volumes. Princeton: Princeton University Press.

Arrington, R. 1983. 'A Defence of Ethical Relativism', *Metaphilosophy* **14**, 225–239.

Arrington, R. 1989. *Rationalism, Realism and Relativism.* Ithaca: Cornell University Press.

Augustine. 1957. *The City of God*, 2 volumes. London: J. M. Dent and Sons.

Augustine. 1961. *Confessions.* Harmondsworth: Penguin.

Austin, J. L. 1962. *Sense and Sensibilia.* Oxford: Oxford University Press.

Back, L. 1993. 'Race, Identity and Nation Within an Adolescent Community in South London', *New Community* **19**, 217–233.

Baldwin-Edwards, M. and Schwain, M. A. (eds.) 1994. 'The Politics of Immigration in Western Europe', Special Issue, *Western European Politics* 17.

Balibar, E. 1991. 'Is There a Neo-Racism?' in Airey, C. and Brook, L. 1986. 'Interim Report: Social and Moral Issues', in Roger Jowell, *et al.* (eds.) *British Social Attitudes.* SCPR. Aldershot: Gower.

Ballard, R. and Kalra, V. S. 1994. *The Ethnic Dimensions of the 1991*

References

Census: A Preliminary Report, Manchester Census Group. Manchester: University of Manchester.

Barry, B. 1989. *Liberty and Justice: Essays in Political Theory*, 2. Oxford: Clarendon Press.

Barry, B. 1995. *Justice as Impartiality*. Oxford: Oxford University Press.

Bauberot, J. 1990. *Vers un nouveau pacte laÏque*. Paris: Le Seuil.

Beitz, C. R. 1979. *Political Theory and International Relations*. New Jersey: Princeton University Press.

Bell, David. 1990. *Husserl*. London: Routledge.

Benhabib, S. 1992. *Situating the Self*. Cambridge: Polity Press.

Berlin,I. 1969. *Four Essays on Liberty*. Oxford: Oxford University Press.

Berlin, I. 1991. *The Crooked Timber of Humanity: chapters in the history of ideas*, ed. Henry Hardy. London: Fontana Press.

Boulton, M. J. and Smith, P. 1992. 'Ethnic Preferences and Perceptions Among Asian and White British Middle School Children', *Social Development* **1**, 55–66.

Braithwaite, R. B. 1971. 'An Empiricist's View of the Nature of Religious Belief', in B. Mitchell (ed.), *The Philosophy of Religion*. London: Oxford University Press.

Brennan, Bernard P. 1968. *William James*. New York: Twayne.

Brentano, Franz. 1966. *The True and the Evident*, ed. O. Kraus, trans. R. Chisholm. London: Routledge and Kegan Paul.

Brentano, Franz. 1973. *Psychology from an Empirical Standpoint*, trans. Antos C. Rancurello, D. B. Terrell and Linda McAlister. London: Routledge and Kegan Paul.

Brown, J. M. 1981–2. 'Right and Virtue', *Proceedings of the Aristotelian Society* **82**, 143–158.

Brown, P. 1967. *Augustine of Hippo: a biography* London: Faber and Faber.

Caney, S. 1995. 'Anti-Perfectionism and Rawslian Liberalism', *Political Studies* **43**, 248–264.

Cheng, Y. 1994. *Education and Class: Chinese in Britain and the US*. Aldershot: Avebury.

Cherniss, H. 1962. *The Riddle of the Early Academy*. New York: Russell & Russell.

Chisholm, Roderick. 1956. 'Sentences about Believing', *Proceedings of the Aristotelian Society* **LVI**, 128–148.

Chisholm, Roderick. 1957. *Perceiving: A Philosophical Study*. Ithaca, NY: Cornell U.P.

Chisholm, Roderick. 1958. 'Intentionality and the Mental', *Minnesota Studies in the Philosophy of Science* **2**.

Churchland, Paul. 1981. 'Eliminative Materialism', *Journal of Philosophy*, **78**, 67–90.

Churchland, Paul. 1984. *Matter and Consciousness: A Contemporary Introduction to the Philosophy of Mind*. Cambridge, Mass.: MIT Press.

Clark, M. T. (ed.). 1974. *An Aquinas Reader*. London: Hodder and Stoughton.

Clark, R. T. 1955. *Herder: His Life and Thought*. Berkeley: University of California Press.

Cohen, G. A. 1986. 'Self-Ownership, World Ownership, and Equality: Part II', *Social Philosophy and Policy* **3**, 77–96.

Cohen, Joshua. 1993. 'Moral Pluralism and Political Consensus', in D. Copp, J. Hampton and J. Roemer (eds.), *The Idea of Democracy*. Cambridge: Cambridge University Press.

Cohen, P. 1988. 'The Perversions of Inheritance: studies in the making of multi-racist Britain', in P. Cohen and H. S. Bains (eds.), *Multi-Racist Britain*. London: Macmillan.

Commission for Racial Equality. 1990. *Britain a Plural Society*. London: CRE.

Condorcet, A. de. 1889. *Projet sur l'organisation générale de l'instruction publique* (1792), in J. Guillaume (ed.), *Procès verbaux du Comité d'Instruction publique de l'Assemblée législative*. Paris: Imprimerie nationale.

Cupitt, D. 1984. *The Sea of Faith*. London: British Broadcasting Company.

D'Costa, G. 1986. *Theology and Religious Pluralism: The Challenge of Other Religions*. Oxford: Blackwell,.

Deane, H. 1963. *The Political and Social Ideas of St. Augustine*. New York: Columbia University Press.

Dennett, Daniel C. 1969. *Content and Consciousness*. London: Routledge.

Dennett, Daniel C. 1987. *The Intentional Stance*. Cambridge, Mass: MIT Press.

Dretske, Fred. 1981. *Knowledge and the Flow of Information*. Cambridge, Mass: MIT.

Dreyfus, Hubert L. and Harrison Hall, (eds.), 1982. *Husserl, Intentionality and Cognitive Science*. Cambridge, Mass: MIT Press.

Dreyfus, Hubert L. 1995. 'Heidegger's Critique of the Husserl/Searle Account of Intentionality'. Paper delivered to the Royal Irish Academy Conference on Heidegger, Dublin.

Dummett, Michael. 1990. 'Thought and Perception: the Views of Two Philosophical Innovators', in D. Bell and N. Cooper (eds.), *The Analytic Tradition*. Oxford: Blackwell.

Dummett, Michael. 1993. *Origins of Analytic Philosophy*. London: Duckworth.

Ehrenberg, V. 1968. *From Solon to Socrates*. London: Methuen.

Elster, J. (ed.) 1986. *Rational Choice*. Oxford: Blackwell.

Emerson, R. W. 1940. *The Selected Writings of Ralph Waldo Emerson*. New York: Modern Library.

Evans, J. D. G. 1977. *Aristotle's Concept of Dialectic*. Cambridge: Cambridge University Press.

Evans, J. D. G. 1987. *Aristotle*. Brighton: Harvester Press.

Evans, J. D. G. 1994. 'Souls, Attunements and Variation in Degree: *Phaedo* 93–4', *International Philosophical Quarterly* **34**, 277–287.

Fodor, Jerry A. 1981. *Representations. Philosophical Essays on the Foundations of Cognitive Science*. Brighton. Harvester.

Føllesdal, Dagfinn. 1969. 'Husserl's Notion of Noema', *Journal of Philosophy* **66**, 680–687.

Føllesdal, Dagfinn. 1990. 'Noema and Meaning in Husserl', *Philosophy and Phenomenological Research,* Supp. **50**, 260–271.

Føllesdal, Dagfinn. 1993. 'La notion d'intentionalité chez Husserl', *Dialectica* **47**, Nos 2–3, 173–187.

Føllesdal, Dagfinn. 1994. 'Objects and Concepts', *Proceedings of the Aristotelian Society,* Supplementary Volume LXVIII.

Foot, P. 1982. 'Moral Relativism', in J. W. Meiland and M. Krausz (eds.), *Relativism, Cognitive and Moral.* Notre Dame: University of Notre Dame Press.

Furth, M. 1988. *Substance, Form and Psyche.* Cambridge: Cambridge University Press.

Galston, W. 1989. 'Pluralism and Social Unity', *Ethics* **99**, 711–726.

Gewirth, A. 1994. 'Is Cultural Pluralism Relevant to Moral Knowledge?', *Social Philosophy and Policy* **11**, 22–43.

Gilson, E. 1961. *The Christian Philosophy of Saint Augustine.* London: Gollancz.

Graham, K. 1986a. *The Battle of Democracy.* Sussex: Wheatsheaf.

Graham, K. 1986b. 'Morality and abstract individualism', *Proceedings of the Aristotelian Society* **87**, 21–33.

Graham, K. 1987. 'Morality, Individuals and Collectives' in J. D. G. Evans (ed.), *Moral Philosophy and Contemporary Problems.* Cambridge: Cambridge University Press.

Graham, K. 1989. 'Class—a simple view', *Inquiry* **32**, 419–436.

Graham, K. 1992. *Karl Marx, Our Contemporary.* Hemel Hempstead: Harvester.

Graham, K. 1994. 'The End of History of the Beginning of Marx?', in C. Bertram and A. Chitty (eds.), *Has History Ended?* Aldershot: Avebury.

Gray, J. 1993. *Post-Liberalism, Studies in Political Thought.* London: Routledge.

Gray, J. 1995. *Isaiah Berlin.* London: Harper Collins.

Guthrie, W. K. C. 1969. *A History of Greek Philosophy,* Vol. 3. Cambridge: Cambridge University Press.

Gutmann, A. (ed.) 1994. *Multiculturalism: Examining The Politics of Recognition.* Princeton: Princeton University Press.

Gutmann A. 1994. 'Introduction' to Gutmann (ed.), 1994.

Habermas, J. 1994. 'Struggles for Recognition in the Democratic Constitutional State', in A. Gutmann (ed.) 1994.

Hampshire, S. 1989. *Innocence and Experience.* Cambridge, Mass.: Harvard University Press.

Hare, R. M. 1952. *The Language of Morals.* Oxford: Clarendon Press.

Hare, R. M. 1963. *Freedom and Reason.* Oxford: Clarendon Press.

Hare, R. M. 1981. *Moral Thinking.* Oxford: Clarendon Press.

Harman, G. 1975. 'Moral Relativism Defended', *Philosophical Review* **84**, 3–22.

Harman, G. 1977. *The Nature of Morality.* Oxford: Oxford University Press.

Harman, G. 1978a. 'Relativistic Ethics: Morality as Politics', *Midwest Studies in Philosophy* **3**, 109–121.
Harman, G. 1978b. 'What is Moral Relativism?' in A. Goldmann and J. Kim (eds.), *Values and Morals: essays in honor of William Frankena, Charles Stevenson, and Richard Brandt*. Dordrecht: D. Reidel.
Harrison, J. 1982. 'Mackie's Moral Scepticisim', *Philosophy* **57**, 173–191.
Haugeland, John. 1990. 'The Intentionality All Stars,' in J. Tomberlin (ed.) *Philosophical Perspectives* 4: *Action Theory and the Philosophy of Mind*. Atascadero, California: Ridgeview.
Hegel, G. W. F. 1952. *Hegel's Philosophy of Right*, trans. T. M. Knox. Oxford: Clarendon Press.
Heidegger, Martin. 1982. *The Basic Problems of Phenomenology*, trans. A. Hofstadter. Bloomington: Indiana U.P.
Heidegger, Martin. 1985. *History of the Concept of Time: Prolegomena*, trans. T. Kisiel. Bloomington: Indiana U.P.
Hick, J. 1985. *Problems of Religious Pluralism*. London: Macmillan.
Hick, J. and Hebblethwaite, B. (eds.) 1980. *Christianity and Other Religions: Selected Readings*. London: Fount paperbacks.
Horton, J. (ed.) 1993. *Liberalism, Multiculturalism and Toleration*. London: Macmillan.
Husserl, Edmund. 1967. *Cartesian Meditations*, trans. D. Cairns. The Hague: Nijhoff.
Husserl, Edmund. 1970. *Logical Investigations*, trans. J. N. Findlay. New York: Humanities Press. 2 Vols.
Husserl, Edmund. 1983. *Ideas pertaining to a Pure Phenomenology and to a Phenomenological Philosophy,* First Book, trans. F. Kersten. Dordrecht: Kluwer. .
Husserl, Edmund. 1989. *Ideas pertaining to a Pure Phenomenology and to a Phenomenological Philosophy*, Second Book, trans. R. Rojcewicz and A. Schuwer. Dordrecht: Kluwer.
Ingram, A. 1994. *A Political Theory of Rights*. Oxford: Clarendon Press.
James, W. 1897. *The Will to Believe*. New York: Longmans.
James, W. 1917a. *Talks to Teachers on Psychology and to Students on Some of Life's Ideals* , eighteenth edition. Boston: Longmans.
James, W. 1917b. *Selected Papers on Philosophy*. London: J. M. Dent.
James, W. 1920. *The Letters of William James*, ed. Henry James. Boston: Atlantic Monthly Press.
Jones, T. 1993. *Britain's Ethnic Minorities*. London: Policy Studies Institute.
Kant, I. 1948. *The Moral Law or Kant's Groundwork of the Metaphysic of Morals,* trans. H. J. Paton. London: Hutchinson.
Kant, I. 1959. *Kant's Critique of Practical Reason*, trans. T. K. Abbott. London: Longmans.
Kant, I. 1978. *The Critique of Judgement*, trans. James Creed Meredith. Oxford: Clarendon Press.
Kant, I. 1991. *Kant: Political Writings*, ed. Hans Reiss, Second enlarged edition. Cambridge: Cambridge University Press.

Kekes, J. 1993. *The Morality of Pluralism*. Princeton, NJ: Princeton University Press.

Kekes, J. 1994. 'Pluralism and the Value of Life', *Social Philosophy and Policy* **11**, 44–60.

Kirwan, C. A. 1965. 'Glaucon's Challenge', *Phronesis* **10**, 162–173.

Kriegel, B. 1985. 'Fonder la citoyenneté', in Storti and Tarnero (eds.), *L'identité française*. Paris: Editions Tierce.

Küng, H. 1986. *Christinaity and World Religions: Paths of Dialogue with Islam, Hinduism and Buddhism*. New York: Doubleday.

Kymlicka, W. 1989. *Liberalism, Community and Culture*. Oxford: Clarendon Press.

Kymlicka, W. 1990. *Contemporary Political Philosophy*. Oxford: Clarendon Press.

Kymlicka, W. 1992. 'Two models of pluralism and tolerance', *Analyse & Kritik* **14**, 33–56.

Kymlicka, W. 1993. 'Reply to Modood', *Analyse & Kritik* **15**, 92–96.

Kymlicka, W. 1995. *Multicultural Citizenship*. Oxford: Oxford University Press.

Larmore, C. 1990. 'Political Liberalism', *Political Theory* **18**, 339–360.

Larmore, C. 1994. 'Pluralism and Reasonable Disagreement', *Social Philosophy and Policy* **11**, 61–79.

Lukes, S. 1989. 'Making Sense of Moral Conflict', in N. Rosenblum (ed.), *Liberalism and the Moral Life*. Cambridge, Mass.: Harvard University Press.

Lycan, William. 1969. 'On Intentionality and the Psychological', *American Philosophical Quarterly*, **6**, 305–311.

Macedo, S. 1993. 'Toleration and Fundamentalism', in R. E. Goodin and P. Pettit (eds.), *A Companion to Contemporary Political Philosophy*. Oxford: Blackwell.

MacIntyre, A. 1981. *After Virtue: a Study in Moral Theory*. London: Duckworth.

MacIntyre, A. 1988. *Whose Justice? Which Rationality?* London: Duckworth.

Mackie, J. L. 1977. *Ethics: Inventing Right and Wrong*. Harmondsworth: Penguin Books.

McManus, I. C. *et al.* 1995. 'Medical School Applicants from Ethnic Minority Groups: identifying if and when they are disadvantaged', *British Medical Journal* **310**, 496–500.

Margolis, J. 1988. 'In Defence of Relativism', *Social Epistemology* **2**, 201–225.

Marx, K. 1976. *Capital,* vol. 1, trans. B. Fowkes. Harmondsworth: Penguin.

Marx, K. 1979. *Collected Works*. London: Lawrence and Wishart.

Meiland, J. 1977. 'Concepts of Relative Truth', *The Monist* **60**, 568–582.

Miles, R. 1989. *Racism*. London: Routledge.

Mill, J. S. 1969. *Essays on Ethics, Religion and Society* in *Collected Works*, vol. X. London and Toronto: Routledge and University of Toronto Press.

Mill, J. S. and Comte, A. 1899. *Lettres inédites de J. S. Mill avec Auguste Comte*, 1841–1847, ed. Lévy-Bruhl. Paris: Alcan.

Mill, J. S. 1978. *On Liberty*. Harmondsworth: Penguin.

Miller, A. 1994. *The Theatre Essays of Arthur Miller*. London: Methuen.

Miller, D. 1995. 'Reflections on British national identity', *New Community* **21**, 153–166.

Millikan, Ruth G. 1984. *Language, Thought and Other Biological Categories: New Foundations for Realism*. Cambridge, Mass: MIT.

Modood, T. 1992. *Not Easy Being British: Colour, Culture and Citizenship*. London: Runnymede Trust and Trentham Books.

Modood, T.. 1993a. 'Kymlicka on British Muslims', and 'Kymlicka on British Muslims: a rejoinder', *Analyse & Kritik* **15**, 87–91 and 97–99.

Modood, T. 1993b. 'Muslim views on religious identity and racial equality', *New Community* 19, 513–519.

Modood, T. 1994a. 'Political Blackness and British Asians', *Sociology* **28**, 859–876.

Modood, T. 1994b. 'Establishment, Multiculturalism and British Citizenship', *Political Quarterly* **65**, 53–73.

Modood, T. and Shiner, M. 1994. *Ethnic Minorities and Higher Education: Why Are There Differential rates of Entry*. London: Policy Studies Institute.

Modood, T., Beishon, S. and Virdee, S. 1994. *Changing Ethnic Identities*. London: Policy Studies Institute.

Modood, T. *et al.* 1996. *The Fourth National Survey of Ethnic Minorities*. London: Policy Studies Institute.

Mohanty, J. N. 1964. *Edmund Husserl's Theory of Meaning*. The Hague: Nijhoff, 1964.

Mohanty, J. N. 1972.*The Concept of Intentionality*. St. Louis, Missouri: Warren H. Green.

Mohanty, J. N. 1981. 'Intentionality and Noema',*Journal of Philosophy* **78**, 706–717.

Mohanty, J. N. 1982. *Husserl and Frege*. Bloomington: Indiana U.P. .

Moore, G. E. 1903. *Principia Ethica*. Cambridge: Cambridge University Press.

Muglioni, J. 1994. 'La république et l'école', *Philosophie politique*, no. 4. Paris: Presses Universitaires de France, 73–87.

Nagel, T. 1986. *The View from Nowhere*. Oxford: Oxford University Press.

Nielsen, K. 1972. 'On Locating the Challenge of Relativism', *Second Order* **1**, 14–25.

Nielsen, K. 1982. 'Problems for Westermarck's Subjectivism', *Acta Philosophica Fennica* **34**,122–143.

Nozick, R. 1993. *The Nature of Rationality*. Princeton: Princeton University Press.

Nussbaum, M. C. 1986.*The Fragility of Goodness*. Cambridge: Cambridge University Press.

O'Connor, D. J. 1967. 'Tests for Intentionality', *American Philosophical Quarterly* **4**,173–78.

Otto, R. 1958. *The Idea of the Holy: an inquiry into the non-rational factor in the idea of the divine and its relation to the rational*, trans. by John W. Harvey. Oxford: Oxford University Press.

Parekh, B. 1982.*Contemporary Political Thinkers*. Oxford: Martin Robertson.

Parekh, B. 1994. 'Decolonizing Liberalism' in A. Shtromas (ed.), *The End of 'isms': Reflections on the Fate of Ideological Politics after Communism's Collapse*. Oxford: Blackwell,.

Parekh, B. 1995. 'Liberalism and Colonialism: a Critique of Locke and Mill' in J. N. Peiterse and B. Parekh (eds.), *The Decolonisation of Imagination: Culture, Knowledge and Power*. London: Zed Books.

Passmore, J. 1961. *Philosophical Reasoning*. London: Duckworth.

Paul, E. F., Miller, F. D. and Paul, J. 1994. *Cultural Pluralism and Moral Knowledge*. Cambridge: Cambridge University Press.

Philllips, A. 1993. *Democracy and Difference*. Cambridge: Polity Press.

Phillips, D. L. 1993. *Looking Backward*. Princeton: Princeton University Press.

Plato. 1961. *The Collected Dialogues of Plato including The Letters*, ed. Edith Hamilton and Huntington Cairns. Princeton: Princeton University Press.

Platts, M. 1979. *Ways of Meaning: an introduction to a philosophy of language*. London: Routledge and Kegan Paul.

Putnam, Hilary. 1991. *Representation and Reality*. Cambridge, Mass.: MIT Press.

Race, Al. 1993. *Christians and Religious Pluralism*. London: SCM Press.

Rawls, J. 1972. *A Theory of Justice*. Oxford: Oxford University Press.

Rawls, J. 1993. *Political Liberalism*. New York: Columbia University Press.

Raz, J. 1990. 'Facing Diversity: The Case of Epistemic Abstinence', *Philosophy and Public Affairs* **19**, 3–46.

Reeves, C. D. C. 1989. *Socrates in the Apology*. Indianapolis: Hackett.

Rex, J. 1985. *The Concept of a Multi-Cultural Society*, Occasional Papers in Etnnic Relations No.3. University of Warwick: Centre for Research in Ethnic Relations.

Rex, J. 1986. *Race and Ethnicity*. Milton Keynes: Open University Press.

Rorty, R. 1989. *Contingency, Irony, Solidarity*. Cambridge: Cambridge University Press.

Rorty, A. O. 1994. 'The Hidden Politics of Cultural Identification', *Political Theory* **22**, 152–156.

Ross, W. D. 1923. *Aristotle*. London: Methuen.

Rousseau, J. J. 1991. *Social Contract* (1762), trans. C. Betts. Oxford: Oxford University Press.

Rushdie, S. 1982. 'The New Empire within Britain', *New Society* 9 December.

Sachs, D. 1981. 'How to Distinguish Self-Respect from Self-Esteem', *Philosophy and Public Affairs* **10**, 346–360.

Scanlon, T. M. 1982. 'Contractualism and Utilitarianism', in A. Sen and B. Williams (eds.), *Utilitarianism and Beyond*. Cambridge: Cambridge University Press.

Scheffler, S. 1994. 'The Appeal of Political Liberalism', *Ethics* **105**, 4–22.

Schnapper, D. 1994. *La communauté des citoyens*. Paris: Gallimard.

Searle, John. R. 1983. *Intentionality. An Essay in the Philosophy of Mind*. Cambridge: Cambridge University Press.

Searle, John. R. 1992. *The Rediscovery of the Mind*. Cambridge, Mass.: MIT Press.

Shklar, J. 1990. *The Faces of Injustice*. New Haven: Yale University Press.

Shklar, J. 1991. *American Citizenship. The Quest for Inclusion*. Cambridge, Mass.: Harvard University Press.

Siegel, H. 1987. *Relativism Refuted*. Dordrecht: D. Reidel.

Sinnot-Armstrong, W. 1988. *Moral Dilemmas*. Oxford: Blackwell.

Skorupski, J. 1985/6. 'Objectivity and convergence', *Proceedings of the Aristotelian Society*, **LXXXVI**, 235–250.

Skorupski, J. 1993. 'The Definition of Morality', in A. Phillips Griffiths (ed.), *Ethics*, Royal Institute of Philosophy Supplement 35. Cambridge: Cambridge University Press.

Skorupski, J. 1995. 'Agent-Neutrality, Consequentialism, Utilitarianism, A Terminological Note', *Utilitas* **7**, 49–54.

Smart, N. 1958. *Reasons and Faiths, an investigation of religious discourse, Christian and non-Christian*. London: Routledge, Kegan and Paul.

Sokolowski, Robert. 1984. 'Intentional Analysis and the Noema', *Dialectica* **XXXVIII**, 113–129.

Sorabji, R. R. K. 1993. *Animal Minds and Human Morals*. London: Duckworth.

Steiner, G. 1961.*The Death of Tragedy*. London: Faber.

Stevenson, C. L. 1944. *Ethics and Language*. New Haven: Yale University Press.

Stevenson, C. L. 1963. *Facts and Values*. New Haven: Yale University Press.

Stich, Stephen 1983. *From Folk Psychology to Cognitive Science: The Case Against Belief*. Cambridge, Mass.: MIT Press.

Stroup, T. 1981. 'In Defence of Westermarck', *Journal of the History of Philosophy* **19**, 213–234.

Stroup, T. 1982 'Soft Subjectivism', *Acta Philosophica Fennica* **34**, 99–121.

Stroup, T. 1985. 'Westermarck's Ethical Methodology' , in E. Bulygin *et al*. (eds.), *Man, Law and Modern Forms of Life*. Dordrecht: D. Reidel.

Taylor, A. E. 1955. *Aristotle*. London: Constable.

Taylor, C. 1994. 'The Politics of Recognition', in A. Gutman (ed.), 1994.

Tillich, P. 1951. *Systematic Theology*, Volume 1. Chicago: University of Chicago Press.

Tillich, P. 1955.*Ultimate Concern*. London: SCM Press.

Tillich, P. 1957. *The Dynamics of Faith*. London: Allen & Unwin.

Tillich, P. 1963. *Christianity and the Encounters of the World Religions*. New York: Columbia University Press.

Toynbee, A. 1953. *Christianity among the Religions of the World*. New York: Columbia University Press.

Van Noort, G. 1961. *Dogmatic Theology*, Volume 3. Cork: Mercia Press .

Van Parijs, P. 1995. *Real Fredom for All.* Oxford: Clarendon Press.

Vawter, B. 1957. *A Path through Genesis.* London: Sheed and Ward.

Vlastos, G. 1994. *Socratic Studies.* Cambridge: Cambridge University Press.

Waldron, J. 1993. *Liberal Virtues: Collected papers 1981–1991.* Cambridge: Cambridge University Press.

Westermarck, E. 1906–8. *The Origins and Development of the Moral Ideas,* 2 volumes. London: Macmillan and Co.

Westermarck, E. 1932.*Ethical Relativity.* London: Kegan Paul, Trench, Trubner & Co.

Westermarck, E. 1934. *Three Essays on Sex and Marriage.* London: Macmillan and Co.

White, F. C. 1986. 'On a Proposed Refutation of Relativism', *Australasian Journal of Philosophy* **64**, 331–334.

Williams, B. 1973. *Problems of the Self.* Cambridge: Cambridge University Press.

Williams, B. 1974–5. 'The Truth in Relativism', *Proceedings of the Aristotelian Society* **75**, 215–228.

Williams, B. 1976. 'Moral Luck', *Aristotelian Society Supplementary Volume* 50, 115–135.

Williams, B. 1985. *Ethics and the Limits of Philosophy.* London: Fontana.

Williams, B. 1993. *Shame and Necessity.* Berkeley: University of California Press.

Wisdom, A. J. T. D. 1965. *Paradox and Discovery.* Oxford: Blackwell.

Wong, D. 1984. *Moral Relativity.* Berkeley: University of California Press.

Wright, C. 1992. *Truth and Objectivity.* Cambridge, Mass.: Harvard University Press.

Wright, C. 1996. 'Truth in Ethics' *Ratio*, **9**, 209–226.

Young, I. M. 1990. *Justice and the Politics of Difference.* Princeton: Princeton University Press.